SHEPHERDS in the

Image of CHRIST

The Centennial History of St. John's ≈ Assumption
Seminary Archdiocese of San Antonio, Texas

October 15, 1915 – October 15, 2015

Mary Diane Langford, CDP

iUniverse LLC
Bloomington

SHEPHERDS IN THE IMAGE OF CHRIST
THE CENTENNIAL HISTORY OF ST. JOHN'S ≈ ASSUMPTION
SEMINARY ARCHDIOCESE OF SAN ANTONIO, TEXAS

iUniverse books may be ordered through booksellers or by contacting:

iUniverse LLC
1663 Liberty Drive
Bloomington, IN 47403
www.iuniverse.com
1-800-Authors (1-800-288-4677)

ISBN: 978-1-4917-3227-4 (sc)
ISBN: 978-1-4917-3228-1 (hc)
ISBN: 978-1-4917-3229-8 (e)

Printed in the United States of America.

iUniverse rev. date: 05/14/2014

THE COVER DESIGN

The cover captures the stained-glass window of Christ, the Good Shepherd in St. Thomas Aquinas Chapel, Archbishop Patrick Flores Residence Hall, Assumption Seminary. The residence was dedicated in 2007, but the stained-glass windows in the Chapel are from a Catholic Church in Philadelphia. They were restored by Cavallini Co., Inc. of San Antonio, TX. Cover design by Catherine T. Maule, graphic artist, Our Lady of the Lake University, San Antonio, TX. Photo by Fred Gonzales.

DEDICATION

I dedicate this work to the nearly 800 men who were prepared at St. John's ≈ Assumption Seminaries and served the Roman Catholic Church as priests and bishops in archdioceses and dioceses throughout the United States and in foreign countries; to the hundreds of men whose spiritual foundation at St. John's ≈ Assumption prepared them for life and for service to their Church as devoted laity; to the priests, religious, and laity whose tireless dedication to the mission of St. John's ≈ Assumption assisted in preparing over a thousand men as priests and dedicated laymen for the Catholic Church.

May those who are enjoying eternal glory intercede for us and our needs. May those who are still serving Church and Society be blessed with ever-greater generosity and peace-filled spirits.

TABLE OF CONTENTS

FOREWORD

Dear Brothers and Sisters in Christ,

Toward the end of his pontificate, St. John Paul II addressed these words to his clergy in Rome: "The apple of the bishop's eye is the seminary, because through the seminary, he sees the Church's future." As a bishop I am constantly reminded of the words of the gospel, "the harvest is great but the laborers are few." Our beloved Assumption Seminary continues to stand as the promise of a bright future for our Archdiocese and the many other dioceses touched by her mission to form priests and leaders for today's Church.

This was certainly in the heart of Bishop John Shaw, fourth Bishop of San Antonio, who on October 2, 1915, dedicated St. John's Seminary on Dwyer Street in San Antonio just a few blocks from San Fernando Cathedral. From that small contingent of faculty and seminarians, over the course of 100 years, St. John's ≈ Assumption Seminary has prepared over 800 Christ-centered men for service to the Church and to God's people. Its mission has continued through good times and difficult times, through moments of great growth and moments of struggle and upheaval in society and in the Church.

I am grateful that my predecessors have continued to value St. John's ≈ Assumption Seminary and have worked diligently to oversee its institutional growth and its mission to form the human, pastoral, intellectual, and spiritual lives of our priests throughout this last century. I am also grateful to the diocesan clergy, the Vincentians, the Sulpicians, the Oblates of Mary Immaculate, the Hermanas Josefinas, and the many committed religious and laypersons who were and continue to be leaders and role models for our seminarians.

I am grateful also to my fellow bishops from the many other dioceses who entrusted to us their future priests for education and formation. St. John's ≈ Assumption Seminary can take pride in the number of priest alumni who are ministering in dioceses throughout Texas and the United States.

The one-hundred year history of this seminary is also a tribute to the many benefactors who over the years have said "yes" to supporting this vital mission. Their generosity and their love for the priesthood of Jesus Christ are greatly appreciated.

I offer my thanks to Sr. Diane Langford, CDP, for skillfully capturing the movements of our providential God in the history of this institution that prepares priests to be instruments of grace to His people.

Lastly, I want to thank God and Pope Benedict XVI for calling me to be the shepherd of the Archdiocese of San Antonio and the opportunity to celebrate this anniversary with my brother priests, the Church, and the community of the City of San Antonio and South Texas.

Through the next one-hundred years, may St. John's ≈ Assumption Seminary continue in its mission, trusting in God and remember the words of our Holy Father, Pope Francis: "The laborers for the harvest are not chosen through advertising campaigns or appeals for service and generosity, but they are 'chosen' and 'sent' by God. The Church . . . is not ours, but God's; the field to be cultivated is his. The mission, then, is primarily about grace." God has graced us by calling men and helping us form them for the priesthood for one-hundred years; may the next century of preparing shepherds in the image of Christ truly be a century of grace.

Through the intercession of St. John, St. Anthony, and Our Lady, Assumed into Heaven,

Most Reverend Gustavo Garcia-Siller, M.Sp.S.

Archbishop of San Antonio

PREFACE

When Msgr. Lawrence Stuebben approached me about writing the centennial history of St. John's ≈ Assumption Seminary, never having worked in pastoral ministries in the Archdiocese of San Antonio, I really did not know "the territory." Although I knew only a few archdiocesan priests, the ones I did know at the time are sterling examples of priestly commitment. And unknown to them, they were a good recommendation for the project!

The former St. John's Seminary was a collection of empty buildings just north of Mission Concepcion in South San Antonio. I had never visited that structure. I had only visited Assumption a few times and the building that I had studied in at the Mexican American Cultural Center, Mary-Catherine Hall, has been razed. To take on this project felt like exploring an unknown land. Nevertheless, I accepted the challenge.

Capturing the history of a one hundred year old institution led me down unexplored labyrinthine paths. But, providentially, I began meeting "old friends" with whom I had become familiar as I wrote *God Has Been God for Us*, the history of the Missionary Servants of St. Anthony.

Once again Bishop Shaw, Archbishop Drossaerts, Archbishop Lucey, Archbishop Furey, and Archbishop Flores whom I had grown to appreciate for their leadership of the Archdiocese came to life. And, Brother Edward Loch, SM of the Archdiocesan Archives, again came to my assistance.

I met colleagues in the "history business": the archivist at De Paul University who supervises the Vincentian collection— Mr. Andrew Rea; the writer-historians, especially Father James Vanderholt who gathered the history of the first seventy-five years, Rev. John Rybolt, CM, a Vincentian historian, and Rev. James D. White, an Oklahoma historian.

And, along the pathways of the past century, I met new friends—both living here and living in eternity—as I combed archives, read histories, interviewed bishops, priests, women and men religious, and dedicated lay people who live throughout the US and hold in their hearts a portion of the story of St. John's ≈ Assumption.

No work of this kind is a solitary project. There are untold people to whom I am now indebted; some of them are listed in the Acknowledgements. But there are others, those who "boarded" me when I was exploring archives or doing interviews; those who gave me "directions" which kept me from ending up at dead ends; those who listened to my tales of weal and woe; and, especially, those who prayed for me.

It has been my privilege to write *Shepherds in the Image of Christ* and now, I, too, will hold St. John's ≈ Assumption Seminary in my heart for the rest of my life.

ACKNOWLEDGEMENTS

I am most grateful to the following whose participation has enhanced this work:

- All those willing to be interviewed
- Mr. Andrew Rea, Archivist and his Staff: Vincentian Archives at DePaul University, Chicago, IL
- Archbishop Gustavo Garcia-Siller, MSpS, for his Foreword
- Artist Michael Lawrence of Tyler, TX, for use of his portrait of Bishop Charles Herzig
- Brother Edward Loch, SM, Archivist of the Archdiocese of San Antonio
- Mr. Chris Munoz, seminarian, for his work on the photos
- Rev. John Rybolt, CM, Vincentian historian at DePaul University, Chicago, IL
- Rev. Joel Rippinger, OSB, Archivist, St. Marmion Abbey, Aurora, IL
- Leadership and members of the Congregation of Divine Providence for their support and prayers
- Ms. Melanie Castillo, Administrative Assistant at Assumption Seminary, for her tremendous technical and archival support
- Ms. Catherine T. Maule, graphic artist, for her beautiful cover
- Mr. Mike Davis, Director of Development at Assumption Seminary for his support, guidance and assistance with photos
- Msgr. Alois Goertz and those "historically-minded" priests, especially Rev. Matthew Gilbert, who preserved the history of seminary life in the Archdiocese of San Antonio since 1915 in *25 Years a Seminary* and *Priest Forever, Breaking Ground,* and *Diamond Jubilee*

xvi   Mary Diane Langford, CDP

- Msgr. James Vanderholt, Diocese of Beaumont, for his work *Called to Serve . . . History of St. John's and Assumption Seminaries, San Antonio, Texas 1915-1990*
- The leadership of the Priests' Alumni Association of St. John's ≈ Assumption Seminaries for their confidence in me to write and produce this history
- The readers of the manuscript for their confidence, support, guidance, critique and prayers: Msgr. Alois Goertz, Msgr. James Henke, Rev. Phillip Henning, Msgr. Jeff Pehl, Msgr. John Peters, Msgr. Lawrence Stuebben, Msgr. John Wagner
- The priests who responded to the 2012 Survey
- And, especially for the Priests' Alumni Association of St. John's ≈ Assumption Seminary which underwrote and guided this project

Priest's titles given in this book are as of the point in time indicated. The information given in the boxes is current to the present time. Titles noted in the listing of alumni are as of the publication date.

The author regrets and apologizes for any error.

Revitalization of the Catholic Church in Texas during Independence and Statehood

The enormous tract of land stretching from Galveston Bay to the mountains of El Paso to the Rio Grande Valley and the plains of what is now Oklahoma, the Prefecture-Apostolic of Texas, was created by Pope Gregory XVI in 1839. Vincentian Father John Timon, Superior of St. Mary-of-the-Barrens, Missouri, was named as the Prefect, a position on par with "bishop". Timon appointed his confrere, Jean-M. Odin, as Vice-Prefect. Charged with inspecting the situation of the Texas Church, Odin, Michael Calvo, Eudaldus Estany, Raymond Sala—all Vincentians—sailed into port at Lavaca Bay on July 12, 1840 (Casteneda, PhD., Carlos E., "Pioneers of the Church in Texas," *Archdiocese of San Antonio, 1874-1949*[1], p. 1-23). The first priests to serve the Church of Texas after the independence of Texas from Mexico were these few French Vincentians[2].

---

[1] *Archdiocese of San Antonio, 1874-1949*, was published by Archbishop Robert E. Lucey in celebration of the Diamond Jubilee of the Archdiocese. The Compiler and Editor, Rev. M. J. Gilbert, is considered one of the "founders" of St. John's Seminary, having served on the faculty from 1916 until 1933 and as rector from 1928 until 1933. Gilbert is the author of "Breaking Ground", an early history of the seminary.

[2] Vincentians, the Congregation of the Missions, pioneered the work of providing for Catholics in Texas during independence and early statehood. Their motherhouse in Perryville, MO, then known as St. Mary-of-the Barrens, prepared many priests, religious and diocesan, for the rigors of life in the wilderness of Texas. In 1940, Archbishop Robert E. Lucey engaged the Vincentians to operate St. John's Seminary.

Odin and his companions discovered that the fledgling Catholic Church of Texas, still under the See of Monterrey, Mexico, was in decay. The See of Monterrey was often vacant; the few priests remaining in Texas were not prepared for the hardships of missionary life in the Wild West; the mission churches established along the San Antonio River near San Antonio were in disrepair. The chaotic government of Texas under President Sam Houston could offer little support (Casteneda, p. 1-23).

The work of the Vincentian missionaries was to re-establish and re-organize the Catholic Church of Texas and they began in earnest. San Fernando Church was cleaned and repaired; Immaculate Conception (Concepción) Mission was re-established; St. Louis Parish was established in Castroville to tend to the Alsatians brought there by *empresario* Henri Castro. The faithful gathered in homes for masses in New Braunfels, Lavaca, and Victoria as they awaited the construction of their churches.

The Holy See elevated the Texas missions to the ecclesiastical status of a Vicariate-Apostolic and Vincentian priest Jean-M. Odin was invested with the authority of a bishop for the vast territory. Odin was unable to rely on Vincentian priests to take care of the Church of Texas and thus decided to appeal to the Catholic communities of the eastern United States as well as the Church of Ireland, the Churches of Paris and Lyons in France, and the Catholic Church of Germany for badly needed priests and monetary resources. Seminarians in these heavily

---

Statistics about the Catholic Church in Texas 1870 -- 1912

- 1870 Population of Texas = 818,579

- 1870 Population of San Antonio = 12,250 with 4 Catholic Churches

- 1874: one bishop; 83 priests, < 100,000 Catholics in the Diocese of Texas

- 1880: 45 priests, 50 churches, 8 chapels, 6 ecclesiastical students (seminarians) and 47,000 Catholics in Texas

- 1896: 66, 000 Catholics; 55 priests, 38 of whom were seculars serving 41 parishes and 73 missions in the Diocese of San Antonio

- 1909: 95,000 Catholics; 118 priests, 64 of whom were seculars; 128 parishes, half of which were missions (Diocese of San Antonio) (*Archdiocese of San Antonio, 1874-1949*, p. 33, 36, 128, 130)

Catholic countries responded to Odin's appeal, and in the spring of 1846, the first small band of French missioners sailed from France to Texas. Often the missioners were acculturated at St. Mary-of-the-Barrens, Missouri, the Vincentian motherhouse, before tackling their ministries in Texas, which had been brought into the Union in 1845.

From 1846 until well into the 20th century, Odin and his fellow missionary successors—including Claude M. Dubuis, the second bishop of Texas; Joan Claude Ncran, the second Bishop of San Antonio; John Anthony Forest, the third Bishop of San Antonio—would all make the same journey back to mother-Europe for more priests, more women and men religious for the growing Catholic Church of Texas.

Having exhausted their resources, the Vincentians withdrew from Texas in the early 1850's. Missionaries from Europe and priests from various orders took their places, continuing the expansion of the Catholic Church in Texas. Conventual Franciscans, Oblates of Mary Immaculate, the Society of Mary, Benedictines from St. Vincent's Abbey in Pennsylvania, and Polish Resurrectionist Priests were in place by the end of the Civil War. Every priest had several parishes to shepherd.

Many parishes in the present Archdiocese of San Antonio owe their foundation and spiritual sustenance to extraordinary missionary priests who were willing to leave home and country for the sake of the Catholic Church of Texas (*Archdiocese of San Antonio, 1874-1949*, p. 22-37).

The First Seminary

The first seminary in the Diocese of San Antonio was established as St. Joseph's College in Victoria, TX, by Fr. A. Gardet, pastor of St. Mary's Parish in Victoria from 1856 until 1891. The college had an unstable beginning and was closed in 1878-1879 due to national economic challenges. Re-opened in 1880, the college was expanded to include a diocesan seminary which was placed under the supervision of the Jesuit Fathers by Bishop Pellicer (*Archdiocese of San Antonio, 1874-1949*, p. 86). However, the Jesuit College in Seguin closed in 1880 and students from that college transferred to the Victoria school (*Archdiocese of San Antonio, 1874-1949*, p. 86). This rudimentary seminary in Victoria provided the first native clergy for the Diocese of San Antonio.

It is not known how many students there were at the inauguration

> of this new and unusual seminary, nor do we know exactly how many priests it numbered among its alumni . . . It is known that at least thirty priests did all or part of their studies there between [1880 and 1902] when it was discontinued (*Archdiocese of San Antonio, 1874-1949*, p. 86).

St. Joseph College, Victoria, Texas, c. 1890 (*Diamond Jubilee*)

The death of Father L. Wyer in November 1902, who had presided over St. Joseph's College and Diocesan Seminary following the death of Gardet in 1891, ended the life of the pioneer seminary.

The Oblates of Mary Immaculate, however, broke ground for their new seminary in San Antonio, St. Anthony Philosophical and Theological Seminary [also known as St. Anthony's Apostolic

Most Rev. John William Shaw of Mobile, Alabama, was educated in the diocesan seminary in Navan, County Meath, Ireland and at the North American College in Rome. Shaw was ordained in Rome in 1888 and returned to Alabama where he was appointed rector of the Cathedral of Mobile in 1892. In 1910, Shaw was consecrated as coadjutor of the Bishop of San Antonio and became the Ordinary of San Antonio upon Bishop Forest's death in 1911. A missionary diocese that covered the western third of Texas, San Antonio Diocese had about 95,000 Catholics. Beginning a seminary was one of Shaw's first endeavors. In 1914, the formation of the new Diocese of El Paso reduced the Diocese of San Antonio to about 60,000 square miles. In 1918, Shaw was appointed Archbishop of New Orleans. (Archdiocese of San Antonio, 1874-1974, p. 25-26; Photo: Archdiocese of San Antonio)

School]. When it opened a year later (October 1903) it received not only Oblate scholastics but also advanced diocesan students.[3] Until the Diocesan Seminary, St. John's, opened in the fall of 1915, men studying for the diocesan priesthood were educated at St. Anthony's until the numbers of students outgrew the Laurel Heights (San Antonio) buildings.

Some students, especially men from foreign countries who had not completed seminary, attended St. Joseph's Abbey in St. Benedict (near Covington), Louisiana, which had been started by the monks from St. Meinrad's Abbey in Indiana in 1889.

Bishop John W. Shaw, the fourth bishop of the Diocese of San Antonio, continued to rely on priests trained outside his diocese and he also turned to his own Irish ancestral roots for English speaking priests for his growing diocese. While studying at the diocesan seminary in Navan, County Meath, Ireland, Shaw became acquainted with Mungret College, a Jesuit school which prepared missionaries for foreign missions in Limerick.

---

[3]   Oblate School of Theology, now in its 105th year in San Antonio, continues to provide the theologate for seminarians who are at Assumption Seminary.

He sponsored five seminarians from Mungret, accepting them for the Diocese of San Antonio sight-unseen. In addition to needing warm bodies to staff his growing parishes, Shaw needed money to support the diocese's many needs, including his seminary dream. In his Christmas letter of 1912, Shaw invited the faithful of his diocese to provide the finances necessary for the future seminary. Hoping that a local seminary would increase the number of vocations, Shaw made a leap of faith in July 1915 and called for the opening of a diocesan seminary in the fall. With few resources, Shaw leaned on the Providence of God and opened St. John's Seminary in September of 1915. His Christmas pastoral letter of 1915 speaks of his deeply-felt responsibility:

> The work of renewing the priesthood and of keeping up the supply of the laborers for the harvest belongs preeminently to the Episcopate. Since our coming to the Diocese we have labored incessantly to increase the number of our clergy and we shall not rest satisfied until we have in our midst a learned and pious priesthood to preach the gospel to every creature, to offer up the clean oblation in every town, village and hamlet, to break the bread of life to famishing souls and to give in the tribunal of Divine mercy that peace which the world cannot give. (*Breaking Ground*, p. 4)

CHAPTER ONE

FOUNDING A SEMINARY

When a desperately poor diocese begins a project as enormous as a seminary, it must resort to a "make-do" philosophy to circumvent the lack of resources. The annual "Pro episcopo" (For the Bishop) collection brought in little cash for the bishop to work with, and so the plans for the seminary were dependent on resources the diocese already possessed.

> Recognizing that a local seminary depends on the beneficence of the laity of the diocese for its success, Bishop John William Shaw wrote the following to his diocese at the end of the first year at St. John's (June 1916).
>
> *"It may interest you to know that the Seminary has a staff of professors that compares most favorably with that of any other institution of the kind in the country. Four of the professors are graduates of old established and renowned European university. In conformity with the wishes of Holy Mother Church, students will be selected from the Diocese as far as possible and irrespective of nationality . . . The Seminary will gladly receive the young Levites and train them to be the future anointed of the Lord."*
>
> *--Breaking Ground*, p. 4

The Hand-Me-Down Residences

A new building was out of the question in the beginning, but in the mind's eye of Bishop John Shaw the property just north of Mission Concepción would be an ideal setting for the future edifice. In the meantime, existing property would have to suffice.

". . . a large three-story stone building had been erected at 310 Dwyer Street by Bishop (John) Neraz in 1885 to serve as the Bishop's residence (*Breaking Ground*, p. 7)." It had been built on a rather grand scale in order to serve as a "diocesan hotel" for priests when they traveled into San Antonio and also to serve as the location for the annual priests' retreat. Shaw, however, found

1

the building to be inconvenient as a residence and chose to live at St. Rose Infirmary instead. At the point of looking for a place for the proposed seminary, the Teresian Sisters were using the Dwyer Avenue house as a temporary home.

> When all the preparations were made it was found that there were accommodations for about twenty students and a resident faculty of three, and that was quite sufficient for the time being. Since the new institution was intended to be only a Minor or Preparatory Seminary, all students of the Diocese who had already entered upon their higher studies (Theology) remained undisturbed in their respective Major Seminaries and not more than twenty new applicants were expected from the grades and high schools (*Breaking Ground*, p. 9).

On October 2, 1915, St. John's Seminary, named in honor of Bishop Shaw's patron saint, opened its doors to thirteen boys. Shortly four others joined them. The seventeen boys who made up the first seminary class came from both San Antonio and the small towns of the sprawling diocese. Like the youngest among them, Sidney Metzger of Fredericksburg, they had come because they "wanted to be priests". The "official photograph" of the staff and student body in 1915 portrays seven boys who were eventually ordained and became pastors and professors at the seminary; one (Sidney Metzger) who became the seminary rector and later a bishop; and other boys who made their mark as laymen in their communities.

Exemplary Faculty

The faculty of the new seminary—anything but hand-me-down—had been culled from the diocesan priests, all of whom knew what it would take to be a pastor in the growing diocese of San Antonio.

Chancery Building, c. 1915; First Seminary
(Photo: *Diamond Jubilee*, p. 184)

Though at first glance, Msgr. William Hume, the first rector might be thought of as a "hand-me-down" since he came to Catholicism from Anglicanism, his credentials were first-class.

Hume had come with Bishop Shaw from the Diocese of Mobile and was an esteemed scholar. Rev. Mariano Garriga had been serving parishes in the western part of the diocese; two were newly ordained Irish missionaries from the Mungret Seminary project—Rev. James F. Cassidy and Rev. Patrick Geehan. These diocesan priests were joined by the Rev. Alphonse Wendling, OSB, chaplain at the Ursuline Convent, and his dog Jack (*Breaking Ground*, p. 11).

A year after the opening, another Irishman, Rev. Matthew Gilbert, came from Mungret, and Rev. Garriga moved on to become a chaplain with the National Guard which was deployed into the regular army during World War I.

First Students and Original Faculty, 1915-1916—L to R, seated:
Rev. James F. Cassidy, Rev. Dan Mullane, CSSR, Very Rev.
William Hume, Most Rev. John W. Shaw, Sidney Metzger (seated
in front of Bishop), Rev. Patrick J. Geehan, Very Rev. Jose M.
Tronscoso, SSJ, Rev. Alphonse M. Wendling, OSB; middle row:
Emil Mitchie, Jerry Sullivan, Emil Baas, Frank Depine, Joseph
Pustka, Martin Maas, Alois J. Morkovsky; back row: Jose Mata,
Leroy Dugger, Peter L. Hanak, Lambert Schiel, Cayetano Romero,
Peter L. Foegele, Cyril Pfeil (Photo: *Priest Forever*, p. 12)

The second year saw a student body that had swelled to
twenty-five boys, among them Henry D. Buchanan, a 29 year
old student for the Diocese of El Paso. Though he never became
a "Latin scholar", Buchanan finished two years at St. John's, his
theology and philosophy at St. Mary's Seminary in Baltimore,
MD, and was the first student from St. John's to be ordained to
the priesthood (*25 Years a Seminary*, p.26; *Breaking Ground*,
p.15).

After finishing their high school preparation and philosophy
at St. John's, those earliest students continued their studies at
the Sulpician Seminary in Washington, DC; at the Benedictine
seminary in St. Meinrad, IN; the North American College in
Rome; and the Vincentian seminary, Kenrick, in St. Louis, MO.

From the earliest years the curriculum included a two-year course of philosophy as Bishop Shaw and Msgr. Hume imagined St. John's becoming a major seminary. However, it would be another twelve years before the Department of Theology was added. In that same year (1928), Rev. Matthew J. Gilbert became the third rector of St. John's, now a Theological Seminary.

Early Traditions

Early on, traditions began which would last for decades. The Irish priests on the faculty soon turned baseball-playing American boys into soccer players and produced several teams that won the city championship. But the first rector, Rev. Msgr. William Hume, "knew that young Americans reveled in the National Game . . . [So] . . . in addition to playing [baseball] and having an impressive record over a period of fifteen years, the students were permitted to attend the opening game of the Texas League, at the expense of the Seminary, and a tradition was born." Later seminarians would see the mighty Babe Ruth "hit the longest home run ever witnessed in San Antonio" (*Breaking Ground*, p. 16-18; *25 Years a Seminary*, p. 21-22, and 31).

The soft-hearted Msgr. Hume was always on the look-out for any activity that would disrupt discipline and spoil the young boys who had chosen the Spartan-styled preparation for priesthood. Traditions that began while he was rector included the annual excursions to the circus and to Landa Park in New Braunfels for the Easter Monday picnic. The trip to Landa Park which required chartering a special train proved to be a memorable occasion that the boys looked forward to year after year.

During the second year of the seminary's existence, the "philosopher's picnic," held for the first time on March 7[4], 1917, was an experience of epic proportions. The philosophy students and their faculty piled into the available automobile and headed for Bandera via the newly-built Medina Dam. In 1917 that was an impossible trip—but the young men preparing for

---

[4] March 7 is the old (pre-Vatican II) feast of St. Thomas Aquinas, patron saint of philosophers; today his feast is on January 28.

Msgr. William Hume was born in 1873 in Isle of Wight. After earning a degree from Winchester College, he joined the Anglican ministry and worked for years in the slums of London. A long interest in Catholicism eventually led to his conversion. Hume then spent several years in Rome studying liturgy and becoming an expert in canon law. After being ordained a Catholic priest, he served at Westminster Cathedral but moved to Alabama because of rheumatism. There he met Rev. John Shaw. He moved with Shaw to San Antonio when Shaw was named the Bishop of that diocese. In San Antonio, Hume established a diocesan chancery, was rector of the newly-formed seminary, served as chaplain to the orphanage and worked on behalf of Mexican refugees who had settled in San Antonio. After serving as the first rector of St. John's Seminary from 1915 to 1918, Hume was called to assist Shaw when he was appointed archbishop of New Orleans. Hume died in 1924 (*Priest Forever*, p. 15-16 and *Diamond Jubilee*, p. 187-188).

the adventure of the priesthood were undaunted by impassable roads, undoable distance, and seemingly unlimited dangers (*Breaking Ground*, p. 17-19).

At the end of his seventh year as the Ordinary of the Diocese of San Antonio, Bishop John W. Shaw was elevated to be the Archbishop of New Orleans and was installed in that position in January of 1918. The pastor of St. Joseph's Parish in Baton Rouge, Louisiana, Arthur J. Drossaerts was named Shaw's successor and consecrated at St. Louis Cathedral in New Orleans on December 8, 1918 (*Diamond Jubilee, 1874-1949*, p. 184, 233).

Shaw had not wanted to live in the Dwyer Avenue house[5] but Drossaerts did and thus the faculty was sent out to look for a new campus (*Breaking Ground*, p. 21). A number of places for housing St. John's Seminary were investigated, including the Mexican

---

[5]   The house on Dwyer Avenue was eventually demolished in 1963 and the stones were re-used in the restoration of Mission San Juan Capistrano (*Priest Forever*, p. 22).

Seminary located on property that had formerly belonged to the Sisters of Divine Providence in Castroville.[6]

Writing in 1928, Fr. Matthew Gilbert, noted that Msgr. Hume was willing to move the seminary to any "habitable shack within or near the confines of San Antonio" and he himself found the new destination—the Garden Academy, a former Episcopalian boarding school located in Highland Park, a newly-developing subdivision just south of downtown San Antonio (*Breaking Ground*, p. 21).

> The property consisted of one large city block on Adele Street [where it was] bisected by the continuation of Rigsby Avenue . . . On this property there were situated three buildings, an administration building, a school building, and another which words fail to describe (*Breaking Ground*, p. 22).

---

[6]   The property, now known as Moye Center, had been the original motherhouse of the Sisters of Divine Providence until 1895 when Our Lady of the Lake College and Convent were built in San Antonio. When the Catholic Church in Mexico was persecuted under President Carranza, the Diocese of San Antonio acquired the property and Mexican seminarians continued to be prepared for the priesthood in Castroville from 1915-1917. The Oblates of Mary Immaculate then took over the building until their new scholasticate was built, and then the Salesians used the building as their novitiate until 1937. The Congregation of Divine Providence bought the property back at that time and subsequently used it as a military school for elementary school-aged boys (1938-1959); as a house of formation from 1959-1985; and since 1985 as a retreat center (Callahan, p 231-232; www.**moyecenter**.org)

The Garden Academy; Second Home to St. John's Seminary,
1918-1920 (Photo: *Diamond Jubilee*, p. 184)

The administration building housed the chapel and the residency for Msgr. Hume, Fr. Alphonse Just, Fr. Patrick Geehan, and Fr. Matthew Gilbert. Other rooms became dormitories. The dank and gloomy basement housed the kitchen, refectory, and store room. An antiquated and inadequate stove and furnace contributed to the frustration of the Hermanas Josefinas and more than once jeopardized the existence of the building itself (*Breaking Ground*, p. 22).

"The so-called school building resembled a large and poorly constructed packing case. It had two floors but the second floor had never been completed, even the flooring was missing in one section" (*Breaking Ground*, p. 22).

> The study-hall, library and classrooms were housed in the school-building as well as an overflow dormitory and bathrooms with less than lukewarm water. The upper floor consisted of one large, barn-like room with a smaller room cut from it near the top of the stairs . . . A ceiling of canvas had been

loosely tacked to the joists and in many placed
the wind had blown it loose from the tacks and it
took on the appearance of a series of hammocks
of widely assorted sizes. There were no walls
(*Breaking Ground*, p. 22-23).

The third building, which, according to Gilbert, defied
description, became the home of the Hermanas Josefinas.

After a back-breaking move involving a wagon borrowed
from St. Peter's Orphanage, Scobey Moving Company, priests'
automobiles, the priest-faculty, the Josefinas, and friends, the
bedding, desks, kitchen equipment, books, chapel necessities, and
the rest of the paraphernalia from Dwyer Avenue was ensconced
on Adele Street.

St. John's Seminary, begun in a hand-me-down building, was
again at home in another hand-me-down structure at the opening
of the 1918-1919 academic year. Nineteen boys were welcomed—
fifteen from the previous year and four new boys.

Gilbert's musings in *Breaking Ground* (p. 24-26) recalled
buildings that needed re-wiring; a temperamental heating
system that threatened the residents with frost-bite; a cesspool,
badly constructed and too small, requiring that the boys muck
it out with regularity—a task that probably won student Alois
Morkovsky his place in heaven; water pressure that left the entire
campus with practically no water by late afternoon; clothes lockers
and dormitories in different buildings; and Highland Park roads
of "undiluted black mud" that were little more than cow trails.
Snakes, mice, and bugs of all varieties were in residence with the
boys and their priest-leaders.

The two years at the Garden Academy were still considered
by Gilbert to be "happy ones for all". Though only a couple of
miles from the center of San Antonio, the campus seemed to be in
open country. Salado Creek was near enough for swimming and
basketball courts, a baseball diamond, and soccer fields satisfied
the need for competitive sports (*Breaking Ground*, p. 23-26).

A Permanent Home

Bishop Arthur J. Drossaerts might be characterized as a "builder-bishop". During the nearly twenty-two years of his episcopate (1918-1940), the growing Diocese of San Antonio saw the erection of sixty parishes and fifty schools and the elevation of the diocese to an Archdiocese. But the first concern of the new bishop was St. John's Seminary. Though the seminarians, many of whom had come from simple living and hard work on farms throughout the diocese, might not have thought negatively about their living conditions at the Garden Academy, Bishop Drossaerts gave his first attention to the needs of the dismally inadequate seminary quarters. Within two years of being ordained bishop, Drossaerts dedicated the newly-built St. John's Seminary, constructed on the grounds of the historic Mission Concepción on Mission Road between Mitchell and Felisa Streets.

The funding of the new seminary project became a joint effort of both clergy and laity. The executive committee for the project, commissioned by Drossaerts, called the first meeting of pastors in September 1919 and asked each pastor to bring "one of the most representative and energetic men of his congregation." Fifteen priests from the parishes in San Antonio each accompanied by a distinguished layman heard the Bishop outline why a new seminary building was an imperative. One of the men in attendance suggested that a similar group of representative women appointed by the pastors be assembled. In the words of Mr. Jose Navarro the campaign for the seminary: "we must either succeed or make ourselves an object of ridicule among non-Catholics who venture greater undertakings and know no failure" (Article in the *Southern Messenger* quoted in *Breaking Ground*, p. 27-29).

The drive was a decided success. Architectural plans for a Spanish cloister-styled structure were drawn up by F. B. Gaenslen but the priests on the building committee rejected the idea of the architect's mission-like edifice. Before being finalized, new plans were reviewed by Rev. Henry Constantineau, OMI, who had a depth of experience in new buildings. Architect-builder Leo M. J.

Dielmann submitted the low bid for construction and the imposing red-brick building that stands to the north of Mission Concepcion today was begun on January 2, 1919. Dielmann was given the impossible task of finishing the main building for the beginning of the school term the coming September.

Construction was still underway when the priest-faculty began to dismantle the Garden Academy in August 1919

> A native San Antonian, **Leo Maria Joseph Dielmann** was a product of the flourishing German-American community of south-central Texas. His father, John Charles Dielmann, a stonemason, immigrated from Germany to Texas in 1872.
>
> Leo M. J. Dielmann was born in 1881. Following his graduation from St. Mary's College in San Antonio in 1898, Leo M. J. Dielmann studied architecture and engineering in Germany. As an architect, Dielmann designed businesses, churches, institutional buildings, residences, and numerous other types of public and private structures throughout Texas. In addition to other commercial structures, his churches and other church-related buildings are particularly noted and include San Antonio's Fort Sam Houston Post Chapel, the Conventual Chapel at Our Lady of the Lake University. Leo M. J. Dielmann died in San Antonio in 1969. (from: www.lib.utexas. edu/ taro/drtsa/ 00011/drt-00011.html)

so as not to have to sign a new lease and continue to squander $125 a month on the rent for a building that might fall down any day (*Breaking Ground*, p.33). Moving was nothing less than an adventure. Carpenters, plasterers, electricians, and plumbers were still working when caravan after caravan of "goods and chattels" made their way down Highland Boulevard, mostly a cow trail, to the mission. Beds, desks, benches, tables, a piano, a barrel of wine, were stashed in the basement since the main floors were still swarming with workers.

The final departure from Highland Park was impressive.

> P. J. G. (Fr. Geehan) in his flivver, hatless, coatless, shirtless, with rivulets of sweat streaming down his noble brow, brought one contingent consisting of some of the Sisters, a cat, sundry bags, boxes, and umbrellas, and Spitz [his dog]. M. J. G. (Fr. Gilbert), attired as P. J. G., only less so, was honored by the company of the remaining Sisters, a few dozen similar boxes, thirteen chickens, and Tosca [his dog].

Things were arranged somehow, nobody remembers how, and blessed night came.

The morning of September 17 [date for beginning classes] was drawing near and there was no sewer, no light, no telephone, no dormitory, no study hall, no kitchen, no refectory, no class rooms, no running water, nothing ready (*Breaking Ground*, p. 34-35).

The new seminary building would become a font of knowledge for hundreds of boys who had left farms and families to serve the People of God. In an interview with the *San Antonio Light*, Fr. Mariano Garriga described the curriculum in 1920.

The course provided embraced "four years of instruction equivalent to that afforded by the best high schools of the country, four years of college work, two years of philosophy, and four years of theology" (*Breaking Ground*, p. 41). Garriga's own words captured the curriculum more specifically.

Bishop Mariano Garriga, considered a founder of St. John's Seminary, was born in 1886 in Port Isabel, TX and educated for the priesthood at St. Mary's, Kansas City, Kansas; and at St. Francis Seminary, Milwaukee, WI. He was ordained in 1911 and began his priestly ministry in parishes in the western part of the Diocese. In 1915 he was recalled to San Antonio by Bishop Shaw who appointed him vice-rector of the new St. John's Seminary. Except for serving as chaplain in the National Guard during World War I, Garriga taught at the seminary until 1936 when he was named Coadjutor Bishop of Corpus Christi, TX. He became the Bishop of Corpus Christi in 1949. Garriga died at age 78 in 1965. (From *Diamond Jubilee*, p. 299)

. . . Latin is essential in all the works and therefore every man starts the study of Latin the very day he beings his schooling. All the lectures are given in Latin, and Latin is used by the students in preparing their work and in examinations.

. . . It would surprise you how soon and how well these young boys acquire and master the dead

Faculty at St. John's Seminary 1915-1941 [All Priests]	
Cassidy, James F.	1915-1917
Drees, Frederick	1925-1926
Ehrhardt, Philip, OMI	1932-1937
Faust, Claude, A.	1939-1942
FitzSimon, Lawrence J.	1921-1925
Garriga, Mariano S.	1921-1936
	1915-1916
Geehan, Patrick J.	1915-1941
Gilbert, Matthew J.	1916-1933
Hubertus, Bruno J.	1937-1942
Hug, Henry	1933-1937
Hullweg, Francis J., OMI	1928-1931
Hume, William W.	1915-1919
Just, Alphonse M.	1919-1924
Kraus, Alexis J.	1936-1941
Lohmann, Albert V.	1937-1939
Metzger, Sidney M.	1928-1940
Mitsch, Edward	1935-1941
	1926-1930;
Morkovsky, Alois J.	1924-1941
Morkovsky, John L.	1940-1941
Murphy, Leo V., SSJ	1930-1941
Robling, John J.	1940-1941
Romero, Cayetano	1937-1942
San German, Juan	1916-1917
Sugranes, Eugene, CMF	1917-1918
Sullivan, Victor A.	1920-1941
Tronscoso, Jose M., SSJ	1915-1916
Valenta, Marcus A.	1940
Wendling, Alphonse, OSB	1915-1917

[From *Priest Forever*, p. 122]

languages . . . English and Spanish are stressed and Ancient and Modern History are taught during the first four years.

Then comes the College work also known as fifth, sixth, seventh, and eighth year Latin . . . These four years give the student a thorough intimacy with the classics, high mathematics, and logic, together with a knowledge of all the subjects associated with and requested of a liberal education . . . Two years of Philosophy follow including generous numbers of hours in psychology, biology, and bacteriology and kindred sciences. Then the future priest is ready for the regular four course (years) in Theology and Religion that precedes ordination. (From a feature article in the *San Antonio Light* on the occasion of the dedication of St. John's Seminary, November 21,1920 in *Breaking Ground*, p. 41-42)

The seminarians who attended St. John's during its first ten years applied not only their brains to the study of an intense curriculum but also their brawn to the surrounding properties that had to be cleared and landscaped. Acres of weeds had to be removed; mesquite trees needed to be hewn and burned; water had to be hauled to the saplings that were planted to beautify the campus. Sidewalks were laid and flowers and shrubs were planted in beds which gave shape to the grounds. Eventually a front entrance was carved out of the "wilderness". Deep-rooted trees required yeoman's strength to dig out but the boys were undaunted. A forest of mesquite was cut down to make room for a pecan grove and a baseball diamond.

In *Breaking Ground* (p. 52), Father Gilbert recalled the extraordinary investment by the boys who

. . . spent many a weary hour with pick and shovel, wheelbarrow and rake, in places where plow and scraper were not necessary, and in making smoother the places where the scraper had done its best. No praise is too high for those who performed these tasks. At least 50% of their recreation time was taken up, they worked as hard as coolies and were sometimes called by that inelegant name, but they seemed to take pride in the work, and most of them actually enjoyed it.

Gilbert's account of the incredible work of the seminarians in the first years after the dedication of St. John's Seminary still causes the reader to be in awe of these future

Rev. Patrick J. Geehan, born in Belfast, Ireland in 1891, completed his studies for the priesthood at the North American College in Rome and was ordained for the Diocese of San Antonio in 1915.

Geehan had been a seminarian at Mungret College near the city of Limerick when Bishop Shaw took a "desperate chance" and "enlisted for future work in San Antonio, five assorted Irish striplings, none of whom had yet started the study of Theology; and not one of them could locate San Antonio on the map of the world." Geehan was one of the five and he came to San Antonio after his ordination in Rome.

Geehan served the Archdiocese at St. John's Seminary for 26 years. He also served as Chancellor and Vicar General of the Diocese, and Chaplain of the Teresian Sisters. (From *Breaking Ground*, p. 2; *Diamond Jubilee*, p. 184-186, 288)

priests who would slave so hard for the beautification of their seminary. The priest-author captured specifically the estimated value of the boys' work.

> . . . to say that the work of the boys saved the sum of $3900 in five years is giving them far less credit than they deserve . . . Two workmen constantly employed could certainly not have done the amount of work done by the boys. Since 1925 work has been carried on almost as continuously as before that time, and we are therefore safe in adding another $2000 making the respectable total of $7000.

Any modern-day observer reading Gilbert's account written in 1928 would ask: Should the seminarians have been asked to work so hard while they were in school? Gilbert addressed that question in the last paragraph of *Breaking Ground* (p. 70):

> There have been some boys and perhaps some parents who thought that manual labor was beneath their dignity, but they were a weak minority. The general good health of the boys, and their no small prowess in athletics owes no small debt to this work. And then there is the question of poverty.

The Seminary could not afford to pay out a sum of twelve or fifteen hundred dollars annually for labor while thirty or forty husky young roughnecks looked on. And finally there

---

The Early Rectors

Msgr. William W. Hume (1915-Feb. 1919)

Rt. Rev. Patrick J. Geehan (1925-1928)

Very Rev. Matthew J. Gilbert (1928-1933)

Rev. Sidney M. Metzger, Pro Rector (1933-1940)

Very Rev. Marcus A. Valenta, Temporary Rector (July 1940-October 1, 1940)

(From *25 Years a Seminary,* p. 16)

is the question of justice. It cost at least $300 to maintain a student for a year in the Seminary, and yet even those who pay in full are asked to pay only the sum of $225 and no one can complain if he is called upon to expend a little honest sweat in exchange for the $75 balance.

There can be no doubt that the priest-faculty at St. John's Seminary provided both the academic excellence and a model of hard work and holiness. They turned out priests who were well-educated, open to adventure, and ingrained with the belief that holiness was more than saying prayers and going to mass. For these first priests who were formed on Dwyer Avenue or on Adele Street or in the shadow of the first shrine of the Immaculate Conception in this hemisphere, holiness included throwing your entire self—body and spirit—into whatever the project required. Following in the footsteps of their esteemed faculty members, they learned that prayer needed to be balanced with hard work, and every hour of study needed at least an hour of manual labor so that blood would continue to flow to the brain.

St. John's Seminary Campus, c. 1925 (Photo:
Archdiocese of San Antonio, 1874-1974)

In 1919, Msgr. Hume, the father of the seminary, had been called into service by Archbishop Shaw of New Orleans and he persuaded Fr. Patrick Geehan to be available for the position of Chancellor of the Diocese. Drossaerts also appointed Geehan as acting rector, a position he held until 1925 when he was named rector.

With Geehan as rector, the student body grew, the seminary grounds were tamed and beautified, and the diocesan clergy began to be more confident that the seminary would be able to provide a locally prepared clergy for the future of the diocese. In 1926, the Apostolic Delegate Pietro Biondi visited the seminary as Apostolic Visitator. Though "he was critical of the institution's extramural athletic activities and its teaching of Philosphy in English instead of in Latin" (*Priest Forever*, p. 33), more importantly, during Geehan's tenure, ten well-prepared men were ordained to serve the Church in the Dioceses of El Paso, Kansas City, MO, and San Antonio.

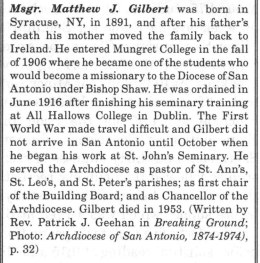

Msgr. Matthew J. Gilbert was born in Syracuse, NY, in 1891, and after his father's death his mother moved the family back to Ireland. He entered Mungret College in the fall of 1906 where he became one of the students who would become a missionary to the Diocese of San Antonio under Bishop Shaw. He was ordained in June 1916 after finishing his seminary training at All Hallows College in Dublin. The First World War made travel difficult and Gilbert did not arrive in San Antonio until October when he began his work at St. John's Seminary. He served the Archdiocese as pastor of St. Ann's, St. Leo's, and St. Peter's parishes; as first chair of the Building Board; and as Chancellor of the Archdiocese. Gilbert died in 1953. (Written by Rev. Patrick J. Geehan in *Breaking Ground*; Photo: *Archdiocese of San Antonio, 1874-1974*), p. 32)

A Major Seminary Emerges

Unforeseen circumstances in 1928-29 brought the dream of Archbishop Shaw and all those founders of St. John's into reality. The major seminaries that usually received the graduates of St. John's for their theology studies (St. Meinrad's (Indiana), Kenrick (St. Louis), Little Rock (Arkansas) were filled and could not receive the St. John's students. The Archbishop decided to recall the men who had been studying at St. Meinrad's and, with those ready to move on to Philosophy and Theology from St. John's, a total of twenty-one men entered St. John's Major Seminary. Another twenty-six students continued in the Minor Seminary.

Newly-ordained Fr. Sidney Metzger, member of the opening class of St. John's in 1915, returned from his studies in Rome with doctorates in Theology and Canon Law in 1928. He was immediately assigned to the faculty of St. John's.

Rev. Matthew J. Gilbert, who had served on the faculty of St. John's since its inception, became the rector in 1928, serving until 1933. With a faculty consisting of Fr. Metzger, Fr. Francis J. Hullweg, OMI, Fr. Garriga (who was also serving as pastor of St. Cecilia's), and Fr. Mitsch, Gilbert began to forge a Major Seminary (*Priest Forever*, p. 34-35).

In addition to their studies, athletics, and work on the seminary buildings and grounds, the seminarians (usually around 75 students) followed a schedule that began at 5:45 A.M. on weekdays for the Major Seminarians and 6:15 A.M. for the Minor Seminarians. Classes began each day, Monday through Saturday, at 8:15 after morning prayer, meditation, Mass, and breakfast. At 10:00 daily, the Minor Seminarians and Philosophers took a fifteen minute break before continuing lessons that would conclude at 11:45 for the noon break which included the Examination of Conscience, dinner, a visit to the Blessed Sacrament and thirty minutes of recreation. Two more hours of studies followed then outdoor recreation (translate: working on the yards!) and showers before studying and saying the rosary before supper which was served at 6:00. Following supper was another forty-five minutes of recreation and a two-hour study hall before spiritual reading at 9:15 and "lights out" at 9:30 (*25 Years a Seminary*, p. 37).

In 1933, having served for seventeen years as a faculty member and rector, Fr. Gilbert resigned from St. John's Seminary. Archbishop Drossaerts, no doubt recognizing the need for strong

> The longest serving archdiocesan priest faculty member at St. John's Seminary was Rev. Victor A. Sullivan who taught at St. John's from 1920 through 1941. A native of Indiana, Sullivan was a "late vocation" who entered the seminary at St. Meinrad Abbey after the death of his wife.—*Priest Forever*, p. 28-29

leadership that knew the Church from the point of view of the Vatican as well as a man with deep roots in the Archdiocese, appointed

Rev. Sidney M. Metzger[7], native of Fredericksburg, TX, as pro-Rector[8] and prefect of discipline (*Priest Forever*, p. 39).

Metzger had been a member of the first seminary class and he was remembered by Garriga as a small boy tugging a large suitcase who announced himself at the door of the Dwyer Avenue house: "I am Sidney Metzger from Fredericksburg and I want to be a priest."

By this time the future priests of St. John's were being exposed to a wide variety of experiences. The choir sang at funerals of dignitaries and at joyous Archdiocesan occasions. The "outside world" found a place inside the seminary when a radio was purchased for the Major House with money the men had earned parking

Archbishop Arthur Jerome Drossaerts (1862-1940), the first archbishop of the Catholic Archdiocese of San Antonio, son of Cornelius and Sophie Drossaerts, was born in Holland in 1862. He studied at a number of seminaries in Holland and was ordained by Bishop Adrian Godschalk of Bois le Duc on June 15, 1889. That same year Drossaerts traveled to the United States at the request of Archbishop Janssens of New Orleans, and served in several Louisiana parishes before he was consecrated Bishop of San Antonio in 1918. During his tenure as Ordinary, Drossaerts built more than sixty churches and fifty schools, the most significant of which was St. John's Seminary. He kept the old Spanish missions alive and went without salary in order to assist poor parishes with expenses. Pope Pius XI honored Drossaerts for his aid to those fleeing from religious persecution in Mexico. Drossaerts died in Santa Rosa Hospital in San Antonio on September 8, 1940."

From: Carlos E. Castañeda, **Our Catholic Heritage in Texas** (7 vols., Austin: Von Boeckmann-Jones, 1936); Catholic Archives of Texas, Files, Austin. And Mary H. Ogilvie, "DROSSAERTS, ARTHUR JEROME," **Handbook of Texas Online** (http://www.tshaonline.org/ handbook/online /articles/ fdr07), accessed December 15, 2010. (Photo: *Archdiocese of San Antonio, 1874-1974*, p. 28)

---

[7] Most Rev. Sidney Metzger's biography is in Appendix I.

[8] This designation is not explained in any of the materials extant.

cars for the various circuses that raised their tents across Mitchell Street. The curriculum continued to provide the young men with all the basics in Latin, as well as consistent work in the Spanish language.

Work on the grounds continued into the 1930's: the distinguishing lily ponds were completed and the seminarians built a grotto to Our Lady.

By 1934-35 there were eighty-three students enrolled at St. John's and Drossaerts Hall was at maximum usage. Archbishop Drossaerts, recognizing the need for expanded facilities, worked with his seminary supporters to find money for a new building. An anonymous benefactor provided Drossaerts with the ability to build Venerable Antonio Margil Hall in 1935.

In its first twenty-five years, St. John's Seminary contributed to the preparation of eighty-five priests, most of whom served the Archdiocese of San Antonio. But men were also ordained for the Church in the Dioceses of El Paso, TX; St. Augustine, FL; Alexandria, LA; Dallas, TX; Corpus Christi, TX; and Lafayette, LA. Of those ordained to priesthood the Most Rev. Sidney M. Metzger, was appointed Bishop of El Paso on January 5, 1940

The close of the decade of the 1930's saw events that would deeply impact the future of St. John's.

Archbishop Arthur J. Drossaerts died on September 8, 1940, having served the Archdiocese of San Antonio for twenty-two years. The legacy that he left behind in terms of St. John's Seminary was reflective of his love for the people of his archdiocese. St. John's stood on a beautiful campus in a sturdy, permanent structure that had already been expanded to accommodate the growth of the student body. A superior faculty that had been educated in seminaries throughout the world offered a challenging curriculum in both the Minor and Major Seminaries. But more importantly, the viability of the seminary had been entrusted to both the priests of the archdiocese as well as competent and resourceful lay people.

The Archbishop had ordained most of the fifty priests who had entered St. John's Seminary from local families to become priests for the San Antonio Archdiocesan Catholic communities. And he had their loyalty and their love.

Although the early accounts of the foundation of St. John's Seminary note Archbishop Shaw, Msgr. Hume and Bishop Garriga as "the founders," a closer look at the first twenty-five years might enlarge the circle. All of the men included in the story of the foundation of San Antonio's first seminary laid the foundation for an institute that has survived for one hundred years. S o m e were teachers; others were confessors and counselors; others were disciplinarians and coaches. Jack, Fr. Alphonse Wendling's dog, and Tosca, Fr. Gilbert's dog, just loved the boys as dogs do.

The priests who came out of St. John's Seminary in its first twenty-five years built dozens of parishes in the Archdiocese of San Antonio, and brought the sacraments to countless individual Catholics. They served in towns small and large. They served as chaplains of hospitals and schools. These men had built up their spiritual muscles while studying and praying; they had built up their physical muscles while tending buildings and the campus.

And the lay women and laymen whom both Bishop Shaw and Archbishop Drossaerts drew into building up the seminary became proud stewards in that first quarter-century, a role the laity would play until the present day.

CHAPTER TWO

LAS HERMANAS JOSEFINAS
≈ A CENTURY OF SERVICE

*During the entire thirty-five years since [the seminary's] foundation, the domestic department . . . has been in the hands of the "Hermanas Josefinas," the Josephine Sisters of Mexico City; and it would be difficult to find a more devoted or hard working group of Sisters. On Dwyer Avenue they occupied a very small house across the street from the Seminary, in Highland Park they were housed in a flimsy shack scarcely worthy to be called a house, and since the new Seminary was built, their home has been a large frame structure formerly used as an annex to St. Joseph's Orphanage, and previous to that as the residence of a large number of refugee priests during the troubled times in Mexico. (**Diamond Jubilee 1874-1949**, p. 186)*

The Founding of Las Hermanas Josefinas

José Maria Aguilera Vilaseca, came to Mexico from Spain as a member of the Congregation of the Missions (known in the US as Vincentians). While a Vincentian, Vilaseca founded missions among various indigenous peoples. He had a deep devotion to St. Joseph; in 1872 he founded the Missionaries of St. Joseph and, with Miss Cesarean Ruiz de Esparza y Dávalos, also founded the Missionary Sisters of St. Joseph (Hermanas Josefinas).

In 1877, Vilaseca left the Vincentians and professed his vows as a member of the Missionaries of St. Joseph.

During the tumultuous years of the 1860's and '70's in Mexico the Catholic Church experienced severe persecution. The

Hermanas Josefinas filled a vacuum in both hospitals and orphanages left by the departure of the exiled Daughters of Charity.

The Josefinas grew substantially over the next forty years and operated hospitals, orphanages, and schools, in addition to staffing the domestic departments in seminaries.

From 1872 until the end of the 19th century the membership of the Hermanas Josefinas expanded. As their numbers increased throughout the twentieth century, so did their ministries. Today, the Hermanas Josefinas are located in Mexico, the US, Central and South America, and Angola. The Sisters minister in preparatory schools (colegios), orphanages, seminaries, parishes, health care institutions, and evangelization projects.

Fr. José Maria Vilaseca, Founder of the Hermanas Josefinas (Photo www. hermanas josefinas. org. mx)

Over the past one hundred and forty years, their understanding of their charism has solidified and deepened. Cesarea Ruiz de Esparza y Dávalos had given up a secular life at age nineteen and professed private vows before meeting Vilaseca. Her writings reveal a spirit imbued with love of God and love of humanity. Conscious of her own frailties, she embraced the least of God's children and those whose outward life suggested that they were sinners. For Cesarea, even the branded sinner was the dwelling place of God.

Cesarea Ruiz de Esparza y Dávalos, Foundress of the Hermanas Josefinas (Photo www.hermanas josefinas. org. mx)

Today's Sisters continue to express their charism in incarnational language: the life of Jesus lives in those who call out to be served. Like St. Joseph, the Josefinas have chosen a hidden life of service to those in need (www.hermanas josefinas.org.mx).

Sor Guadalupe Mondragón who has been at Assumption since 1965 noted[9] that the Josefinas are not cloistered, but that in addition to St. Joseph of Good Counsel, their two patrons are St. Teresa of Avila and St. John of the Cross, both Carmelites. The descriptive word that she used for their way of living religious life is not monastic, but "cartujo" which references a "life of prayer, devotion to community, and service lived close to home" in the tradition of the Carthusians. The Sisters experience their community life of prayer and caring for one another as the well-spring from which they are able to serve those in need (Mondragón Interview, July 2013).

Coming to San Antonio[10]

In the years following the founding of Las Hermanas Josefinas, Mexico experienced a relatively quiet political period under President Diaz. However, the early years of the twentieth century were filled once again with political tension which led to revolution. The Catholic Church came under direct persecution during the presidency of Venustiano Carranza (1915-1920) with dozens of bishops, priests, and religious fleeing to the US, many to the Archdiocese of San Antonio. The Superior of the Missionaries of St. Joseph (the Josephite Fathers), Rev. José Maria Tronsoco, SSJ, established himself and his community members in San Antonio where he served on the first seminary faculty until he returned to Mexico in 1916. During this time period, a group of Las Hermanas Josefinas found themselves isolated in Monterrey,

---

[9]   Interview with Sor Guadalupe Mondragón: July 2013

[10] The material in this section and the following ones include material from two essays on the Hermanas Josefinas by unknown authors. Both are housed in the Archdiocesan Archives. One of the two short papers, "A History of How the Josephine Sisters Arrived in San Antonio, Texas," was written in 1972; the other paper, "Hermanas Josefinas," is undated.

unable to be in contact with their motherhouse in Mexico City. Msgr. William Hume, Bishop John Shaw's chancellor, learned of their precarious situation and interceded with the American Consul in Monterrey on their behalf. The American Consul sent his own son to rescue the eight nuns in Monterrey and bring them to the US. Their first temporary shelter was with the Ursulines on the northern edge of downtown San Antonio, but the Bishop later moved them to Our Lady of the Lake Convent, the recently built motherhouse of the Sisters of Divine Providence on Elmendorf Lake.

At this time, Shaw was developing his vision for a diocesan seminary and he had decided to put the Josefinas in charge of the domestic department of the new institution for priestly formation. When the seminary opened on October 1, 1915, on Dwyer Avenue, four of the eight Sisters who had come from Mexico were settled in a house across the street and the other four Sisters were sent to Nicaragua.

Thus began a one hundred year relationship between the seminarians and faculty members at St. John's and Assumption Seminaries and Las Hermanas Josefinas.

First Residence of Hermanas Josefinas on Dwyer
Street (c. 1915) from Assumption Archives

The first Sisters experienced a number of early challenges. The rationing policies during World War I made providing three meals a day for hungry seminarians and priests difficult. Just as the war was ending, the newly appointed bishop of the Diocese of San Antonio, Arthur J. Drossaerts, decided he wanted to live in the Episcopal Residence which Bishop Shaw had abandoned for the use of the fledgling seminary. Therefore, in the summer of 1918 the seminary was moved to Highland Park, described in archival documents as "a dark, desolate spot filled with brush, very dusty during the dry season and a veritable mud-hole during the rainy one."

While the priest-faculty did its best to upgrade the tumble-down Garden Academy for dormitory space and classrooms for the seminarians, the Josefinas were relegated a three-room broken-down house which "bore out the saying that 'what is not a crack is a skylight.' In the winter it was a freezer, and in the summer, an oven. They frequently found inside the house a variety of animals: snakes, rats, rabbits, and once, even, a coyote" ("A History of How the Josephine Sisters Arrived in San Antonio, Texas", p. 1).

Working conditions for the Sisters at the Highland Park seminary were horrible. "A tunnel which existed under one of the large houses served as kitchen and dining room. They cooked in a huge place which sapped more of their energy, and they made a fire in a stove so small that you could only use splinters and very small pieces of wood . . . when it rained, the kitchen was flooded with three inches of rain so that the cooks were often in the resulting humidity as well, day in and day out" ("A History of . . . the Josephine Sisters", p. 2).

Archbishop Drossaerts focused diocesan resources on building an adequate seminary and by the end of August 1920, the main building, eventually called Drossaerts Hall at St. John's Seminary at the corner of Mitchell and Mission Road was inhabitable. The home for the Sisters was little better than the one in Highland Park. At more than one time, due to challenging work conditions, the Superiors of the Josefinas asked that this mission be closed. But that was never to be.

When the Congregation of the Missions (Vincentians) took over St. John's Seminary in 1941, they found the Josefinas on duty. Though not formally related to the Vincentians, the Sisters later staffed several Vincentian seminaries, including DeAndreis Seminary in Lemont, IL, which trained Vincentian priests. And they are considered members of the Vincentian "family"—though as "cousins."

In 1963 *The DeAndrein* (Vol. 33, Feb. 1963), a Vincentian publication, carried an article by a Vincentian priest in celebration of the ninety years (1872-1963) of service to the Church by the Josefinas since their founding. The unnamed author's reflections on the Josefinas

> *They give us that extra push . . . an encouraging word when you think you're at your wit's end.*
>
> --Miguel Moreno, Seminarian for the Archdiocese of San Antonio (2012)

reveal the love and esteem that the Sisters called forth from the seminarians at DeAndreis Seminary. Generous to a fault, the Sisters spent the late night hours in the laundry washing, ironing, and folding the seminarians' clothes after having provided breakfast, lunch, and dinner for them throughout the day. The author remembers listening to them sing hymns in Spanish while they worked.

The author, at the time of writing, pondered "how could they do it all? What was the source of all their strength?" In his reflections, he answered his own questions. "Perhaps the best summary of their daily life is the perfect joining of the works of Martha with the prayers of Mary" (*The DeAndrein*, Vol. 33, Feb. 1963, p. 10).

The prayer life of the Josefinas not only supports their vocations and their ministries, but it gives them a fulcrum-like center upon which to balance the many difficulties of the day.

In the 1950's and 1960's it was usual for the various religious communities to ask the Archbishop for specific permission for benediction of the Blessed Sacrament in their conventual chapels. In February 1957, Archbishop Lucey gave the Josefinas at Assumption Seminary the following general and particular days when they could experience Benediction of the Blessed Sacrament.

1. All Sundays and Holydays of Obligation
2. All Doubles of the First and Second Class
3. All days of retreat—annual and monthly
4. All First Fridays
5. On the 12th and 19th of each month (in order to celebrate through the year their patronage under Our Lady of Guadalupe whose feast is December
   12th and St. Joseph whose feast is March 19th)
6. Thursday of each week (the day traditionally dedicated to the Blessed   Sacrament because of the institution of the Eucharist on Holy Thursday)
7. On each day of Church Unity Octave (the Feast of the Chair of St. Peter [January 18] through Feast of St. Paul [January 25])

8. On each Friday during Lent
9. On the anniversary of the Election of Pope Pius XII (March 2)
10. On each day of May in conjunction with special devotions in honor of the Blessed Virgin Mary
11. On each day of the Novena for the Feast of the Assumption in August
12. On the Feast of the Exaltation of the Holy Cross (September 14)
13. On each day of October up to and including November 2nd
14. On each day of the Novena for the Feast of the Immaculate Conception
15. On each day of the Novena for the Feast of the Nativity of Our Lord (Christmas)

The ritual of Benediction requires the presence of a priest, ritual prayers and singing, and assumes that the Blessed Sacrament had been exposed in a monstrance for prayer for a segment of time before the ritual blessing.

This focus on prayer before the Blessed Sacrament—a modern day image of sitting at the feet of Jesus—underscores that the works of a "Martha" are empty without the quiet prayer of a "Mary".

The Sisters continued to serve at the St. John's location until it was closed in 1970; they began serving at Assumption at its opening in 1952.

Assumption Seminary

Their first home at Assumption Seminary was the "President's House," which faced Ashby Place near the corner of Epworth Street, and unfortunately did not live up to its "title". This edifice had been built prior to World War II for the president of Westmoreland College and later became the home of the President of Trinity University while Trinity occupied the Woodlawn location. The house was just a step away from uninhabitable, but, as they had done for so many years before, the Sister made do. Stories reveal that the Sisters were not the only residents of this building. Rats, snakes, squirrels, and possums also occupied parts of the building, often keeping the Sisters awake at night with their nocturnal scurryings.

In the 1950's and 1960's the Sisters were young and they were told not to talk to the seminarians. But as they realized that the young men were often lonely and afraid, they made them individual pies on Saturdays as a treat, expressing their care without words.

Today, Las Hermanas Josefinas who serve Assumption Seminary, all of retirement age, live in two convents on seminary property at the same location where the President's house stood. They are within a short walking distance from the kitchen-dining hall, which has been named St. Joseph Hall in their honor. These houses were built in the early 1970's when the close of St. John's Minor Seminary brought the sophomore, junior, and senior classes to Assumption. This change consolidated all of the Josefinas at Assumption. Sisters who could not be employed at Assumption after the close of St. John's were assigned to the Alexian Brothers Medical Center in Elk Grove, IL, where they joined the dietary department.

Madre Esperanza Ponce, HJ

On April 11, 1954, Madre Esperanza died, the first Josefina Sister to die in San Antonio. Mother Esperanza had come to St. John's Seminary in 1939 and "soon endeared herself to all by her deeply religious spirit and her quiet sense of humor. She was the founding superioress of the Josephine Sisters at Assumption" (Priest Forever, p. 62).

At her death, Assumption Seminary's rector, Rev. Gilmore H. Guyot, CM, purchased four cemetery plots at San Fernando Cemetery for the use of the Josefinas. This investment solidified the plan that the Josefinas would not be returning to Mexico, their homeland, even at death. They had come to know that their missionary character required them to remain in the mission country where God had put them as ministers even after death.

The stone for Mother Esperanza's grave was purchased by the seminarians who were at her bedside as she was dying.

At this time the remains of five other Hermanas Josefinas have been interred at San Fernando Cemetery: Sor DeAngeles, Sor DeJesus, Sor Carmelita, Sor Margarita, and Sor Marta.

The present convents for those who serve Assumption Seminary are simply furnished with a small chapel dominating the living arrangement. Sor Mondragón pointed out that the people of the area have come to know them and some ask to have their children make First Communion in the convent chapel. Some older couples want to renew their marriage vows as they celebrate an anniversary. Other people just come to join them at Mass.

Their care is evident at all times whether it is mending ripped pants or a ripped ego. They have come to know my family . . . they offer me good advice . . . a pat on the back keeps us going.

--Freddie Perez, Seminarian for the Diocese of San Angelo

As Las Hermanas Josefinas come to an end of a century of service to seminarians, faculty and staff at St. John's-Assumption Seminary, Sor Guadalupe Mondragón reflected on their reality. She acknowledged that the ones at the seminary now are "the last ones." Though they are looking for vocations to their special ministry here, their Sisters in Mexico want to evangelize in Oaxaca or serve the poor in Angola.

With bright twinkling brown eyes, Sor Mondragón said that she and the others have become family for the young men who come to study for the priesthood. "We meet their families when they come; we make them soup when they are ill; we pray for their vocations along the way; we rejoice with them at their ordinations."

With a broad smile, Sor Mondragón relished her forty-plus years at Assumption: "The young men made me young," she confessed.

Over 600 priests have been touched by the Mexican Sisters who fed both their spirits and their bodies. Msgr. Lawrence Stuebben spoke with heart-felt emotion at a recent (2012) gala in honor of Las Hermanas Josefinas: "By example—a life of service, prayer, joy, and smiles they have been a blessing to faculty and to the seminarians. We learned from them what we could not have learned in books; we saw God in them and we were blessed" (Speech given at 2012 fundraiser for the retirement needs of Las Hermanas Josefinas).

In Retirement

In addition to the Sisters pictured below who have ministered at Assumption in recent years, another dozen Sisters who served the seminary in the past are in retirement in their convent on John Adams Street near St. Paul Catholic Church. Beginning in 2012, a project to enlarge the convent on John Adams Street and create a retirement endowment for the Hermanas Josefinas was begun by the Archdiocese.

Las Hermanas Josefinas at Assumption, December 2013

Seated: L to R—Sor Rosa Saldivar, Sor Bernardita
Garduño, Sor Rosa Aguinaga, Sor Bernarda Zuniga, Sor Celia
Aceguedo, Sor Irma Vazquez, Sor Mariada Refugio Cerda

Standing: L to R—Sor Lucia Anaya, Sor Francisca
Chávez, Sor Catallina Garcia, Sor Guadalupe Mondrigón,
Sor Maria de Jesus Cruz, Sor Josefina Hernandez,
Sor Guadalupe Trujillo, Sor Josefina Ruiz

(Photo by Christopher Munoz, Seminarian,
Archdiocese of San Antonio)

The Mission of Las Hermanas Josefinas

Aware of being sent by the Father and with openness to the Holy Spirit, we present Jesus Christ and his Gospel in the Church. Responsible with the laity, with the inner life force, and through constant updating, we collaborate in order to evangelize all peoples. As did St. Joseph, we care for the Life of Jesus in others through various ministries, preferably to the poorest among us. We discern our apostolic presences in light of the gospel and the signs of the times, choosing our ministerial locations to better serve our brothers and sisters. (from the website of Las Hermanas Josefinas)

CHAPTER THREE

BUILDING UP SACRED GROUNDS

The Continuing Development of the Campus Buildings at St. John's

> **Antonio Margil de Jesus** was ordained a Franciscan priest in 1682 in Spain and the next year was sent as a missionary to New Spain where he was assigned to the College of the Holy Cross in Queretaro, Mexico. In 1706 he founded the College of Our Lady of Guadalupe of Zacatecas and from there did missionary work in Texas. In 1716-1717 Margil worked in East Texas, at the missions established there, but due to conflicts between the Spaniards and the French, the missions were soon abandoned. Margil moved to San Antonio where in 1720 he founded Mission San Jose. He died in 1726 in Mexico City. One of the most legendary missionaries in New Spain, Margil is under consideration for sainthood. His death is observed on August 6th in the Church calendar. Donald E. Chipman, "MARGIL DE JESUS, ANTONIO," **Handbook of Texas Online** (http://www.tshaonline.org/handbook/online/articles/fma45), accessed December 10, 2012. Published by the Texas State Historical Association.

Bishop Robert Emmet Lucey, the Bishop of Amarillo, Texas, was named Archbishop of San Antonio on January 23, 1941. He inherited a large and growing archdiocese that had already spawned the Diocese of Corpus Christi in 1912; the Diocese of El Paso in 1914; and the Diocese of Amarillo in 1926. It reached from south Texas to north of the Hill Country and from the Colorado River on the east to the Rio Grande in the west. Under Archbishop Lucey, the Province of San Antonio included the Dioceses of Oklahoma City, Dallas, Amarillo, Austin, Galveston, Corpus Christi, and El Paso (*Diamond Jubilee*, p. 303).

The new Archbishop also inherited a growing seminary. From its humble beginnings on Dwyer Street with seventeen seminarians and a faculty of four, St. John's Seminary, now a

After a period of slow growth during the 1930s, San Antonio's population increased by 61 percent during the wartime boom of the 1940s, to reach 408,442 in 1950. . . In the 1950s the city grew by almost 44 percent to reach 587,718 in 1960. [from T.R. Fehrenbach, "SAN ANTONIO, TX," **Handbook of Texas Online**(http://www.tshaonline.org/ handbook/ online/ articles/hds02), accessed December 13, 2012. Published by the Texas State Historical Association.]

major seminary located just north of Mission Conception, had a student body of nearly one hundred and a faculty of eleven archdiocesan priests. By the end of the 1930's the seminarian population had even outgrown Drossaerts Hall. The faculty could no longer live on the campus even though a second residence building, Margil Hall, had been erected in 1935-1936 with the help of an anonymous donor. The new building was named for Fray Antonio Margil de Jesus.

In the fall of 1941 St. John's started its second quarter-century under the auspices of the new Archbishop. Over the summer of 1941, Lucey had contracted with the Congregation of the

Archbishop Robert E. Lucey, a native of Los Angeles, California, brought a wealth of experience to the Archdiocese of San Antonio when he became its sixth Ordinary on March 27, 1941. He organized the Catholic Welfare Bureau, the Catholic Action Office; called the Vincentian Fathers to staff St. John's Seminary and focused his efforts on Social Justice issues. He established the Confraternity of Christian Doctrine on an archdiocesan basis and established the Office of Catholic Schools. Lucey was nationally recognized for his efforts on behalf of Hispanic Americans and African Americans. In 1950 he was appointed to President Harry S. Truman's Commission on Migratory Labor in 1950 and in 1953, a year before Brown v. Board of Education, Archbishop Lucey integrated all of the Catholic schools in his Archdiocese.

Though a social liberal, Lucey was an ecclesiastical conservative and he found himself entangled with his priests over justice issues regarding farm workers in the Rio Grande Valley in 1965 and later there were disagreements over the war in Vietnam.

His priests challenged Lucey and requested his resignation. An investigation by Rome ensued and Lucey resigned in 1969. (from en.wikipedia. org/wiki/ Robert_Emmet_Lucey; Photo: *Archdiocese of San Antonio, 1874-1974*, p. 30)

Missions, also known as Vincentians[11], of Perryville, MO, to take over St. John's Seminary. Due to population growth in San Antonio and the rest of the Archdiocese, the San Antonio clergy were needed in Archdiocesan ministries.

In addition, during the Second World War, as other dioceses began to send their major seminarians to San Antonio, the buildings at St. John's became more inadequate. Lucey wanted to look for property that could accommodate a new facility for the major seminary while maintaining the minor seminary at the St. John's campus. However, the war effort siphoned off all possibility of investing in a new complex.

The people of the Archdiocese remained very loyal to the future of the seminary despite the challenges of World War II and its aftermath. A fundraising campaign to acquire monies to build a new major seminary was quite successful, but post-war construction costs made launching the project cost-prohibitive. So, as a stop-gap measure that would offer relief to the bulging campus buildings at St. John's, Lucey and his advisors made the decision to add another building to the southside campus.

St. Mary's Hall, completed in 1947 and named for Archbishop Lucey's mother Mary Lucey, consisted of an auditorium and several classrooms.

Use of the St. John's Seminary buildings by both the major and minor seminaries continued, but Lucey and his advisors had not lost the dream of re-locating the major seminary.

---

[11]   The Congregation of the Missions was founded by St. Vincent de Paul in 1624.

St. John's Seminary Campus, c. 1950; Assumption Archives

Another "Hand-Me-Down Facility"

During its ten years (1942-1952) on what their history calls "the Woodlawn Campus," Trinity University's enrollment had reached 2,000 students, largely due to returning veterans and the growing population of San Antonio. Established in 1869 in the small village of Tehuacana, Texas, forty-six miles east of Waco (www.texas escapes.com/CentralTexasTowns North/Tehuacana-Texas/accessed on December 14, 2012), the Presbyterian-affiliated university had moved to its second location in Waxahachie in 1902. Waxahachie was more accessible but that location also provided little growth potential and so, in 1941 . . .

. . . Trinity accepted an invitation from the San Antonio Chamber of Commerce to establish a strong Protestant institution of higher learning in the Alamo city. San Antonio business leaders

promised financial support and facilitated a merger
of Trinity and the University of San Antonio, a
small Methodist institution . . . (www.**trinity**.edu/
accessed on December 19, 2012)

The merger gave Trinity facilities on the near West side of
San Antonio.

Westmoreland College, the Methodist-owned school on
Woodlawn Avenue, had begun as a two-year college for women
in 1894. Then in 1936 it had changed its name to the University
of San Antonio before it was subsumed by Trinity University in
1941 (*Called to Serve*, p. 27-28). During and after the war, the
growing Presbyterian university added military barracks and
Quonset huts to the Administration Building, the President's
house, and Mary-Catherine Hall. Between the barracks and
the permanent structures, Trinity was able to accommodate
their growing post-war student body into the early 1950's (www.
trinity.edu/ accessed on December 14, 2012).

Mary-Catherine Hall, date unknown; Assumption Archives

The Archdiocese was still looking for a location for its
major seminary when the property occupied by Trinity became

available. "After burying miraculous (sic) medals[12] about the campus of Trinity (University), prayers were answered when . . . the Archdiocese . . . at last was able to buy the university and immediately plans were begun to convert Trinity into a seminary" ("The Preface," *1952-1953 The Student Diary*, archived at Assumption Seminary). The Archdiocese purchased the Trinity property on Woodlawn Avenue in 1952 for $265,000 and opened Assumption Seminary, a major seminary of the Roman Catholic Church in September of 1952 with eighty-five students (*Called to Serve*, p. 28).

With prayer, much was accomplished between May and September of 1952. The dedication took place on September 24, 1952, in the presence of 5,000 people with Cardinal Samuel Stritch of Chicago blessing the buildings. Among the dignitaries in attendance were Bishop Sidney Metzger of El Paso, an alumnus and former rector of St. John's; and Bishop Mariano Garriga of Corpus Christi, a founder and former faculty member of St. John's Seminary (*Called to Serve*, p. 28-29).

Retrofitting a Campus: a Fifty-Year Project

The campus at Woodlawn Avenue and West French was built around the four-story administration building on West French which was eventually taken down because the top floors had been condemned and only the ground floor was usable. Mary-Catherine

---

[12]   Catherine Labouré (1806-1976), a nursing sister with the Daughters of Charity of St. Vincent de Paul at the Visitation Convent on Rue de Bac in Paris, was a visionary who had multiple experiences of the Blessed Virgin Mary. In these encounters, the Blessed Virgin asked her to have a medal struck that is today called the Miraculous Medal (en.wikipedia.org/wiki/Catherine_Labouré).

Hall[13] which had been a women's dormitory at Trinity was re-dedicated under the patronage of the Blessed Virgin Mary and St. Catherine Labouré. It served as a dormitory for 84 seminarians and six of the Vincentian Fathers who conducted the seminary ("Preface," *1952-53 The Student Diary*). In recent years, Mary-Catherine Hall was taken down to provide space for new structures.

Another building, the President's House for Trinity University, became the home of the Hermanas Josefinas who would continue their services at both the Assumption campus and the St. John's campus (*Called to Serve*, p. 60).

A gymnasium, various military barracks and four Quonset huts completed the property. These buildings served as classrooms and residence space for faculty and students. The largest Quonset hut which had housed the library for Trinity University was retrofitted to serve the seminary as its chapel ("The Preface," *1952-1953 The Student Diary*).

Though all of the original buildings provided enough space for classrooms and living quarters, they were old and in poor condition. The Archdiocese began to improve the campus almost immediately. In 1954, a swimming pool and a handball court were constructed giving the men, who seldom left the campus, some recreational opportunities in addition to working on beautifying the lawns.

In 1955, ground was broken for St. Alice Residence Hall which was partly financed by the Catholic Extension Society. Archbishop William O'Brien, the Society's president, dedicated the residence

---

[13] Mary Catherine Hall, a 24,000 square feet building in Spanish eclectic style, had been designed by Adams and Adams, the architects who designed Thomas Jefferson High School located on Donaldson at Wilson Ave. Mary Catherine Hall was built by Mr. and Mrs. R. M. McFarlin as a tribute to Mrs. McFarlin's mother, Mary Catherine Bernard. The seminary used the building as a dormitory for some years and then the building was taken over by the Mexican American Cultural Center in 1972 until the Center moved into its new quarters in 2000. (Richelieu, "Survey would assess historic S.A. buildings", *San Antonio Express-News*, Nov. 18, 2000, p. 1B/3B) The building has since been torn down.

in February 1956 under the patron saint of his mother, Alice O'Brien. The $320,000 building contained sixty-five rooms, each housing two students (*Called to Serve*, p. 30-31).

In addition to upgrading the living quarters for the seminarians, the Archdiocesan plan included improvements to classrooms. Four new classrooms, a dining hall (refectory) and kitchen were begun in late 1956.

The classroom building, named in honor of St. Anthony de Padua the patron saint of the City and the Archdiocese, had facilities for science and speech labs[14]. This building cost the Archdiocese more than $200,000, but the growing numbers of seminarians in the mid-1950's warranted the investment. By 1958 there were 172 students at the seminary and nineteen men were ordained that year (*Called to Serve*, p. 29-39).

Improvements to the campus of Assumption continued throughout the third quarter century of St. John's/Assumption Seminaries. An old wooden-structured gymnasium on the west end of the campus (where the present swimming pool is located) had been used for clergy days. However, it was uncomfortable, the floor squeaked and it was an eye sore. Another building that had little usefulness was the administration building. "It was not in good shape and was a hazard. The sisters were frightened because it was invaded by strangers and prowlers by night" (*Called to Serve*, p. 39). Both buildings were taken down in the mid-1960's.

New buildings taking the place of the administration building were Shaw Hall, named for Bishop John W. Shaw, the bishop of San Antonio at the time of the seminary's founding; and a Student Union Building, both dedicated on October 9, 1966. The Student Union Building (known familiarly as the SUB) was dedicated Padua Hall in honor of the patron saint of San Antonio, but that name has never been used (*Called to Serve*, p. 38).

---

[14]   At this time, Assumption Seminary was both a college seminary and a major seminary and specialized classrooms and labs were still needed.

St. Edith and St. Florence Chapel ≈ Our Lady's Chapel

Since the beginning of their occupation of the former Trinity University campus, Assumption seminarians used a Quonset hut, which had served Trinity as a library, for a chapel. The seminarian (unknown) who wrote the "Preface" in the *1952-1953 The Student Diary* saw the Quonset hut chapel with kind eyes.

> The Chapel is extremely simple, and yet, extremely beautiful. This simplicity can never grow old nor lose its beauty. The altar is the focal point of the chapel. As everything in the chapel the altar is plain, simple and beautiful. The table of the altar extends forward and sideways several feet from its base and is adorned in the center of the base with a silver Franciscan Cross . . . The Sanctuary is covered with asphalt tile and has no altar rail. The pews, walls, floors and altar blend comfortably in their light tans, cream, brown and gray shades . . . directly behind the altar is the sacristy . . . Beyond the sacristy is a large room containing six altars for private masses of the faculty and visiting clergy.
>
> We are justly proud of our Chapel because of the honor and glory it must give to the Prisoner of Love Who is our motivating force on [sic] the holy Priesthood (*1952-1953 The Student Diary*).

Later alumni do not carry such fond memories of the old Quonset hut chapel. They remember stifling heat and roaring fans in a building that did not have the potential to be a prayerful liturgical space. In the meantime, as Assumption had moved into the 1960's, the student body had grown to more than 140 students, with more than 40% being transfer students from dioceses throughout the US (*Called to Serve*, p. 44).

However, the physical inadequacy of the Quonset hut chapel was not the only impetus for a new chapel. The Second Vatican Council (1962-1965) had opened the Church to new liturgical practices and most parishes were remodeling their churches and sanctuaries in terms of the Council directives. After the Council, the seminarians learned to say Mass in English or Spanish. Liturgies included much larger participation of the laity. And sanctuaries had to be reordered so that Mass could be celebrated with the presider facing the congregation.

The Quonset hut chapel would not accommodate the post-Vatican changes needed. The altar could not be turned in order to allow the presider to face the assembly. Though there was no uniform thinking on the placement of the tabernacle immediately after the Vatican Council, of concern to Archbishop Lucey was the fact that the presider would have his back to the tabernacle while saying Mass. The sanctuary did not have sufficient space to allow for the Bishop's Chair. And there were significant difficulties with an altar for exposition of the Blessed Sacrament (Correspondence: Box of Files on Seminary Building, Archdiocesan Archives, San Antonio). A liturgical space designed for the priests of the future Church was needed.

Funds for the chapel had been bequeathed to the Archdiocese by John Cotter Sullivan, a well-known Catholic from a pioneer San Antonio family who had died in 1966. Sullivan's desire was that the chapel be built in memory of his wife, Mrs. Edith Florence Fletcher Sullivan who had preceded him in death in 1962.

O'Neil Ford was born in Pink Hill, Texas, on December 3, 1905. After the death of his father in 1917, Ford moved to Denton, Texas. He attended Northeast State Teachers College in Denton for two years, but was unable to continue his formal education due to financial difficulties. "Instead, he earned an architectural certificate by mail from the International Correspondence Schools of Scranton, Pennsylvania." After his certification, Ford began a long and distinguished career in architecture throughout Texas. His works incorporated bricks, glass, and wood and was deeply rooted in the beauty of Texas. "He was appointed to the National Council on the Arts by President Lyndon B. Johnson, and in 1974 Ford himself was designated a National Historic Landmark by the Council (the only human to ever be given that title)."

In addition to significant works in the Denton area, Ford's architectural achievements in San Antonio include the renovation of La Villita, a number of buildings including the tower at Trinity University, the University of Texas Main Campus in San Antonio, and the Tower of the Americas at Hemisfair Plaza.

Ford died in San Antonio in 1982 at age 76. (en.wikipedia.org/ wiki/O'Neil Ford)

Though Archbishop Lucey had sufficient financial resources for the seminary chapel, the project required a great deal of preparation. O'Neil Ford, well-known San Antonio architect, was engaged to do the design. He asked for another San Antonio architect, Nicanor Salas, to work with him on details. Due to liturgical changes that would be required, Archbishop Lucey wanted a trained Catholic presence to participate in the design of the chapel (Correspondence on the erection of the seminary chapel on file, Catholic Chancery Archives, San Antonio).

The rector of the seminary, Msgr. Roy Rihn, was asked to provide a treatise for Ford which would define the liturgical underpinnings for the chapel. He chose to invite a seminarian for the Diocese of Oklahoma City-Tulsa, James D. White[15], to collaborate with him on the document that would serve as a theological guide for Ford (James D. White, "A Memoir", unpublished).

---

[15]   Rev. James D. White, retired from the Diocese of Tulsa, OK, was very generous in providing the author with a detailed account of his memory of the design of St. Edith and St. Florence Chapel. The author is most appreciative of his memoir-like account which he wrote from his retirement residence in the Diocese of San Bernardino, CA.

Msgr. Rihn also retained Frank Kacmarcik to provide liturgical guidance and artistic expertise. Kacmarcik had been trained at the Benedictine University of St. John's in Collegeville, Minnesota, where he was on the faculty. His education also included studies in Paris after the Second World War. In his treatise on the future chapel, Rihn described Kacmarcik: "a specialist in the liturgical arts, [he] is a stage designer for the sacred mysteries and should be made to account for the specific principles involved in every [needed accouterment]" ("New Chapel for Assumption Seminary: A Program for the Guidance of the Architects," Box on Seminary Buildings, Archdiocesan Archives).

Paul Philibert, OP, in his book *From Seeing and Believing* (Pueblo Books, The Liturgical Press, 1995) wrote of Kacmarcik:

> No one has had a greater influence on the development of American religious architecture and art in the past four decades than Frank Kacmarcik. He is a rare personality who possesses understanding, experience, and vision concerning every aspect of church design, furnishings, ritual space, and art.

Coincidentally, James D. White had made the acquaintance of Kacmarcik while he was at Mundelein Seminary in Chicago prior to coming to Assumption Seminary. He thus served the Archdiocese as an unofficial liaison between the local architects and the liturgical artist (White, "A Memoir").

Due to the number of voices in the design of the new chapel, it took over a year to come to final determinations before work could begin. Ground-breaking took place on April 20, 1969. By that time, Msgr. Rihn had been relieved of his duties as rector and the chapel was completed a year later under Msgr. Edward F. Bily, who was named rector following Rev. Carlos Quintana in 1970[16].

Abbot John Klassen, OSB, of St. John's Abbey where Kacmarcik lived out his days as a Benedictine Oblate, said of his work: "There's no architectural cuteness, fluff or fads. Some people would be taken aback by the starkness of a Kacmarcik design, but he believed the uniqueness of each person in the gathering completed the space" (mail.architexturez.net/+/Design-L.V1/archive/msg21319.shtml, accessed on February 25, 2013).

Our Lady's Chapel Today

While generally maintaining the integrity of O'Neill Ford's building and with deference to Frank Kacmarcik's original liturgical environment, the Archdiocese renovated Assumption's chapel in 2013-2014. Directed by Archdiocesan Architect Robert E. Morkovsky, the renovation included re-locating the sanctuary and adding a "retalbo" which stands behind the sanctuary. A new altar which incorporates the altar donated by the Sulpicians in 2005, a new ambo and other liturgical art grace the re-designed sanctuary. New sacristies, a new baptistery/holy water font, improved lighting and sound, new flooring, and new pews ensure a unified worship space in the historic chapel which still holds the mark of O'Neil Ford.

The newly-renovated chapel has been renamed Our Lady's Chapel and was rededicated on March 25, 2014. The dedication plaque recognizes the generosity of the Sullivan family who provided the initial capital for the 1969 St. Edith and St. Florence

---

[16] Rev. Carlos Quintana was the immediate successor of Msgr. Roy Rihn. Quintana resigned in March 1970. At that juncture St. John's was closed and Msgr. Edward Bily who had been the rector at St. John's became the rector of Assumption and the boys of St. John's moved to Assumption to complete their high school education. Quintana transferred to Guatemala where he entered a Benedictine monastery and eventually became involved in seminary work as a Benedictine of Marmion Abbey in that mission country (Vanderholt, *Called to Serve*, p. 51-52).

Chapel. The plaque also recognizes the original designers, Ford, Powell, and Carson with Nicanor Salas and Guido Brothers Construction; Bucheli Religious Architects; Morkovsky & Associates; and J. C. Stoddard Construction. Many, many supporters have provided this striking place of worship for the seminary community (Information from Msgr. Pehl, February 23, 2014).

Sanctuary, Our Lady's Chapel, Assumption
Seminary, 2014 (Photo: Robert Galvan)

The hundreds of men who have prayed in Assumption's chapel as they sought God's will for their lives surely learned in that space that their lives, well-lived as priests or laymen, would indeed serve to add to the "design of the Church".

1969—Archbishop Francis J. Furey

The appointment of Francis J. Furey as Archbishop of San Antonio following the resignation of Archbishop Lucey in 1969 brought a new era to Assumption Seminary.

The upheaval at Assumption generated by Archbishop Lucey discharging the administrators of the seminary was experienced by a drop in enrollment. In the fall of 1969, Assumption had received 146 seminarians from San Antonio and the southwest. But in January of 1970 only 80 students returned for the spring semester, and by 1973 the student body had dropped to 60 students (*Called to Serve*, p. 51 and following).

The decreased number of students meant that the campus was very adequate—even spacious—for those enrolled. Only the convent for the Hermanas Josefinas needed to be improved. Since 1952 they had lived in the brick residence that had been the President's

---

The Mexican American Cultural Center (MACC) began with conversations at a gathering of the Chicano priests group PADRES in 1971. A proposal was presented to Archbishop Francis Furey and then formally developed by the Texas Catholic Conference (of Bishops). Primarily for priests and religious, MACC dealt with issues related to ministry to Hispanics from developing Spanish-language resources for the US Church to providing workshops for dioceses and parishes on cultural and diversity concerns in the ecclesial community.

For thirty-three years, MACC was blessed with the ministry of Sister Rosa Maria Icaza, CCVI who began as a teacher in 1979. Other outstanding contributors include Rev. Virgilio Elizondo, one of the founders. Visiting professors included South American liberation theologians Fr. Gustavo Gutierrez and former priest, Leonardo Boff. Other visitors over its history were Jesuit priest Pedro Arrupe and labor-leader Cesar Chavez.

Dwindling funds led to an evaluation of MACC's future and at the same time Archbishop José Gomez was considering a specialized college that would provide pastoral degrees for those interested in serving the Hispanic Church. The Mexican American Catholic College opened in 2008, embracing the original purpose of the Cultural Center and expanding its potential.

Seminarians, religious and priests from all across the US prepared for ministering to the Spanish-speaking Church in the US at MACC over its 36 year history. ("Nun's new challenge: Mexican American Cultural Center" www. thefreelibrary.com accessed Feb 27, 2013; Lopez, Katherine Jass, Sister Rosa Maria Icaza, CCVI, Leaves 33-year Legacy of Learning at MACC, *Today's Catholic*, July 27, 2012; "Mexican American Cultural Center evolves into Catholic college" www.catholicnews.com accessed Feb. 27, 2013)

House for Trinity University. With the closing of the St. John's campus at the end of the 1970 school year, sophomores, juniors and seniors who wished to finish their high school as seminarians came to live in Mary-Catherine Hall at Assumption. The Hermanas Josefinas who lived at St. John's moved to Assumption as well. Two homes for the Josefinas were completed in June of 1972. For the first time in their almost fifty years of service— since the beginning of the seminary in 1915—the Hermanas Josefinas had a residence which was designed to accommodate their needs (*Called to Serve*, p. 60).

Utility of the various buildings at Assumption began to shift. After his installation as Archbishop in August of 1969, Archbishop Furey resided in Shaw Hall, the seminary's administration building. This began thirty years of Shaw Hall serving as the residence for the Archbishop.[17]

The Mexican American Cultural Center

In 1972, the seminary began to share its facilities with the Mexican American Culture Center.

> An adult education program oriented toward people preparing for bi-cultural ministry, [the Mexican American Cultural Center's] students were mostly professed and ordained religious who already had much experience in ministry. Though there was some difficulty and inconveniences in arranging the schedules of the seminary and MACC, its presence helped create an atmosphere of ministry on campus (*Called to Serve*, p. 60).

With an international staff, the Mexican American Cultural Center served the archdioceses and dioceses throughout Texas

---

[17]   Archbishop Patrick Flores also lived in Shaw Hall after he became the Archbishop. Archbishop Gomez began his tenure by living at Shaw, but had a residence built on the seminary grounds where the present Archbishop lives.

and the Southwest as well as students from South American, Canada, Australia, and Europe. Classes were held bilingually in order to maximize the ability of students to serve the growing numbers of Hispanic Catholics throughout the United States.

By the end of the twentieth century, Mary-Catherine Hall was no longer able to be maintained and was torn down in 2000 in order to accommodate a new facility for the Mexican American Cultural Center[18].

As the Archdiocese moved into the twenty-first century, it experienced a resurgence of vocations to the priesthood. Seminarians lived in St. Alice Hall which only accommodated 55 students as the originally double-rooms had been retrofitted for single occupancy. Fifty-nine students were expected in the fall of 2003 and Stuebben Residence Hall, a residence for six seminarians and a faculty member named for Msgr. Lawrence Stuebben, former rector of the Seminary (1981-1987) and then vicar general for the Archdiocese, was blessed in the fall of 2003 ("Residence hall blessed, new faculty welcomed," *Today's Catholic*, Oct. 3, 2003).

Recognizing that growing numbers of seminarians could not be housed piece-meal, the Seminary Advisory Board announced a $26 million capital campaign in 2004. Rev. Gerald L. Brown, SS, rector-president of Assumption (2000-2004), said at the launch of the campaign that the seminary was receiving men from eleven countries and he believed numbers would continue to grow.

Archbishop Patricio Flores was very supportive of the campaign and made an initial donation of $100,000 from his personal funds.

---

[18] The decision to raze Mary-Catherine Hall brought significant challenge to the Archdiocese from the San Antonio Conservation Society who wanted the building, an original building from the earliest days of Trinity University and its predecessor institution Westmoreland College, to be restored. The city, however, did not pursue historic designation for the building (Richelieu, David Anthony, "Archdiocese gets OK to demolish 1925 building," *San Antonio Express-News,* Nov. 16, 2000, p. 7B).

The capital campaign was divided into six phases:
Phase I: a new residence hall for 80 students and four faculty with appropriate lounges, kitchenettes, visiting rooms, laundries, and chapel. This phase was completed with the blessing of Archbishop Flores Hall by Archbishop José

Archbishop Patrick Flores Residence Hall, built
in 2007 (Photo by Mike Davis, 2014)

Gomez, Archbishop Patricio Flores (retired), both of San Antonio, and Cardinal Francis E. George of Chicago on August 15, 2007 (McMorrough, Jordan, "New hall a symbol of increased vocations," *Today's Catholic*, August 31, 2007, and McMorrough, Jordan, "Assumption Seminary announces new $26 million capital campaign," *Today's Catholic*, Feb. 7, 2003, p. 4).

In the last decades, the Seminary Board has consistently worked with **Robert E. Morkovsky**, the Archdiocesan architect, on the upgrading of Assumption Campus. Morkovsky grew up in the shadow of St. John's Seminary and his two uncles, Bishop John Morkovsky and Msgr. Alois Morkovsky, served on the seminary faculty when he was a boy. In addition to many other archdiocesan projects involving more than a dozen parishes, Mr. Morkovsky's firm began working with seminary projects when he first remodeled St. Alice Hall in the mid-1970's. He is responsible for the design and building of the new facility for the Mexican American Cultural Center (2002), now the Mexican American Catholic College; the Archbishop's Residence (2009); Archbishop Flores Hall (2007); Msgr. José Lopez Hall [formerly St. Alice Hall] (2012); and the remodeling of Our Lady's Chapel (2014). (Interview with Robt. E. Morkovsky, July 2012)

Phase II: the second renovation of St. Alice Hall completed in the summer of 2012. At the dedication of the newly-remodeled building, the contemporary residence now houses more than twenty college seminarians in addition to providing new meeting rooms, handicap accessible public restrooms, and various upgrades to conform to city codes. The residence hall was renamed Msgr. José A. López Hall in memory of "Fr. Joe" (d. 2011) who was a formator and spiritual director for the Seminary and a professor at the Oblate School of Theology.

Msgr. José Lopez Hall, erected 1955, remodeled 2013

Phase III: the renovation of Shaw Hall, the administration building.

Phase IV: renovations of the Chapel and the Student Union Building.

Phase V: upgrading the grounds, swimming pool area, bell tower, walkways, interior roads, and parking lots.

Phase VI: renovations of the Dining Hall (Refectory Building).

Robert E. Morkovsky, the architect for seminary projects since the mid-1970's, noted in a July 12, 2012, interview that a master plan for the buildings at Assumption was created during Father Brown's tenure as rector.

Morkovsky indicated that future projects at the seminary will have to take into consideration a type of soil that demands very expensive "suspended" foundations, but all buildings will be continually stewarded in light of future concerns. Some will be able to be retrofitted for future needs, and others will be deemed to have outlived their ability to serve.

The campus of the future will welcome seminarians who come from various cultures and professional backgrounds, and quarters for living and studying must support their vocations for the Church.

For one hundred years the development and care of the campuses of St. John Seminary and Assumption Seminary have reflected a hand-in-glove relationship between the Archbishop and the loyal and generous Catholic laity of the Archdiocese. Stewarding the seminary campus into the twenty-first century will depend on a future-minded Seminary Board and the vision of Archdiocesan leadership.

St. Thomas Aquinas Adoration Chapel, Flores
Hall (Photo by Melanie Castillo)

St. Thomas Aquinas Adoration Chapel in Archbishop Flores Hall melds the past and future Church. The works of artisans of the past and artisans of today are blended together to surround the Sacramental Presence with antique stained-glass windows from a church in Philadelphia and new stained-glass windows crafted by Cavallini Stained Glass Studios in San Antonio.

The chapel epitomizes that Christ must forever be the central relationship for those called to serve the Church as priests. As they offer the holy sacrifice of the Mass, the priests ordained from Assumption recognize that they serve in the shadow of all the priests who have gone before them and they provide a model for all those who will come after them.

The prayer garden, also part of Flores Hall, provides a "new Eden" where the Lord "walks in the cool of the evening" today as surely as He did with our parents of millions of years ago.

In the stillness that permeates the seminary campus, those who are preparing for a lifetime of service to the Church in the priesthood can listen to the whispers of God's loving voice calling them to be people who in their own lives mirror the presence of Christ in today's world.

CHAPTER FOUR

THE VINCENTIANS

Archbishop Robert E. Lucey was installed as the second Archbishop of San Antonio on March 27, 1941. At a small reception that followed the ceremonies of installation, he took the Rev. Marshall Winne, CM, "Visitor"[19] of the Congregation of the Mission (Vincentians) in the United States, who had been a student at St. Vincent's College in Los Angeles with Lucey[20], aside and asked him in confidence if the Vincentians would be able to assume supervision of St. John's Seminary for the coming academic year. Lucey indicated in the conversation that he had not yet explored the concerns of the seminary, but he felt that he "might require some professors."

A confidential meeting between Winne and the Archbishop followed in mid-June 1941, and at the end of June, the Vincentians accepted St. John's Seminary. Rev. William Brennan, then ministering at St. Vincent's in Los Angeles, was selected by the Vincentians as rector.

---

[19] The Congregation of the Mission refers to their Superior as the "Visitor".

[20] Lucey had studied at both St. Vincent's College in Los Angeles and St. Patrick's Seminary in Menlo Park under the confreres of the Congregation of the Mission as part of his own preparation for ordination. While he was the Bishop of Amarillo (1934-1941), Lucey engaged the Vincentians to pastor Holy Souls Parish (now St. Vincent de Paul) in Pampa in 1940. (Saul E. Bronder, "LUCEY, ROBERT EMMET," **Handbook of Texas Online** (http://www. tshaonline.org/ handbook/ online/articles/flu14), accessed April 24, 2013, published by the Texas State Historical Association; and www.amarillo diocese.org)

The material from the archives at DePaul University, indicate that once arrangements were in place, Lucey wrote to the Apostolic Delegate informing him of the upcoming transition.

The Vincentians supplied a faculty and administration of ten priests (Materials from Special Collections and Archives, DePaul University, Chicago, IL; accessed August 21, 2013).

A number of reasons have been suggested as to why Lucey made this change—and made it so abruptly—only months after he had been installed as Archbishop. Perhaps it had been more and more challenging for the Archdiocese to staff the seminary with archdiocesan priests and maintain commitments to parishes and archdiocesan offices. Perhaps the priests of the Archdiocese who were assigned to seminary duties were too often distracted by other pastoral commitments. Perhaps preparing seminarians with an appropriate seminary education in "modern times" required costly specialized skill sets. And perhaps, the winds of war in early 1941 boded a need to prepare for an unknown future for the Archdiocese which was centered in San Antonio, a basically military town at that time.

The Congregation of the Mission

The Congregation of the Mission, founded in 1625 by St. Vincent de Paul in Paris, France, is one of two communities of men religious established in France for the purpose of organizing and operating seminaries (*cmglobal.org/en/*; en.wikipedia.org/ wiki/ **Congregation_ of_the_Mission**; and *American Vincentians*, p. 97).

> The seminary apostolate first brought the Vincentian Community to the United States [from France], and this apostolate remained one of its principal works until recent times. The Vincentians were also one of the few communities that came to the United States for the explicit purpose of establishing a diocesan seminary (Rybolt, CM, John, ed., *The American Vincentians: A Popular History of the*

Congregation of the Mission in the United States 1815-1987 (1988), p. 97; Vincentian ebooks @ http:// via. library. depaul.edu/vincentian_ ebooks/18 [hereafter noted as *American Vincentians]*).

The Sulpicians, the other French order which had a seminary apostolate, established the first American seminary in Baltimore in 1791 while the Vincentians established their first house at The Barrens (now Perryville) in Missouri in 1818.

From there, the Vincentians were instrumental in beginning and staffing diocesan seminaries, parishes, schools, and colleges throughout the United States frontier (Louis J. Franz, C.M., "VINCENTIAN FATHERS," **Handbook of Texas Online** [http://www.tshaonline.org /handbook/online/articles/ixv01], accessed May 02, 2012. Published by the Texas State Historical Association).

Both the Sulpicians and the Vincentians have had a tremendous impact on priestly formation in the United States.

According to various Vincentian publications, the Congregation had an upswing in vocations in the 1930's. The Western Province of the Congregation of the Mission ordained some of its largest classes and had ample personnel for the venture in San Antonio (*American Vincentians*, p. 78-79; and

---

Brennan, Msgr. William M. (1885-1970) was born in Marysville, Kansas. He entered the Apostolic School of the Vincentians in Perryville, MO, and attended St. Mary's Seminary, also in Perryville. Brennan entered the novitiate of the Congregation of the Missions in 1905, took his vows in 1907, and was ordained to the priesthood in 1915. He obtained his JCD from Collegio Angelico in Rome in 1915. Before serving as rector of St. John's Seminary, Brennan was on the faculty at DePaul University in Chicago, and four seminaries including Kenrick in St. Louis and St. Thomas in Denver.

After his tenure as first rector at St. John's (1941-1945), he was the superior at St. Mary's in Perryville and served at other seminaries. He died at Kenrick Seminary in St. Louis, Missouri. -- *Information supplied by the Vincentian Archives, DePaul University*

"Personnel Catalogues"[21] @ http://via. library.depaul.edu/
per_cat/).

At the time the Vincentians took over St. John's Seminary,
they had a long history of seminary work in the United States
and were operating eleven diocesan seminaries (both major
and minor) across the country. Their own universities and
seminaries for their men included Niagara University, a
major seminary and university, founded in 1856; St. Mary's
Seminary (for Vincentians) in Perryville, MO, founded in 1818,
St. Vincent's Seminary in Germantown, PA, founded in 1867
("Personnel Catalogues," Vols. 1853 and following).

The first Vincentian rector in the fall of 1941 was Msgr.
William M. Brennan, CM, JCD, PhD. He led a faculty of eight
for the ninety-eight seminarians. With the exception of Thomas
Kavanaugh, who was newly ordained, all of the faculty were
experienced seminary educators. The Vincentians provided
courses in dogma and preaching, history, Latin, patrology
(sic), English, apologetics, moral and canon law, scripture,
sociology, mathematics, rhetoric, philosophy, and Greek (*The
DeAndrein*, Vol. 12, Oct. 1941, p. 3 and 4, http://via.library.
depaul.edu/andrein).

Three Archdiocesan priests remained on the 1941-42
faculty: Father Bruno Hubertus who continued to oversee
finances, Father Claude A. Faust who was professor of
Gregorian Chant, and Father Cayetano Romero who taught
Spanish. In 1942, the Vincentian leadership added five more
faculty members, and the Archdiocesan priests were reassigned, giving the Vincentians complete charge.

---

21   The "Personnel Catalogues" are the listings of placements of
     Vincentian priests throughout the world in a given year. They
     are arranged by country and province. However, since the
     assignments were not always made prior to the publication of the
     "Catalogue" in Paris, a given "Catalogue" may not be completely
     accurate. The author has chosen not to note any page numbers
     or volumes in her citations. The "Catalogues", Volumes 1853
     through 1941 and 1947 through 1960 are online at http://via.
     library. depaul. edu/per_cat).

When the Vincentians began their ministry at St. John's "most of the students [were] native Texans, preparing to work in the Archdiocese, but there [were] a number from Dallas and Corpus Christi." In its first quarter-century, eighty-five men had been ordained from St. John's (*The DeAndrein*, Vol. 12, October 1941, p. 1).

In October of that first year under the Vincentians, the Apostolic Delegate, Archbishop Amleto Giovanni Cicognani[22], visited St. John's. He was in San Antonio to invest Archbishop Lucey with the pallium[23] and consecrate Bishop Laurence FitzSimon, a native San Antonian, as the successor of Archbishop Lucey as Bishop of Amarillo (*The DeAndrein*, Dec. 1941, p. 2; *en.wikipedia.org/wiki/Laurence_ Julius_ FitzSimon*).

Presumably, his visit to the seminary was arranged so that he might observe the operations of St. John's under the supervision of the Vincentians.

Educational Background of Vincentian Priests

During the twenty-five years that they operated St. John's and Assumption Seminaries, the Vincentians sent highly educated men to teach and mold the seminarians.

Most of the Vincentians sent to St. John's had been prepared for the priesthood at St. Mary's Seminary at Perryville, MO. A number of them had higher degrees from the Catholic University of America, a pontifical university, in Washington, DC, which at that time admitted only men to classes for priests. Several had studied in Rome at the Pontifical Biblical Institute, the Angelicum, and the Leonine College. And a number also had studied at their

---

[22] Some Vincentian materials suggest that a visit by the Apostolic Delegate earlier had led Archbishop Lucey to change the leadership at the seminary from Archdiocesan priests to the Vincentians who were better trained to oversee seminaries (*American Vincentians*, p.152).

[23] The pallium is a small stole of lamb's wool worn by the pope, metropolitan archbishops and primates, signifying their relationship to Christ the Shepherd.

university, DePaul, in Chicago.

St. John's Under the Vincentians

Through the 1940's the enrollment at St. John's climbed: 1942—thirty-six in the Major Seminary; sixty-six in the Minor Seminary; 1943—a total of 114 students; 1947-140 students; 1949—eighty-five students in the Minor Seminary and eighty-five in the Major Seminary.

> **Did you know?**
>
> In 1945 seven members of the Goertz-Bartsch families of Rockne, Texas, were enrolled at St. John's. Those ordained in 1952 were Rev. Bernard C. Goertz, Rev. Victor M. Goertz (Austin Diocese); Msgr. Alois Goertz was ordained in 1948 and Msgr. Edward C. Bartsch was ordained in 1949 for the Archdiocese of San Antonio (*Priest Forever*, p. 56 and Seminary Records of Ordinands).

Seminary Activities

The Margil[24] Unit of the Catholic Students' Mission Crusade (C.S.M.C.) had been organized at the Seminary in 1937. This organization "pursued a three-fold program: prayer, education and

> **Stakelum, CM, Rev. James W.** (1904-1972) was born in New Orleans, LA, where he attended elementary school in New Orleans. He went to high school at St. Vincent's College in Cape Girardeau, MO. After his novitiate at St. Mary's in Perryville, he took his vows in 1924. Following his ordination in 1937, Stakelum served as assistant director of novices at Perryville. He then studied in Rome at the Angelicum and in 1937 he received his Ph.D. Besides serving in seminaries, Stakelum was the Provincial Superior (Visitor) for the Western Province from 1950 until 1962. He was the rector of St. John's in San Antonio from1945-1950 He died in St. Louis at age 67. (*Information supplied by the Vincentian Archives, DePaul University*)

> *"The Well-dressed Theologian"*
>
> "Philosophers and Theologians should come to the seminary provided with cassock, biretta, two plain linen surplices (Roman style), and sufficient changes of winter and summer clothing . . . The seminary dress consists of the cassock, Roman collar, and biretta. The street dress for Theologians consists of black suit, rabat, Roman collar, and straw or black felt hat according to the season." (from *1945-1946 Catalogue*, p. 12)

sacrifice for the missions." By 1939 the seminarians had incorporated a Mission Correspondence Course, a program instituted by Vincentians at Perryville, which reached non-Catholics "who either have not time, courage, or

---

[24] Named for Fray Antonio Margil de Jesus, the Franciscan friar who had established the San Antonio Missions.

an opportunity of taking instructions [to become Catholic] from a priest, and also those Catholics who may have scanty knowledge of their faith" (*25 Years a Seminary*, p. 46-47 [noted as *25 Years* hereafter]). The Vincentians supported the Mission Crusade whole-heartedly and in 1945, "all student activities and organizations . . . were incorporated under the jurisdiction of the C.S.M.C . . . thus centralizing, strengthening, and simplifying the student government of the seminary" (*The DeAndrein*, Dec. 1945, p. 4).

Since the inception of the Correspondence Course at St. John's until 1943, the seminarians had worked with "156 students who had answered the first test, 72 had graduated, and 40 converts had been made." In 1943 "12 soldiers were enrolled among the active members" and eleven students enrolled from Prairie View College, a historically black college northwest of Houston, now called Prairie View A & M (*The DeAndrein*, Vol. 13, Jan.—Feb.1943, p. 5; *en.wikipedia.org/wiki/Prairie_View_ A%26M_ University; Catalogues of St. John's Seminary* 1941-1952, "1944-45 Catalogue", p. 19 et al.).

The Margil Unit also provided focused study through discussion groups, study clubs, and guest speakers. Various events, organized for the seminary by the seminarians themselves, engaged topics including the study of the Labor Encyclicals of Leo XIII and Pius XI; catechetics for first communicants; Christianizing America, street preaching, Catholic Action, credit unions, convert-making, and parish activities. (*25 Years*, p. 49).

The campus newsletter, ***The Bulletin***, was issued in print format for the first time in October 1943 and the 1943-44 ***Bulletin*** under the co-editorship of William Botik and Erwin Juraschek "received the coveted 'All-Catholic' award from the National Catholic School Press Association" (*Priest Forever*, p.54).

Eventually the ***Bulletin*** was replaced by the ***Magnificat*** when the seminarians in the major seminary transferred to Assumption (1952). In 1957 the ***Eaglet*** was published in mimeograph form to record events at St. John's while the ***Magnificat*** became the publication of Assumption Seminary.

The "Falso Bordoni", often called upon to sing for funerals of clergy and other Archdiocesan events, developed a number of traditional Latin works such as the *Laetentur Coeli* and the

Magnificat, both sung in four-part harmony (*The DeAndrein*, Vol. 13, Jan. 1943, p. 5).

A dramatics club, established in the fall of 1941 under the Vincentians, presented "A Christmas Carol" before the seminarians went home for the holidays that year. In 1943 the Genesian Society, named for St. Genesius the Comedian[25], was organized for the purpose of presenting plays and in 1943 the Christmas play was "You Can't Take It with You." Over the years a variety of plays were produced by the seminarians. Productions included selected scenes from Shakespeare's "A Midsummer Night's Dream," "As You Like It," and "The Merchant of Venice" in 1944 (*The DeAndrein*, Vol. 13, Jan. 1943, p. 5; Vol. 14, Jan. 1944, p. 4). Various light comedies followed—"Brother Pansy," directed by Mr. Thomas Collins and "Three Men on a Horse" directed by Mr. Edward Bartsch in 1947. In 1948-1949 the curtain rose on "Shadow and Substance," directed by Mr. Carlos Quintana; "Murder in a Monastery," directed by Mr. Paul Prove; and "George Washington Slept Here," directed by Mr. Robert Walden. Directing and performing in plays continued into the 1950's until Assumption Seminary was opened. At St. John's the major seminarians played both male and female roles and built the needed stage scenery for all productions.

The Genesian Society also had a puppet theater, "Il Piccolino" ("Catalogues" in *Catalogue St. John's Seminary 1941-1952*).

One might suppose that these many performance-oriented endeavors developed men who were quite comfortable before an assembly years before they said their first Masses!

---

[25] "Saint Genesius of Rome (died c. 286 or c. 303) was a comedian and actor who worked in a series of plays that mocked Christianity. One day while performing in a work that made fun of baptism he received sudden wisdom from God, realized the truth of Christianity, and had a conversion experience on stage. He announced his new faith, and refused to renounce it, even when ordered to do so by emperor Diocletian. He is the patron saint of actors, lawyers, barristers, clowns, comedians, converts, dancers, epileptics, musicians, printers, stenographers, and torture victims. His feast day is 25 August" (*en.wikipedia.org/wiki/ Genesius_of_Rome*).

Spirituality

Devotion to Mary

The Vincentians have a strong Marian spirituality and they promote Our Lady of the Miraculous Medal. St. Catherine Labouré (1806-1870), a Daughter of Charity of Vincent de Paul who nursed in Paris, received visions of the Blessed Virgin at Visitation Convent on Rue de Bac. Our Lady asked her to have the Miraculous Medal created and gave her explicit instructions on how it should be struck. Since that time, the

Congregation of the Mission has promoted the Miraculous Medal and the simple prayer that is engraved on it: *O Mary, conceived without sin, pray for us who have recourse to thee (en.wikipedia. org/ wiki/Catherine_Labouré).*

Since 1929 the Vincentians have maintained the National Shrine of Our Lady of the Miraculous Medal at their motherhouse in Perryville, MO. In 1942, seventy-six seminarians at St. John's were enrolled into the Miraculous Medal Association (*The DeAndrein*, Vol. 13, Jan. 13, p. 5, and *www.amm.org*).

An annual novena in preparation of the Feast of the Immaculate Conception, October devotions, and communal praying of the rosary served to strengthen the seminarians' devotion to Mary.

St. John's Chapel, St. John's Seminary, c. 1952

Prayer and Other Devotions

In addition to all liturgical feasts, annual events offered the

"Solemn Mass and Vespers are celebrated every Sunday and on many of the greater feasts. Benediction with the Blessed Sacrament is given on all Sundays, feasts of the Blessed Virgin and of the Apostles and on all solemnities when permitted by the Most Reverend Archbishop." --from "1947-1948 Catalogue", p. 5

"Under the head of 'Discipline' are included not only the rules by which order, regularity and conduct are enforced, but that **Spirit of the Seminary** which results from the strict observance of the rule and conscientious discharge of duty. The written rules are few and simple and are such as the priest should try to observe in his afterlife on the mission. Their observance accustoms the student to regularity of life, to self-restraint, to proper regard for his companions, and to prompt and cheerful obedience to authority . . . The spirit of honor and gentlemanliness is inculcated, and if necessary, enforced" (*Catalogue St. John's Seminary 1941-1952*, various pages).

seminarians a way to deepen their personal and communal

Eucharistic spirituality. The Forty Hours Devotion, a popular three-day mini-retreat during the 1940's and 1950's focusing on the Eucharist was celebrated at the seminary in Lent.

A week-long retreat in strict silence preached by a Vincentian priest brought in from Perryville or some other Vincentian-directed facility gave the seminarians ample time for prayer and recollection (*Catalogues of St. John's Seminary* 1941-1952).

A Missionary Consciousness

The Vincentian community of the United States had two very interesting missionary endeavors. One was a mission of the Western Province of American Vincentians in the Vicariate of Yukiang in Northern Kiangsi, China, where, since 1922, the American Vincentians pastored parishes and missions, ran seminaries, hospitals, clinics, and orphanages ("V1947" (1947). Personnel Catalogues. Paper 86 @ http://via.library. depaul. edu; *The DeAndrein*, Vol. 30, May 1960, p. 2-3). The annual celebration of "Pekin Day" which focused on the cultural world of China stretched the seminarians' consciousness of global reality. Regular correspondence between the Vincentian missioners and St. John's faculty also provided the seminarians with a close look at experiences in the foreign missions.

The Motor Mission effort, two or three Vincentians travelling throughout rural America in the summer months and doing street preaching, gave the St. John's seminarians an opportunity to enter into a very unique experience of evangelization.[26] Seminarians were invited to participate in preaching Motor Missions of the Vincentians during the summers. Rev. Mr. Anthony Costantino and Rev. Mr. Robert Schmidt, both ordained in 1944, spent their

---

[26]   Eventually, in the 1960's, Rev. Stephen A. Leven (1905-1983) of Oklahoma would be elevated to the position of Auxiliary Bishop of San Antonio. As a priest in the Oklahoma City-Tulsa Diocese, Leven himself was a "street-preacher" (1933), well-known for his captivating evangelization efforts in Oklahoma small towns where Catholics were in a distinct minority (en.wikipedia.org/wiki/ Stephen_Aloysius_Leven).

diaconate summer of 1943 preaching throughout Texas with Rev. Raymond O'Brien, CM. Younger seminarians were often sent to remote and isolated missions to teach religious education with the Confraternity of Christian Doctrine (*Priest Forever*, p. 54).

Speakers brought to the seminary underscored the emphasis on a missionary mentality. Msgr. Thomas O'Donnell, National Director of the Society for the Propagation of the Faith, spoke at St. John's in the fall of 1943. "The gist of his talk is best captured into one sentence which he spoke: 'The people will not learn to love the Missions unless you, the priests of tomorrow show them by prayer and example to 'Make disciples of all nations'" (*Catalogue of St. John's Seminary 1941-1952*, "1943-44 Catalogue," p. 30).

According to the "Chronicles" in the 1941-1952 Catalogues, the seminarians heard Msgr. Luigi Ligutti, promoter of Catholic Rural Life; Rev. Aloysius Heeg, SJ, on teaching catechism; Rev. Victor M. Villeneuve, OMI, on the Jocist Movement[27]; Bishop Fulton J. Sheen, who spoke at Municipal Auditorium on "Men of Good Will"; Mr. William Smith, Radio Chairman for the National Council of Catholic Men; Rev. Albert Smith, MM, on Guatemala; Rev. Roy Rihn, associate pastor at St. Cecilia Parish, also on the Jocist Movement; and many others.

Though the young men might have felt that they were basically living "in captivity" on Mission Road, the Vincentians promoted

---

[27]   After World War I, Father Joseph Cardijn founded a movement that expanded throughout Belgium and France. Known as Young Christian Workers or in French Jeunesse Ouvrire Chritienne (JOC) [the latter is where the "jocist movement" name comes from], the movement is the forerunner of Young Christian Students (YCS) and the Christian Family Movement (CFM) which developed in the US in the 1940's. Gospel-based small communities, YCS and CFM were popular in the early 1950's and 1960's in Catholic parishes in the US. Meetings consisted of studying the gospel so as to interface it with problems of the times. "See, Judge, Act" were the operative actions for the group: "See" the problem . . . "Judge" it in terms of the gospel . . . decide on an "Action" to be taken communally (en. wikipedia.org/wiki/ Young_Christian_Workers; and the author's personal experience of YCS and CFM in her home parish, Sts. Peter and Paul, Tulsa, OK)

their exposure to both national and international experts. The "Chronicles" reveal that speakers addressed a variety of subjects including life in rural America, the challenges of the race question, Mexican art, China, the mission to the Native Americans, and the work of the Catholic press to note a few.

These aspects of Vincentian spirituality no doubt instilled in priests ordained from their seminaries devotion to Mary, sensitivity to the needs of rural Catholics, the challenge of representing Catholicism in locations that are decidedly non-Catholic, and a practical knowledge of imparting Catholic teachings. In addition, ordinands from St. John's had a broad understanding of the apostolic work of a priest regardless of where he was assigned.

Athletics

In its first quarter-century, St. John's students enjoyed baseball, soccer and handball. Having the winners' names inscribed on the Metzger Cup, the coveted prize of the spring handball tournament signaled the prowess of fitness, skill, and survivability of the last team standing. In the second quarter century, recreation continued to mean playing baseball and soccer as well as landscaping the ever-changing campus on Mission Road.

During the tenure of the Vincentians, the Athletics Director was a major seminarian. His job was to coordinate basketball, touch football, baseball, and soccer games, and plan for tournaments.

After the Major Seminary was moved to Assumption in 1952, St. John's athletics program became more intramural oriented. The boys eventually engaged in track and baseball with other Catholic schools through the Texas Catholic Interscholastic League (TCIL). In 1957, St. John's Seminary participated in the Texas Catholic Interscholastic track meet held in Dallas where the seminarians took third place (*The DeAndrein*, Vol. 27, May 1957, p. 5).

Campus Development

Also under the Vincentians the campus at St. John's was expanded and improved. In the fall of 1941 the chapel was re-decorated in the liturgical style of the day. To serve the growing student body, the refectory (dining room) was eventually doubled in size and redecorated, the study hall was enlarged, and the kitchen was extended (*Priest Forever*, p. 54). By the end of the 1940's the tennis courts had been asphalted, and repairs to the faculty house were made (*The DeAndrein*, various issues: 1942 through 1947).

In 1943, the enrollment of 114 seminarians necessitated housing thirty sophomores and juniors at St. Peter's and St. Joseph's Orphanage located two blocks from Drossaerts Hall and operated by the Sisters of Charity of the Incarnate Word. The need for a dormitory prompted the generous response of the Catholic faithful of the archdiocese and though the Second World War delayed construction, St. Mary's Hall was completed in 1947 (*Priest Forever*, p. 54-55).

Continued growth in numbers of seminarians in the Minor Seminary in the late 1950's and early 1960's necessitated further new construction. A study hall-library, a classroom building, a dining hall-kitchen, and chapel were added to the Mission Road seminary property. Drossaerts and Margil Halls were converted into dormitory space and an administration-faculty building respectively (*The DeAndrein*, Vol. 27, Nov. 1956, p. 7 and 8). The construction of four new buildings at once and the renovation of Drossaerts and Margil Halls reflects the energy that the Vincentians had for sustaining and improving St. John's Seminary as well as the commitment of the archdiocese.

The Curriculum at St. John's

The curriculum at St. John's for the high school, the college, and the theologate were standard for the time.

The "1944-1945 Catalogue" listed the following courses for those in Philosophy and Theology: philosophy (five courses); Sacred Scripture (six courses); Church History (five courses, including the works of the Fathers of the Church); Languages (English and Spanish); Public Speaking (three courses); Gregorian Chant and Music (eight courses); Ascetical Theology (three courses); Dogmatic Theology (four courses); Moral Theology (five courses); Pastoral Theology (two of the five courses were oriented to preparing the priests for pastoral work in Spanish and Czech); Canon Law (four courses); Liturgy and Ceremonies (four courses, including one on the Breviary); Sociology. These courses were taken over a four-year time frame. Most of the texts noted for the courses were in Latin.

> *"In an endeavor to meet the ever increasing demands for more priests throughout the Southwest, St. John's Seminary introduced, for the first time in its thirty years, an accelerated course. Thus on June 19th the new 1944-45 scholastic year began. By 4:00 p.m. fifty-nine students had been registered for the Major House, filling the room capacity to overflowing."* --from "Chronicle 1944-1945," 1945-1946 Catalogue, p. 40; Catalogue St. John's Seminary 1941-1952*

Prior to the ordination of the candidate in the various orders (Minor and Major), examinations were held on the afternoon before the retreat for Orders. Candidates were aware of the content of each exam as taken from *Specimen Examinis Ordinandorum*. Candidates for the Major Orders (subdeacon, deacon, priest) took both written and oral examinations on assigned theological tracts.

Two Seminaries—Two Campuses

In the fall of 1952 the doors of two seminaries opened in San Antonio. St. John's Minor Seminary under the leadership of the Very Rev. John P. Tackaberry, CM, rector, and a faculty of nine Vincentians received 102 high school and collegian seminarians at the Mission Road campus. The Very Rev. Gilmore H. Guyot, CM, rector, and a faculty of seven Vincentians received eighty-five philosophers and theologians at the Woodlawn Avenue campus.

Guyot, CM, Rev. Gilmore H. (1907-2000) was born in Perryville, MO, where he attended St. Vincent's Elementary and High Schools. From there he continued his education at DePaul University in Chicago before returning to St. Mary's Seminary in Perryville for his novitiate and seminary studies. Guyot took his vows in 1928 and after ordination in 1934, he studied at the Angelicum Pontifical University in Rome, earning a Licentiate in Sacred Theology and at the Biblical Institute in Rome where he obtained a Bachelor in Sacred Scripture. Before being assigned to St. John's/Assumption in San Antonio in 1950, Guyot served at the seminaries in St. Louis, MO. While serving as rector at Assumption, Guyot was President of the Catholic Biblical Association in 1950-1951. -- *Information supplied by the Vincentian Archives, DePaul University*

Tackaberry, CM, Rev. John (1916-2001), a native of St. Louis, MO, entered the novitiate of the Vincentians at St. Mary of the Barrens in Perryville, MO, in 1933 and professed his vows in 1935. He was ordained in 1941.He taught in various seminaries for thirty-nine years, usually teaching Latin. He is remembered in the Vincentian community for his dedication to creating Latin scholars of his students. Tackaberry was always available to help in parishes and ended his priestly career as a priest-presenter at Marriage Encounter Retreats in Cape Girardeau, MO. Rev. Tackaberry was the rector at St. John's from 1952 until 1955 and a faculty member at Assumption from 1955 through 1963. -- *Information supplied by the Vincentian Archives, DePaul University*

The Curriculum at Assumption

In 1954 the Faculty at Assumption experimented with a new class schedule, more European in nature, which allowed the seminarians to have Wednesday as a study day. The Vincentian seminary at Perryville followed that plan and other Vincentian seminaries picked it up (*The DeAndrein*, Vol. 24, Jan. 1954, 9. 3).

In 1961, the leadership at Assumption Seminary collaborated with St. Mary's University located only two miles from the Woodlawn campus and seminarians began attending classes at the nearby university (*The DeAndrein*, Vol. 32, Dec. 1961, p. 7). This cooperation with St. Mary's University afforded the seminarians a wider variety of degree programs and a larger spectrum of courses than could be offered at Assumption.

Seminarians were well-prepared for further studies in Rome or at the Louvain in Belgium and many dioceses sent their men abroad for their Theology courses.

Other Contributions to the Archdiocese by Vincentian Priests

Hogan, CM, Rev. Jeremiah P. (1918-1981), was born in of Astoria, New York. He entered the novitiate at Perryville from Chicago after attending St. Vincent's College in Cape Girardeau, MO and took his vows in 1940. He was ordained in 1946. In addition to being the rector at St. John's in San Antonio from 1961-1962, Hogan served at St. John's from 1950 through 1955, teaching social studies and prefecting students. Other assignments included St. Louis Preparatory Seminary, St. John's in Kansas City, MO, DePaul University Academy in Chicago. He died in Chicago.

Leonard, CM, Rev. Lawrence Joseph (1913-1999), a native of Everett, Washington, entered the Vincentians in 1940 from Chicago after attending DePaul University. He was ordained in 1948 at St. Mary's in Perryville. Leonard served as superior and principal at St. John's Seminary from 1955-1961 and beginning in 1964, Leonard was a spiritual director at Assumption Seminary. -- *Information supplied by the Vincentian Archives, DePaul University*

The Archbishop spent a social evening with the Vincentians at least annually throughout the twenty-five years they served the Archdiocese. These collaborative relationships led to many instances of pastoral involvement by the Vincentian faculty members in parishes, schools, and other venues in the Archdiocese. It is evident from their own publications that the Vincentians maintained a very close relationship with local parishes and local priests in the Archdiocese of San Antonio.

The faculty members regularly

- o Preached the Forty Hours devotions in parishes throughout the Archdiocese;
- o Taught at Blessed Sacrament Academy;
- o Contributed articles to the *The Register* (Catholic paper);
- o Helped at parishes during Christmas, Lent and Easter Seasons;
- o Provided retreats for communities of women and men religious (Benedictine Sisters, Sisters of Divine Providence,

CICM priests, Sisters of the Incarnate Word and Charity, the Presentation Sisters, etc.);

o Preached retreats at the local Catholic colleges;

o Provided retreats and speakers at the Catholic high schools throughout the Archdiocese, including commencement addresses;

o Gave retreats at Fort Sam Houston, Kelly Air Force Base, Brooks Air Force Base, and Lackland Air Force Base;

> **McOwen, Rev. James** (1914-year of death not known), a native of California, was educated at Los Angeles College (Vincentian) in the Diocese of Los Angeles before entering the Vincentians at St. Mary's Seminary in Perryville, MO, in 1934 and professing his vows in 1936. He was ordained in 1941. McOwen continued his studies after ordination at Catholic University in Washington, DC and complete a Licentiate in Theology. From 1942 until 1955 he was assigned to various positions (Director of Students, Novice Director) at Perryville before becoming the rector of Assumption Seminary from 1955 to 1963. After his tenure at Assumption, McOwen taught at Cardinal Glennon College in St. Louis and served in Bujumbura, Burundi, Africa. -- *Information supplied by the Vincentian Archives, DePaul University*

o Preached Days of Recollection at Archdiocesan parishes;

o Preached the *Tre Ore* (a Good Friday service) at San Antonio parishes.

o Two priests—Fr. John Walker and the Very Rev. William Brennan, CM served on the Archdiocesan Marriage Tribunal.

o Vincentians judged oratorical contests at local Catholic schools.

o Fr. Thomas Kavanaugh, at the request of the Archbishop, instituted a course in Spanish for the young priests of San Antonio, many of whom had come from Ireland, and was involved in inter-faith dialogue in San Antonio.

o They offered classes that supported catechetics in the Archdiocese.

o Rev. Jeremiah Hogan, CM and Rev. Thomas Kavanaugh, CM, both taught at Our Lady of the Lake College.

o Rev. Daniel Martin, CM and Rev. James Fischer, CM with Rev. Paul Decker, OMI, collaborated to write a two-booklet series published by the Archdiocese for high school students entitled *Searching the Scriptures* (1954).

o   Rev. James Towns, CM, (Assumption) was appointed a member of the Archdiocesan Liturgical Commission (1956).

In addition to being highly educated, the confreres who had been assigned to St. John's and Assumption distinguished themselves and the Vincentians in other ways.

> **Derbes, CM, Rev. Louis** (1924-1995) was a native of New Orleans, LA. Before entering the Vincentians, he taught in elementary and secondary schools in New Orleans and Portland, OR. He entered the Vincentian novitiate after teaching for two years at St. Vincent's College in Cape Girardeau, and professed his vows in 1945. Derbes was ordained in 1951. In addition to holding the position of rector and teacher at St. John's Seminary from 1962 to 1966, Derbes taught at several high school seminaries in Illinois, Missouri, Oklahoma, and Arizona.
>
> *-- Information supplied by the Vincentian Archives, DePaul University*

> **Lee, Rev. Albert H.** (1930-1977), the last Vincentian rector at St. John's, was born in Oak Park, IL and entered the Vincentians from there in 1948. He was ordained in 1957 at St. Mary's Seminary in Perryville. In addition to serving as Rector, Dean of Studies, and math teacher at St. John's from 1966-1968, Lee served in other seminaries in California and Missouri. He was teaching at St. John's Seminary in Kansas City, MO, when he died. *Information supplied by the Vincentian Archives, DePaul University*

> **Kammer, Rev. Edward J.** (1908-1975), the last Vincentian rector at Assumption, was born in New Orleans, LA. He entered the Vincentians in 1925 and took his vows in 1927. Kammer held an MA and a PhD from Catholic University of America. In addition to serving as rector at Assumption from 1963-1967, Kammer taught at St. Mary's Seminary in Houston, served several parishes, and worked in several positions including the Associate Vice-President at DePaul University. He died while serving at St. Joseph's Church in New Orleans. *Information supplied by the Vincentian Archives, DePaul University*

o   Two served as Provincial Superiors of the Western Province: Rev. James Stakelum, CM and Rev. James Fischer, CM

o   Very Rev. John R. Cortelyou became the president of DePaul University

o   Two were authors: Rev. Edward Danagher, CM who wrote *Son, Give Me Your Heart*, and Rev. Carl Schulte, CM who wrote *A Guiding Star*

o   Rev. E. J. Kammer, CM, served as the Vice-President of DePaul University before coming to Assumption

The Vincentian Faculty at St. John's and St. Assumption Seminaries 1941-1963[28]

Brennan, CM	Msgr. William	1941

Bayard, CM	Rev. Ralph K.	1941
Bagen, CM	Rev. John	1941
Brennan, CM	Rev. George	1941
Brosnan, CM	Rev. John J.	1941
Burke, CM	Rev. Michael J.	1941
Cortelyou, CM	Rev. William T.	1941
Dolan, CM	Rev. George E.	1941
Kavanaugh, CM	Rev. Thomas	1941
Vidal, CM	Rev. William X.	1941
DeWitt, CM	Rev. Allan	1942
Dolan, CM	Rev. George	1942
Gaughan, CM	Rev. William	1942
Zimmerman, CM	Rev. Lee	1942
Zimney, CM	Rev. Robert	1942
Cannon, CM	Rev. Edmund	1943
Fischer, CM	Rev. James	1943
Gibbons, CM	Rev. Marion	1943
Kane, CM	Rev. Maurice	1943
O'Brien, CM	Rev. Raymond	1943
Sharpe, CM	Rev. John	1943
Darby, CM	Rev. Emmet	1944

Rev. Thomas C. Kavanaugh, CM, was newly-ordained when he began his long career at St. John's ≈ Assumption Seminary in 1941. Assigned after ordination to missions in China, Kavanaugh was unable to enter that mission field because of the onset of World War II. He was then assigned to St. John's in San Antonio. From 1941 until 1967, Kavanaugh, known to the seminarians as "TK" taught Spanish. Msgr. Arnold Anders of the Diocese of Corpus Christi ('50) remembers "TK's" favorite saying: "Easy does it, Buzz"—wise words for those going into the complications of ministerial life! After the Vincentians left Assumption, Kavanaugh served at St. Leo's Parish, Our Lady of Grace Parish, and Our Lady of Mt. Carmel Mission. Kavanaugh died at Padua Place in 2005. (Archdiocesan Archives; Anders' response to Survey of Priests, 2012))

---

[28] The listing of faculties has been compiled from *The DeAndrein* (various volumes, 1941 through 1952) and *Personnel Catalogues*. The year listed is the year the priest was assigned to St. John's. Materials are housed at the Vincentian Archives at DePaul University and can be accessed through "http://via.library.depaul. edu ". The author apologizes for any error or omission due to different formats of the listings.

Degan, CM	Rev. Bernard	1944
Riley, CM	Rev. Edward	1944
Walker, CM	Rev. John	1944
Burroughs, CM	Rev. Joseph	1945
Fallon, CM	Rev. Donald	1945
Gervononik, CM	Rev. Francis	1946
Martin, CM	Rev. Daniel	1945
McNeil, CM	Rev. Donald	1945
Stakelum, CM	Rev. James	1945

Hagan, CM	Rev. John	1947
Jourdan, CM	Rev. Jerome	1947

Frommell, CM	Rev. Peter	1948
Meik, CM	Rev. Thomas	1948
O'Brien, CM	Rev. Patrick	1948
Schucker, CM	Rev. Thomas	1948

Danagher, CM	Rev. Edward	1949
Johnson, CM	Rev. Jacob	1949
Owen, CM	Rev. Quigley	1949
Schulte, CM	Rev. Carl	1949
Winkelmann, CM	Rev. Wilbain	1949
Eirich, CM	Rev. George	1950
Guyot, CM	Rev. Gilmore	1950
Miller, CM	Rev. Norbert	1950

Did you know?

Before the Second Vatican Council seven rituals celebrated the steps to priesthood. Today three remain.

Tonsure—the "beginning"—ritual of cutting the candidate's hair reminding him of his servitude

Porter—in the early Church this position informed the faithful of the time and place for liturgy, unlocked the church doors and rang the bell that called the community to prayer

Exorcist*--was another position of servitude, providing those attending the prayers with the service of washing of hands and feet, a prelude of cleansing Christians of Satan's wily ways and leading them to holiness

Lector*--This position still exists and formally entrust the candidate with the Word of God which will guide his life

Acolyte*--This position also still exists and when bestowed on a candidate enables him to assist at liturgical functions and prepare the altar

Assumption Faculty 1952-1964

Guyot, CM	Rev. Gilmore	1952
O'Brien, CM	Rev. Frank	1952

Miget, CM	Rev. Robert	1952
Zimmerman, CM	Rev. Lee	1952
Germovnik, CM	Rev. Francis	1952
Barr, CM	Rev. Morgan	1952
Eirich, CM	Rev. George	1952

Gagnepain, CM	Rev. Francis	1953
Kavanaugh, CM	Rev. Thomas	1954
Parres, CM	Rev. Cecil	1954
Kwanitael, CM	Rev. William	1954
McOwen, CM	Rev. James	1955
Dicharry, CM	Rev. Warren	1955
Menard, CM	Rev. J. Godden	1955
Daspit, CM	Rev. Joseph	1955
Fischer, CM	Rev. James	1956
Towns, CM	Rev. James	1956
Martinez, CM	Rev. Frederick	1957
Kenneally, CM	Rev. Wm.	1957
Zimmerman, CM	Rev. Lee	1957
Gieselman, CM	Rev. Richard	1958
Zimmerman, CM	Rev. Francis	1958
Martin, CM	Rev. Daniel	1958
Pansini, CM	Rev. Francis	1958
McHardy, CM	Rev. James	1959
Navas, CM	Rev. L	1959
Falanga, CM	Rev. Anthony	1961
Lynch, CM	Rev. William	1961
DeVries, CM	Rev. Bernard	1963
Kammer, CM	Rev. Edward	1963
Gibbons, CM	Rev. Marion	1964
Leonard, CM	Rev. Lawrence	1964

Subdeacon—The position, abolished by Paul VI, entrust the candidate with the responsibility of praying the Divine Office of Liturgy of the Hours

Deacon—Once ordained a deacon, the candidate is bound to celibacy and may serve the priest at the altar, proclaim the gospel, preach, and administer baptism (Vanderholt, *Called to Serve*)

These positions are ritualized steps to ordination, not to be confused with various ministries of the laity in today's liturgy or defined ministries by priests of a diocese/archdiocese.

*These are the years that the Vincentians listed were appointed to Assumption.

Conclusion: About the Vincentians

Just before the close of the Second Vatican Council, novitiates and seminaries were bulging with vocations. In the mid-1960's St. John's averaged 160 seminarians. When the Vincentians released the minor seminary back to the Archdiocese there were over 150 seminarians at St. John's (*The DeAndrein*, Vol. 34-35, 1964-65). And in 1967 there were 143 students enrolled at Assumption (*Called to Serve*, p. 45).

As the Church underwent self-examination in the early 1960's, she recognized that her structures had begun to distance her from the realities of modern life. Those who operated seminaries began to question whether the institutionalized life that so many young seminarians had embraced in their teen-age years had become counterproductive. In response to anticipated changes in the Church and in hopes of providing seminarians with an opportunity for greater personal maturity, the Vincentians at Assumption changed the diaconate program substantially beginning in 1962.

Studies had suggested that young priests were unwilling to "carry their share of the work, . . . [were] more interested in seeking their own wills than the will of God." The Vincentians decided that it was "obvious that a deeper sense of responsibility must be engendered in the young clergy." Thus the main purpose of the change in the program for deacons, as described in *The DeAndrein* (cited below), was to instill this sense of responsibility, indicating a **pioneering spirit in seminary work**.

Instead of being on a strict common schedule, the deacon was given the chance to arrange his own daily plan. "The only restrictions placed on him are that he keep silence according to need, that he be on time for Mass in the morning, that he be present at the noon and evening examens[29], and that he receive

---

[29]   A formal examination of conscience, usually done daily, sometimes as a public devotion.

oral permission to leave the grounds. The time for rise and retiring, for making meditation, and for his other duties is left entirely up to him."

Many of the young men had never had (outside of vacation time) an opportunity to "test their mettle" in less-structured circumstances. The horarium had governed every minute of their day for years, leaving little decision-making opportunities for them. They had never had to choose a spiritual or devotional life since communal prayers were built into the day.

In order to facilitate more independence for deacons at Assumption they lived together in what was known as "deacon-ville", a small house out by the old gym from the Trinity campus. This may have been their first and only experience of self-directed living.

The 1964 article in *The DeAndrein* (Vol. 34, April 1964, p. 4, 11) notes that the experiment of two years had not been given enough time to be properly evaluated. But some results could be seen. The spiritual life of the deacons was not as solid as the deacons thought. Devotional practice slid, meditation was often omitted, visits to the Blessed Sacrament became erratic. Deacons noted that they often did not get enough sleep. However, the deacons did learn that becoming a priest is dependent first on becoming a responsible man (*The DeAndrein*, "Aggiornamento, San Antonio Style," Vol. 34, April 1964, p. 4, 11).

These changes, at first glance, seem to reflect a new way of training priests for the future Church. However, the long history of the Congregation of the Mission reveals four characteristics which serve well the Vincentian priests into whose hands bishops and archbishops entrusted their future priests.

Another characteristic is **dependence on Providence**. *American Vincentians*, the history of Vincentians in the US edited by Rev. John Rybolt, CM, recounts any number of instances when the leadership at Vincentian seminaries and colleges (Niagara University, St. Mary's at Perryville, St. Vincent's in Cape Girardeau, DePaul University in Chicago, for example) stepped out on thin ice when he/they determined that real change required an enormous investment of energy and/or capital. Often the decision required money that did not exist and the leadership borrowed to the hilt in order to press ahead into the future. The authors of *American Vincentians* are quite critical of the leaders (particularly those in the 19th and early 20th centuries) who more than once brought the Province to the brink of fiscal disaster in order to improve the future of one institution.

But most religious communities have similar stories of leaders from the past who were willing to take amazing risks in order to move forward. At the time of the risk, the risk-takers would have acknowledged the jeopardy, but also they would have said that **dependence on Divine Providence** "saw them through."

The third is a **willingness to do hard work**. Every evidence—the building of Niagara University, DePaul University, and St. John's in New York, accepting pastorates of poor and fragile parishes, taking on weak seminaries—indicates that Vincentians were priests who were not afraid of hard work, both physical and mental. Campuses with inadequate facilities and funds required that both the faculty and the seminarians had to pitch in with "handy man" chores, landscaping, and janitorial work. Parish priests often had to physically build or repair dilapidated churches. And it would seem that the Vincentians never said "no" to any request from local pastors or bishops who needed a speaker.

Creative endeavors—plays, choruses, puppet-theater, prizewinning in-house newsletters—encouraged the development of talents of every kind in the young men who studied at their seminaries.

And **Vincentian ingenuity**—taking what you have and molding it for the good of the Church—set the seminarians "in charge" of tasks from landscaping to directing athletics, from directing plays to editing the **Bulletin,** from binding books to educating converts.

Addendum:
The Pastoral Work of the Vincentians in the Archdiocese

In addition to St. John's Seminary and Assumption Seminary, two parishes and several missions came under the pastoral leadership of the Vincentians during the episcopacy of Archbishop Lucey.

In 1942 Rev. Michael Ries, CM, became the pastor of Sacred Heart Parish in Cotulla, Texas. Upon Ries' arrival in the spring of 1942, parish affairs were in a completely unorganized condition. The church was ill-equipped and dilapidated. Ries' leadership as pastor brought the church building to a safer condition, repaired and painted the inside, and put in altars and confessionals.

As pastor, Ries established the Confraternity of Christian Doctrine and engaged the Sisters of the Sacred Heart of St. Jacut from San Antonio to staff catechetical programs in the parish missions.

In 1956 Archbishop Lucey asked the Vincentians to pastor St. Leo's, one of San Antonio's largest parishes. The work of the Vincentians at St. Leo's began with visiting the 806 parish families. Parishioners who had been away from the sacraments were helped to "get straight with God." Those who were afraid of the Sacrament of Confession "came to know the peace and joy of a good confession" no matter how many years they had been away from the sacrament.

Daughters of Charity provided a catechetical and social center at Losoya. From El Carmen Mission the Daughters of Charity served four parishes, two of them with Vincentian pastors.

Vincentian pastors in parishes in the Archdiocese of San Antonio were Rev. Michael M. Ries, CM; Rev. Raymond F. O'Brien, CM; Rev. Jan Van Lare, CM; Rev. Oscar Huber, CM; Msgr. Ray Ruiz, CM; Rev. Leo Ebisch, CM; Rev. Jose Mejac, CM; Rev. Marin Braspenning, CM; Rev. Herbert Vandenberg, CM; Rev. John Bagen, CM; Rev. Joseph Daspit, CM, and Rev. Thomas Kavanaugh (Vincentian *Personnel Catalogues* @ http:// via.library. depaul.edu/cgi/ and Archdiocesan archives).

At the time of this writing, Rev. Kevin Fausz, CM, is the pastor of Holy Redeemer Parish and serves as campus minister at Our Lady of the Lake University (Archdiocesan Directory, 2011, p. 244).

To live in the midst of the world without seeking its pleasure;

To be a member of each family, yet belonging to none;

To share all sufferings; to penetrate all secrets;

To heal all wounds; to go from men to God

and offer Him their prayers;

To return from God to men to bring pardon and hope;

To have a heart of fire for charity, and

a heart of bronze for chastity;

To teach and to pardon, console and to bless always;

My God, what a life! And it's yours, O priest of Jesus Christ!

--Jean-Baptiste Lacordaire, OP (1802-1861), French priest

CHAPTER FIVE

ST. JOHN'S SEMINARY: THE FINAL YEARS

At its beginning in 1915, St. John's was a "preparatory seminary." Its purpose was to prepare young men of high school or early college age for seminary and in its first year, St. John's had neither a philosophy department nor a theology department. Bishop Shaw did, however, anticipate that the preparatory seminary would be expanded to include a philosophy department in the near future (*25 Years a Seminary*, p. 7). Shaw's intention followed the words of Pope Benedict XV who lauded the native priest who "by birth and temperament, by sentiment and interests, is in touch with his people." The class of seventeen boys which entered in October 1915 were in their teens or early twenties, Sidney Metzger of Fredericksburg being the youngest (*25 Years a Seminary*, p. 7).

As a preparatory seminary, its goals were to develop discipline in the boys, give them an educational foundation which would support the study of philosophy and theology in Greek and Latin, and introduce them to a structured spiritual life which would prepare them for the priesthood. The first curriculum included English, Greek, Latin, Spanish, history, religion, elocution, and mathematics. In 1916 a philosophy program was added to the seminary curriculum so that as students finished the basic curriculum they could begin their philosophy studies (*25 Years a Seminary*, p. 13).

The Development of Aspirancies and Preparatory Seminaries in the US

In the nineteenth century it was common for congregations of women religious to recruit teen-aged girls and educate them toward teaching or nursing at their motherhouses, schools, and hospitals or infirmaries. Similarly, dioceses accepted teen-aged boys for the priesthood and placed them in seminary or with priest-tutors for training until they were prepared for ordination.

Recognizing that training for priesthood demanded more standardization, the First Plenary Council of Baltimore (1852) required every province in the US to have a seminary. The Second Plenary Council of Baltimore (1866) initiated preparatory (minor) seminaries. The Third Plenary Council of Baltimore (1884) insisted that

> "Preparatory seminaries should be instituted. The pupils should be taught Christian Doctrine, English, and at least one other language according to the necessities of the diocese. They must learn to speak and write Latin. Greek is also to be taught. The usual branches of profane learning, not omitting the natural sciences, as well as music and the Gregorian chant are to be part of the curriculum."

In addition, the curriculum and testing procedures for major seminaries were strengthened ("Plenary

I went to St. John's as a 9th grader from St. Cecilia's (San Antonio) Parish in 1943 and stayed until my senior year. After I graduated from Central Catholic, I returned for one more year of seminary at St. John's. We slept on the south end of the 2nd floor of Drossaerts Hall and had a Solemn High Mass every Sunday. I really liked that. The subjects we took were high school subjects, but we had lots of Latin.

I appreciate my years at St. John's. From there I went into the Air Force and then a service-oriented profession. I became a social worker.

The seminary provided me with a firm faith foundation. I was able to teach my own children and show them a spiritual way. I still go to daily Mass and am grateful for my years at St. John's.

--**Paul Brinkman**
Interview, July 9, 2012

Councils of Baltimore," (en.*wikipedia.org/wiki/ Plenary_*
Councils_of_Baltimore).

By the early twentieth century, guided by the Councils, bishops such as John Shaw were doing their best to provide proper training for their future clergy.

During the fifty-five years of the existence of St. John's Minor Seminary, most religious communities of women and men as well as most dioceses in the US accepted teen-aged candidates for religious life and the priesthood. It was a time when many young people in the US did not automatically go to high school or did not complete a high school curriculum because of family needs. And, since the high school curriculum used in smaller rural high schools may not have provided an adequate foundation for the major seminary curriculum or higher education, the academic preparation in the extended postulancy and the minor seminary were important.

Students in these high school preparatory experiences often came from large families who lived in small towns or rural communities. In the early part of the twentieth century, the curricula of the minor seminary or high school postulate prepared the young men and women for college, but they did not always receive a high school diploma.

When preparatory structures for women and men religious were reorganized after World War II, high school aged candidates for women's communities were educated in aspirancies, accredited high schools which also initiated young women into religious life. For both women's and men's communities, postulancy was a college-oriented period during which high school graduates were immersed into the culture of religious life.

Men's communities and dioceses separated their minor seminaries from their major seminaries. Minor seminaries were no longer commonly connected with the facilities for their major seminaries, and they, too, began issuing high school diplomas.

The Discontinuation of Aspirancies and Minor Seminaries

Congregations of women religious began to discontinue their aspirancies in the late 1960's after the Second Vatican Council. Men's communities and dioceses continued their minor seminaries a bit longer, but by the late 1970's, most of these had also been discontinued[30].

During the years immediately after the Second Vatican Council (after 1965), many communities of religious women and men as well as dioceses experienced large numbers of sisters, brothers, and priests asking to be dispensed from their vows in order to marry or pursue a professional life. Further examination indicated that aspirancies and minor seminaries had not provided the type of developmental environment needed by adolescents in the latter part of the twentieth

Vincentian Faculty at St. John's 1952-1967*		
		Year of Appt.
Tackaberry, CM	Msgr. John	1952
Stack, CM	Rev. Robert	1952
Lange, CM	Rev. Douglas	1952
Van Lare, CM	Rev. Jan	1952
Hogan, CM	Rev. Jeremiah	1952
O'Connor, CM	Rev. John	1952
Jourdan, CM	Rev. Jerome	1952
Miller, CM	Rev. Norbert	1952
Danagher, CM	Rev. Edward	1952
Kavanaugh, CM	Rev. Thomas	1952
Ruiz, CM	Rev. Ray	1953
Miller, CM	Rev. Rudolph	1953
Mullin, CM	Rev. Edward	1954
Leonard, CM	Rev. Lawrence	1955
Miller, CM	Rev. Norman	1955
Vidal, CM	Rev. John	1956
Hoernig, CM	Rev. Alphonse	1956
Grass, CM	Rev. Kenneth	1956
Dilberto, CM	Rev. Peter	1958
McHardy, CM	Rev. James	1958
Lamy, CM	Rev. Robert	1958
Villarroya, CM	Rev. Peter	1959
Stack, CM	Rev. Robert	1961

---

[30] Though most dioceses and religious communities have closed their minor seminaries, an exception is the Capuchin Franciscans of Milwaukee who operate St. Lawrence High School Seminary in Mt. Calvary, WI. This high school seminary is one of the last in the US (*www.capuchinfranciscans.org/* and www.**stlawrenceseminary**.org; "St/ Lawrence High School Seminary" (in Wikipedia Encyclopedia, *en.wikipedia.org/wiki/ St._Lawrence_Seminary_High_School*).

century. Often the issues of adolescence (learning to negotiate with the opposite sex, separating from/rebelling against parental supervision, learning to accept adult responsibilities, and developing other life-skills, for example) remained unaddressed. When the religious women or priests entered

Hogan, CM	Rev. John	1961
Derbes, CM	Re. Louis	1962
Herbst, CM	Rev. Charles	1963
* Lee, CM	Rev. Albert H.	
Rice, CM	Rev. Robert E.	
Gregor, CM	Rev. Joseph	
Grace. CM	Rev. Thomas A.	
Discon, CM	Rev. Warren J.	
Kavanaugh, CM	Rev. Thomas	
Melito, CM	Rev. August	
Rev. Douglass	Lange, CM	

*Rev. Albert Lee and following were on the 1966-67 faculty at St. John's. The year of their appointment is not in file. Vincentian records are not consistent

into their late thirties or forties, unaddressed adolescent issues reappeared.

The decision by many congregations of women religious, as well as many dioceses, to close their aspirancies and minor seminaries in the late 1960's and early 1970's resulted as well from shifts in the US culture. Fewer young people of high school age wanted to begin religious life or study for the priesthood as teenagers. Parents were less willing to let their children make life-changing decisions at such an early age. And the lifestyle of American teenagers began to change

A Day in the Life of a St. John's
Seminarian—1968

6:30	Rise
6:50	Morning Prayers
7:05	Breakfast
7:20-7:55	Domestic Duties, Study, Free
7:55	Bus leaves for school
8:20	Classes
3:10	Bus returns from school
3:30-4:00	Domestic duties, recreation
4:00-5:00	Recreation
5:00	Clean-up
5:30	Mass
6:10	Supper followed by recreation
7:15	Spiritual reading, Rosary
8:00	Study period
8:45	Break
8:50	Study period
9:35	Night prayer
10:00	Lights out for lower classes
10:45	Lights out for upper classes

--From *1968-1969 St. John's Seminary Catalogue*, p. 19

drastically. Communities of women religious and priest-formators were uninterested in dealing with various adolescent crises that had become common in the US[31].

St. John's Seminary during the 1960's

In 1952 when Assumption Seminary opened as the major seminary for the Archdiocese of San Antonio, the Archdiocese continued the operation of its minor seminary, St. John's, at the original location on Mitchell Street. Vincentians continued to operate both seminaries for the Archdiocese.

St. John's Under Archdiocesan Leadership

Toward the end of his tenure as archbishop, Archbishop Robert E. Lucey and the Vincentians dissolved their contractual arrangement. In 1967, the Vincentians left Assumption and the following year, they concluded their services at St. John's. Both seminaries were placed under archdiocesan administrations. Indecisive about the future of St. John's after the establishment of Assumption, the Archbishop created a committee to determine how best to continue with St. John's. Laymen with educational backgrounds including Harold Wren, PhD, professor of education at Our Lady of the Lake College, and Victor Rodriguez, a principal in the San Antonio Independent School District, along with several priests assisted the Archbishop in deciding to continue the operation of St. John's under diocesan priests. It was

---

[31] This same general development led to the closure of most Catholic boarding schools, orphanages, and reformatories.

further decided to arrange with Central Catholic High School[32], a Marianist school, to educate the high school seminarians (*Called to Serve,* p. 53).

For the school year 1968-1969, the Archbishop appointed Rev. Balthasar Janacek as rector, Rev. Charles Herzig as vice-rector and dean of students, and Rev. Jack O'Donoghue as spiritual director. Rev. Gilbert Cruz and Rev. Lawrence Stuebben were also on the staff (*Called to Serve,* p. 54).

> **Msgr. Balthasar Janacek (1926-2007),** known affectionately as Father Balty, was ordained for the Archdiocese of San Antonio in 1950 after being prepared at St. John's Seminary in San Antonio. Father Balty served as rector of St. John's Minor Seminary during the 1968-69 school year. In addition to this ministry, he served St. Agnes Parish in Edna, St. Cecilia's Parish, Christ the King Parish, St. Lawrence, Parish, San Fernando Cathedral, and San Francesco di Paolo, all in San Antonio. Other work in the Archdiocese included being the spiritual director for the Cursillo Movement, director of the Old Spanish Missions, campus minister at Our Lady of the Lake University, and campus minister for the Archdiocese. (From www.victoria advocate.com and the author's personal knowledge)

The changes at St. John's drew appreciation from the Catholic community and the student body enrollment for 1968-69 was just under one hundred boys. Catholic laity believed that the new system at St. John's had brought morale to an "all time high" and that Central Catholic High School had been a excellent choice for the boys (*Called to Serve,* p. 54).

The controversy regarding the resignation[33] of Archbishop Lucey brought a change to the administration of St. John's.

"All of the priests on the staff, with the exception of one, had signed the public letter that called for the resignation of the

---

[32]   Archbishop Lucey actually preferred Antonian High School, a new high school [at that time, for boys; since 1990, co-ed] established by the Christian Brothers in 1964 (www.**antonian**.org). However, "the Archbishop deferred to the recommendation of the committee" (*Called to Serve,* p. 53-54). The author conjectures that Central Catholic was chosen because of its long history in San Antonio (established in 1852 by the Society of Mary), its reputation with Catholic families, its location since 1932 just north of downtown San Antonio, and the fact that it has always been a boys' school (*www. cchs-satx.org/*).

[33]   Chapter Six holds more on this critical episode.

archbishop. As a result, most were replaced at the end of the first year. Father Edward Bily was named rector beginning in 1969. Father Alton Rudolph was named vocation director. Both Fathers Herzig and O'Donoghue continued to serve on the staff" (*Called to Serve*, p. 56).

The Well-Dressed High School Seminarian

Every student is expected to be neatly and properly dressed at all time . . . A seminarian has no need for ties other than black. Each seminarian will need as a minimum: 2 black jackets, 3 pairs black trousers, black shoes with rubber heels . . . , 12 changes of underwear, 8 white shirts . . . , 12 handkerchiefs, 5 bedsheets, 3 pillowcases, 2 black ties, 1 bathrobe, 1 pair house slippers, 12 pairs black socks, 2 pairs of pajamas, 6 towels, 2 laundry bags, 1 drinking cup, 1 soap dish.

--From *1967-68 St. John's Seminary Catalogue, p. 10*

Msgr. Edward F. Bily was born in Praha, TX (near Schulenburg) in 1926. He entered St. John's Seminary to prepare for the priesthood at age 12 and was ordained in 1951.

Before serving as rector of St. John's Minor Seminary (1969-70), Bily had been the Associate Pastor at the newly-formed St. Pius X Parish in San Antonio and had also served at Espada Mission. In addition, he served as rector of Assumption Seminary from 1970-1975, after the resignation of Rev. Carlos Quintana. Vanderholt notes that "Bily brought stability to Assumption. He was always present and very accessible to the students. They found him to be a very good listener who had much pastoral experience" (p. 59).

A much beloved pastor, Bily served parishes in South Texas including St. James in Gonzales. His last assignment was as associate pastor at Sts. Peter and Paul Parish in New Braunfels.

Msgr. Bily died April 20, 2006.

("Obituary of Msgr. Edward F. Bily", *San Antonio Express-News*, 21 Apr 2006; Vanderholt, *Called to Serve* (p. 59)

In the spring of 1969, just before his resignation, Archbishop Lucey appointed another committee to determine the future of St. John's. The committee which included Rev. Edward Bily, St. John's rector; Rev. Carlos Quintana, the rector of Assumption and other priests, recommended that St. John's be closed. Before a decision could be made, however, Archbishop Francis J. Furey became the Archbishop of San Antonio and Lucey retired (May 13, 1969). Lucey had left a recommendation for Furey that St. John's students should be enrolled in St. Anthony's Seminary, the local minor seminary of the Oblates of Mary Immaculate. Quintana, on the other hand, suggested that future high school seminarians should enroll in the minor seminary of the Diocese of Corpus Christi which was administered by diocesan priests, but had a faculty of Jesuits (*Called to Serve*, p. 55).

Program for St. John's (1969)

Basis:

1) Boys, during 4 of the most impressionable years of their lives
2) who will mature from "little boys" to "young men" under our guidance,
3) who have in mind the priesthood as a remote goal

Our hope:

1) to FORM them
   a) into a Christian Community (serving, loving, worshipping)
   b) as the People of God
   c) as leaders
2) to HELP THEM MATURE in a novel way
   a) spiritually
   b) emotionally
   c) culturally
   d) intellectually
   e) socially
3) to FOSTER AND NOURISH their inclination to the priesthood
   a) through our personal interest in them
   b) by presenting the ideal and image of the priest
      (1) as servant
      (2) as worshipper
      (3) as witness
      (4) as prophet

--From "St. John's: The Last Year, August 22, 1969—May 27, 1970", Archives of Assumption Seminary

---

When St. John's opened at the Mitchell St. Campus for the 1969-70 school year there were sixteen seniors, twelve juniors, twenty-seven sophomores, and twenty-five freshmen. Seventy-seven of the students were from the Archdiocese of San Antonio; three were from other dioceses in Texas.

On March 21, 1970, the Archdiocese announced that "St. John's Minor Seminary would be closing at the end of that school year. No freshmen would be accepted." Applicants were referred to Corpus Christi Seminary. Sophomores, Juniors and Seniors would reside at Assumption Seminary for the 1970-71 school year and continue classes at Central Catholic High School. For high school boys who wanted to continue to discern a vocation to the priesthood and live at home, the archdiocese adopted a "home apostolic program" under Rev. Jack O'Donaghue.

The 1970-71 school year began with the St. John's boys living in Mary-Catherine Hall on the campus of Assumption Seminary (*Called to Serve*, p. 55 and *The Alamo Messenger*, March 20, 1970).

In its final year, 1971-1972, St. John's (on the Assumption campus) had nine seniors, and seven juniors. Sophomores and Freshmen had been phased out (*San Antonio Express/News,* Saturday, May 6, 1972, p. 5-B).

The Last Students

In the last years (1965-1969), the student body at St. John's Minor Seminary ranged from 153 students in 1965, just above 100 students in 1967-1968, to sixteen juniors and seniors[34] in 1972. In the various "Catalogues", student lists show that though the greater percentage of students were from the Archdiocese of San Antonio (+/- 70%), other dioceses (Dallas, San Angelo, Austin, Galveston-Houston, Oklahoma City, and Beaumont) also sent their high school seminarians to St. John's.

The students from the Archdiocese of San Antonio were about evenly split between those from small town parishes and those from parishes in San Antonio itself. Many of the boys from the other dioceses were from small towns, and the overwhelming majority of the boys of the 1966-67 class were non-Hispanic.

Though attrition statistics for St. John's Minor Seminary were not tracked in its fifty-five year history[35], most of the hundreds of boys who attended the minor seminary were not ordained.

Of the twelve high school seminarians in the Senior Class of 1968 who were from the San Antonio Archdiocese, two were eventually ordained: Michael J. Boulette of Fredericksburg, Texas, and James M. Kotara from Karnes City. At this writing, Msgr. Boulette is at Notre Dame Parish in Kerrville, TX and is also the director of St. Peter-Upon-the-Water Retreat Center in Ingram, TX. Rev. James Kotara is presently the pastor of St. Thomas More Parish in San Antonio, TX.

---

[34]   There is not a listing of these young men. The author presumes that they are included in the student listings of Central Catholic High School.

[35]   According to Vanderholt's *Called to Serve* (p. 57), "No complete records have been kept of the alumni of Saint John's who were not ordained."

CHAPTER SIX

REFOUNDING THE SEMINARY: A NEW VISION

The sixteen documents which resulted from the Second Vatican Council had been in print less than two years when Rev. Roy Rihn was appointed as rector of Assumption Seminary in the summer of 1967. Father Rihn and his confreres, Rev. Robert Walden, the new vice-rector; Rev. Louis Michalski, the dean of students; Rev. Virgil Elizondo, academic dean; Rev. Vincent DelaRosa, director of music and spiritual director; and Rev. Ray Henke, spiritual director—all archdiocesan priests—now had the task of re-shaping the seminary according to the vision of the Second Vatican Council (Vanderholt, p. 41-42).

The academic development of the theologians was in the hands of the Graduate School of Theology of St. Mary's University. Nationally-known theology professors at St. Mary's, Marianist priests George Montague, Willis Langlinais, and Charles Neumann anchored this aspect of the seminary program.

> *Msgr. Roy Rihn* (b. 1918) was educated in his home parish school, St. Louis in Castroville, TX; St. John's Seminary; the Gregorian University in Rome, Italy; and Catholic University of America in Washington, DC. He was ordained for the Archdiocese of San Antonio in 1942, served at St. Cecilia's Parish, and is the founding pastor of St. Pius X Parish. After serving as rector of Assumption Seminary from June 1967- October 1968 (15 months), Msgr. Rihn was the Associate Director of Campus Ministry at Oklahoma University; and pastored St. Patrick's Parish, Bloomington, TX; St. Mary's Parish in Victoria, TX; and was the parochial vicar at St. Paul's Parish in San Antonio. His other ministries include archdiocesan vocation director, preaching retreats for priests and laity, offering spiritual direction, and writing. [From Msgr. Rihn's "Curriculum Vitae", 2012]

Collegians also attended St. Mary's. Because the seminarians attended a regular university, each seminarian could pursue a degree of his choice and graduate with a college degree.

The new seminary catalogue for the academic year 1967-1968 incorporated statements from Vatican documents. When an article in the *Alamo Messenger*[36] was picked up by the National Catholic News Service, Assumption received national recognition as

the first United States seminary to offer a complete program in an environment drawn from the Vatican II documents. It was the first complete post-Conciliar seminary. The staff no longer ate at a separate table in the refectory but ate two meals a day with the students. They ate the third meal alone as that afforded time for a daily staff meeting. The students were kept busy on campus without having strict rules and many new apostolic programs were introduced.

The discipline did not stress externals . . .

> *Discipline is not merely external conformity* to rules. The idea of discipline is returning to its original definition: a learning situation where we develop into men. It is a period of discipleship. "By wisely planned training, there should be developed in seminarians a due degree of human maturity, attested to chiefly by a certain emotional stability, by an ability to make considered decisions, and by a right manner of passing judgment on events and people. In general, seminarians should learn to prize those qualities which are highly regarded among men and speak well of a minister of Christ. Such are: sincerity of heart, a constant concern for justice fidelity to one's word, courtesy of manner, restraint, and kindliness in speech."
> [*Assumption Seminary Catalogue, 1968-1969* and Vatican II, "Decree on Priestly Formation", 4.11, quoted on page 9 of the Catalogue]

There were no bells and no formal night prayer. There was no designated period of study as the student had to regulate his own life. Periods of

---

[36] The *Alamo Messenger* was the name of the newspaper of the Archdiocese of San Antonio established in 1957 when the *Southern Messenger*, published by the Menger family, merged with the *Alamo Register*. In 1972 the archdiocesan newspapers became known as *Today's Catholic* (from 1874-1974 Archdiocese of San Antonio).

silence were encouraged to create the atmosphere of study and prayer (Vanderholt, p. 43-44).

Father Rihn and the faculty welcomed 143 students—eighty-eight in college and fifty-five in theology—in the fall of 1967. Over forty percent of the students were transfers from other dioceses and half of the students were for the Archdiocese of San Antonio. "Other dioceses represented were Oklahoma City; Santa Fe; Saginaw, Lansing, and Grand Rapids in Michigan; Santa Rosa in California; Alexandria in Louisiana; Denver; and Arecibo in Puerto Rico" (Vanderholt, p. 45).

In the first year of the return to archdiocesan leadership for the seminary, plans were laid for the construction of St. Florence and St. Edith Chapel based on a paper on the philosophy of Catholic liturgy written by Father Rihn (See Chapter Three: Building Up Sacred Ground). Father Bob Walden developed a field education program for the seminarians in order to give them some practical experience in parish life. Programs for students were re-designed annually in order to maximize their effectiveness in terms of student needs. Msgr. Rihn remembers the seminarians being highly politicized, actively participating in the very volatile national election of 1968. Seminarians also took part in anti-war demonstrations, a position in opposition to the Archbishop's posture of holding the war in Viet Nam as justified by Catholic social doctrine (Interview with Msgr. Roy Rihn; Vanderholt, p. 46).

Challenges in the Archdiocese[37]

In 1968 frustrations among the Archdiocesan priests with the leadership style of Archbishop Lucey reached their zenith. Without faulting Lucey's contributions to the archdiocese in the past, the priests' complaints were focused on his relationship with the Priests' Senate, the transfer of priests, and his positions

---

[37] Much of the material in this section is from Vanderholt's *Called to Serve*, pages 45-52. If the material is from elsewhere, the citation is noted.

on social justice issues. After several failed attempts by the priests to dialogue with the Archbishop in the winter of 1967-68, the archdiocesan priests wrote a letter to Archbishop Lucey requesting that he retire. Written by Father Sherril Smith[38] and Father Roy Rihn, the letter, signed by more than fifty priests, was eventually sent to Rome on September 16, 1968. The priests who signed noted that if they had not heard from Rome by a given date, they would make the letter public.

Archbishop Lucey's response targeted the seminary faculty and he arranged for an investigation of the seminary in October.

> The investigation at Assumption came off on "Black Monday," October 21, 1968. At 1:00 in the afternoon, the archbishop, with four priests and four laymen, made an unannounced visit to the seminary. With one priest guarding a group of seminarians waiting only to be questioned, and another priest standing in front of the interrogation room, Lucey's committee grilled individual students on seminary discipline, including reports of drinking, dating, and disregard to traditional spirituality. The inquisition ended only with Rihn's arrival and a sharp exchange with the archbishop (Bronder, Saul, *Social Justice and Church Authority*, page not cited)[39].

Though the Archbishop had indicated that he was favorable to the various changes at Assumption by the archdiocesan priests in leadership, the faculty itself had come to see that the system

---

[38]   Msgr. Sherril Smith (d. 2012) was a political activist who marched for racial equality in the 1965 Selma-to-Montgomery March with Dr. Martin Luther King; he also "championed the poor, the unborn, civil rights, labor and racial justice, which many times landed him in jail" [http://www.legacy.com/obituaries/ sanantonio/obituary].

[39]   . This exact piece from Bronder's biography of Archbishop Lucey is quoted on page 48 of Vanderholt's work *Called to Serve*. *Social Justice and Church Authority* was published in 1982 by Temple University Press in Philadelphia (Vanderholt, p. 185).

needed to be tweaked. They wanted to continue to offer the seminarians appropriate freedom to mature and at the same time curb the abuses by the more immature candidates.

The priests had not heard from the Vatican by the date given in their letter and on October 24, 1968, three days after "Black Monday," they called a press conference and released the contents of the letter. Nearly eighty per cent of the 161 students at Assumption signed the priests' letter—now public. That same week over half of the seminarians demonstrated at St. Pius X Parish where Archbishop Lucey was administering the Sacrament of Confirmation. In those post-Vatican II times, changes from Rome still moved slowly and the seminarians carried some unreal expectations of how the Church would respond to challenges such as this one.

The four members of the faculty at Assumption who had signed the letter to Rome, Msgr. Rihn, Fathers, Walden, Henke, and Michalski, were removed from their appointments in October 1968. They declined their assignment to live at Padua Place[40] and took a leave of absence (Interview with Msgr. Rihn).

Father Carlos Quintana was appointed rector in the fall of 1968. In the first year he was assisted by Father Robert Kownacki, Father Joseph James, Father Alton Rudolph, Father Austin Lindsay, CSV. Other priests who joined the faculty the next year (1969-70) were Father Charles Grahmann, Father Bernard Mullaney and Father Lambert Bily.

> *Rev. Carlos Quintana, OSB* (1924-1998) had studied at St. John's Seminary in preparation for being ordained a priest of the Archdiocese of San Antonio in 1949. Prior to serving as rector of Assumption Seminary, Father Quintana had been the pastor of St. Phillip of Jesus Parish and the editor of *La Voz*. After resigning as rector in March 1970, Quintana was sent by the Archdiocese to do mission work in the Diocese of Huehuetenango in Guatemala where he worked as a pastor and with seminarians. It was there that he met the Benedictines of St. Marmion Abbey, who have a mission, San José Priory, in Guatemala. He professed his monastic vows in January 1978. Quintana remained in Guatemala and was instrumental in re-locating the priory from Solalá to its present location in the Diocese of Quetzaltenango. He taught in the seminary there, did spiritual direction and pastoral work. After a decline in his health, Fr. Carlos died in Quetzaltenango in 1998; he is buried there. [from Vanderholt, p. 49; interview with Rev. Joel Rippinger, OSB, St. Marmion Abbey, Oct. 1, 2013]

---

40   Padua Place is a private facility for infirm priests in San Antonio owned and operated by the Missionary Servants of St. Anthony.

The 1968-1969 academic year focused on attempts to stabilize life at Assumption but student unrest continued. The staff, at the direction of Archbishop Lucey, moved slowly in dismissing students who seemed to be the leaders of dissatisfied seminarians. Morale was low among both the seminarians and the faculty.

Archbishop Robert E. Lucey submitted his resignation to the Vatican on December 10, 1968, and it was accepted in May 1969. In early summer, the appointment of Bishop Francis Furey of San Diego was announced and his installation in August of 1969 signaled a new era for Assumption. The new archbishop, faced with financial challenges, decided to live at the seminary and sell the historic Episcopal residence in the Monte Vista area in which Archbishop Lucey had lived for most of his episcopacy.

Challenging Years

For the academic year 1969-1970, many dioceses withdrew their seminarians, some seminarians were asked not to return, and some withdrew believing they did not have a vocation to the priesthood. By January of 1970, the student body which had begun at 146 in September 1969 was reduced to eighty. Thirty-one of these were theologians; the rest were college students. This downturn in enrollment caused a great financial difficulty for the archdiocese, and in February 1970, "Father Quintana sent a report to Archbishop Furey that 'the faculty was unanimous that Assumption should close. The San Antonio students could move into the empty rooms at the Scholasticate[41] at St. Mary's University but continue to take their classes locally'. Archbishop Furey did not accept this" (Vanderholt, p. 51).

A month later Father Quintana resigned as rector, and later transferred to the San José Benedictine Priory in Guatemala, a mission of Marmion Abbey in Aurora, IL.

---

[41]   The Scholasticate is the residence on the St. Mary's University campus for men who are studying to be Brothers of Mary (Marianists) or priests of that same order.

Father Edward Bily[42], the rector of St. John's, was named the rector of Assumption and held that post until 1975.

The challenges of those post-conciliar times were felt in Assumption Seminary no differently than in the Catholic Church as a whole. Laity and priests alike, longing for the more predictable days of the pre-Vatican II Church, were critical of changes that had taken place at the seminary since the Vincentians departed. Faculty complained about the freedoms that seminarians had, suggesting that the environment at Assumption had become too lax.

As rector, Father Bily sought to bring stability to the major seminary. Bily was in the last year of phasing out St. John's students who now lived on the Assumption campus. In 1970, under Bily, undergraduate collegians remained at St. Mary's while graduate theologians were transferred to Oblate School of Theology. Efforts were made to broaden the education of seminarians. For example, Michael Boulette, was given permission to pursue his master's degree in psychology at Trinity University while he was in the formation program at Assumption; David Garcia finished his theology at Notre Dame; Norman Ermis studied at the Theological College

Archbishop Francis Furey (1905-1979) was born in Summit Hill, PA, and attended St. Charles Borromeo Seminary in Overbrook, PA, and the Pontifical Roman Seminary in Rome. Furey was ordained in Rome in 1930. After returning to Pennsylvania, he was the secretary to Cardinal Dennis Dougherty, Archbishop of Philadelphia; president of Immaculata College; and rector of St. Charles Borromeo Seminary. From 1958 until his appointment as Auxiliary Bishop of Philadelphia in 1960, Furey served as pastor of St. Helena Parish there. In 1963, he was named Coadjutor Bishop of San Diego and served as bishop of that diocese until 1969 when he became the third Archbishop of San Antonio. While serving as Ordinary of San Antonio, Furey supported the Farah strike in October 1973 and the lettuce boycotts on behalf of the Texas Farm Workers Union. His national offices included chair of the Committee for the Campaign for Human Development. [From en.wikipedia.org/wiki/ Francis_ James_ Furey; "Era of Archbishop Furey, 1969—", *1874-1974: Archdiocese of San Antonio, p. 34-36*]

---

[42]   See a biography of Msgr. Edward Bily in Chapter Five—The Final Years.

(Sulpicians) in Washington, DC (Interview with Msgr. Michael Boulette, Summer 2013; information from Msgr. Lawrence Stuebben).

As programs developed to meet the needs of the future priests, the environment at Assumption began to crystallize.

Collegians in the first two years of college met with Father Charles Herzig for spiritual growth and development; third and fourth year collegians met with Father Bernard Mullaney on the theme of Christian commitment. First and second year theologians pursued the theme of "vocation" with Father Jack O'Donaghue; Father Bily met with third and fourth year theologians to develop pastoral skills. Self-discipline, self-knowledge, serving others, and "developing a safe life in all of this especially with their commitment to the church and celibacy" focused the seminarians and the faculty (Vanderholt, p. 59-60).

Development of the campus continued as homes were built for the Hermanas Josefinas and Mary-Catherine Hall was retrofitted to accommodate the Mexican American Cultural Center (MACC) which opened in the fall of 1972. The presence of the MACC students, women and men from all over the US who were expanding their pastoral skills so as to be of service to the growing Latino population in the US, served to broaden the world of the seminarians (Vanderholt, p. 60).

> *Father Charles Kram, Jr.* (1929-2000), St. John's Class of 1953, was ordained on December 5, 1975, at age 46 by Archbishop Furey. Kram was stricken with polio while home on vacation in 1952. After months of rehabilitation, he returned home to Shiner, TX, a paraplegic. Though he had not been ordained, Kram was voted into the Priests Alumni Association in 1960. Pope John Paul II gave his special permission in 1975 for Kram to be ordained. Though confined to a wheelchair, Father Kram continued a ministry in pastoral care at Yoakum Catholic Hospital for many years. In the Fall 1984 Assumption Newsletter, Kram wrote: "For me, pastoral ministry is a ministry of strength and consolation to the sick and their loved ones, . . . the bonds of love and grace remain unbroken." [from various internet sources, *Assumption Newsletter* and Vanderholt, p.157]

Guest-professors at Oblate School of Theology also brought a wider perspective of Church and society to Assumption seminarians. During the 1970's these professors included Father Luke Richard, an Oblate from Weston Theological School in Boston; Father Bernard Lee, SM; Father David Power,

OMI, from Catholic University; Father Joachim Pillai, OMI, a biblical theologian from Sri Lanka (Vanderholt, p. 61).

In 1973, Assumption began the fall semester with sixty students: thirty-eight collegians and twenty-two theologians. Most of the seminarians were for the San Antonio Archdiocese.

Others who served on the staff in the 1970's included Father James Janish (1974), who was a spiritual director. Father Janish had a Master's Degree in Spirituality from the University of San Francisco at Berkley, a Jesuit school.

Oblate School of Theology (formerly Oblate College of the Southwest), founded in San Antonio in 1903, was initially the seminary for vocations to the Missionary Oblates of Mary Immaculate who were preparing for missionary work in Texas, New Mexico, Louisiana, Mexico, and the Philippines. Today, by integrating theological study and pastoral experience, the School of Theology prepares seminarians from religious congregations and dioceses from all over the US, women and men from Roman Catholic parishes and other Christian denominations for a variety of ministries. Oblate continues to understand that faith is imbedded in culture and that "preparation for mission and ministry [is] the actual integration of pastoral experience and theological study." In an arrangement with St. Paul University in Ottawa, Canada, OST offers an ecclesiastical degree: the STB, Baccalaureate in Sacred Theology. In addition to the seminary curriculum, Oblate offers other programs: Ministry to Ministers is a four-month intensive experience for women and men religious and priests who have been in ministerial assignments for a number of years; the Lay Ministry Institute and the *Instituto de Formacion Pastoral* prepare the laity for professional ministry in the Church; the Oblate Renewal Center offers programs in spiritual growth and retreats; the Sankofa Institute for African American Pastoral Leadership offers academic and cultural support for pastoral leaders for the African American Christian community.

A highly-credentialed faculty of women and men, religious and lay, who have terminal degrees from prestigious institutions in the US and abroad, provides course work, pastoral supervision, and spiritual guidance to the seminarians who study at Oblate. [From: Oblate School of Theology, *www. ost.edu]*

Financial stress because of continued low enrollment at Assumption pressed Archbishop Furey to investigate other options. In 1975 talks between Assumption and Oblate in San Antonio, and St. Mary's Seminary in Houston began to evolve. Suggestions included creating a theologate at one seminary and a college seminary at another. Miscommunication between Archbishop Furey and Bishop John Morkovsky of Galveston-Houston resulted in a decision by both Ordinaries to maintain their own seminaries as they had been doing (Vanderholt, p. 63).

Father Edward Bily had resigned the position of rector in the spring of 1975, effective in the summer. When the talks for merging the two seminaries in San Antonio and Houston broke down, Archbishop Furey announced that he was engaging a new rector, Father James Vanderholt from the Diocese of Beaumont (Vanderholt, p. 63).[43]

The last years of the episcopate of Archbishop Francis Furey, with Vanderholt as rector, were re-building ones for Assumption Seminary.

Immediate changes in the fall of 1975 included the designation of a room on the second floor of St. Alice Hall as a Blessed Sacrament Chapel in order to promote group and individual prayer. And, seminarians at Assumption, now

Msgr. James Vanderholt (b.1932), a native of Beaumont, TX, attended St. Mary's Seminary in Houston and was ordained for the Diocese of Galveston-Houston in 1957. When the Diocese of Beaumont was created in 1966, Vanderholt served in a variety of ministries in that diocese. Vanderholt was engaged as rector of Assumption Seminary by Archbishop Furey in 1975. After six years in that position, he returned to the Diocese of Beaumont where he edited the diocesan newspaper, wrote the history of Assumption Seminary from its inception until 1990, and pastored both rural and African-American parishes. In 1991, Vanderholt received the Texas Catholic Historical Society's Carlos Eduardo Castañeda Award for the promotion of Catholic historical study in the Texas. He is now pastor-emeritus in residence at St. Mark the Evangelist Parish in Silsbee, TX. [From Vanderholt's vitae; *Called to Serve*; Vanderholt, Father James, "Rector recalls time at Assumption Seminary," *Today's Catholic*, August 17, 2007; Interview, Nov. 2012]

Recollections

The seminarians gathered outside Fr. Vanderholt's room for *Las Mañanitas* on a September morning shortly after he became the rector. But the early morning festivities were interrupted by a skunk who believed them to be in his pre-dawn space. The men were sprayed! When the incident was reported to the Archbishop with a notation that "something needed to be done about the skunks," Furey responded, "Be kind to them, Father Jim. They seem to be the only ones on campus who dress in clericals!" (Vanderholt, p. 64).

students at Oblate School of Theology, were required to earn a Master's Degree in Divinity. Not

---

[43] Father Vanderholt's book, *Called to Serve*, related this incident familiarly from his own point of view on pages 63 and 64. He had expected to join the faculty and staff at Assumption in the summer of 1975 as a spiritual director, but a "failure to communicate" left him without the knowledge that the Archbishop was expecting him to take on the position of rector (Vanderholt, p. 63).

only was the new requirement for the master's degree bringing Assumption into compliance with the agenda of the US Catholic Conference of Bishops for seminarians, but it also gave the seminarians a more solid footing for their ministerial life.

Assumption continued to offer a balanced program of spiritual direction, psychological development, community living, scholarship, and connection to the larger Church.

Innovative Programs

A student intern program which had been developed at Southern Methodist University in Dallas was initiated at Oblate for the Oblate and Assumption seminarians. Designed to assist seminarians to transition successfully from the world of academics to the work of pastoral life, the program was both practically based, professionally supervised, and had an ecumenical flavor (Vanderholt, p. 64-66).

In the 1980's, Msgr. Charles Grahmann, the pastor of St. Gregory's Parish in San Antonio, initiated an alternative seminary program at the parish. Seminarians were allowed to live at the parish and attend classes at Oblate School of theology. Five priests were ordained from this program (Most Rev. Charles Grahmann's written memoirs, Feb. 1, 2012).

Enlarging the World of the Seminarian

Seminarians at Assumption became acquainted with the global concerns of the Church as they interacted with students at the Mexican American Cultural Center. Both the priests of the growing Vietnamese Catholic Community and PADRES, a national organization of Mexican-American priests, opened offices across the street from Assumption. Though the students did not have much contact with these offices, their presence served to alert the seminarians to the future Church whom they would serve as priests.

Other events and circumstances at Assumption during the late 1970's and early 1980's expanded the world in which the seminarians were being trained.

o In May of 1976, Mother Teresa of Calcutta spoke at the Municipal Auditorium in San Antonio.

o Runaway teens at an emergency home at the former Peacock Academy on Woodlawn who took their meals at Assumption became a daily reminder of the breakdown of society and the needs that follow.

o Rev. Pedro Arrupe, SJ, then Master General of the Society of Jesus, celebrated the Eucharist at Assumption while visiting San Antonio.

o Rev. Adrian van

> **Rev. Stanley Rother** (1935-1981), born in Okarche, OK, an alumnus of St. John's and Assumption (1953-1959) and St. Mary's Seminary in Emmitsburg, MD (1959-1963), had been ordained for the Diocese of Oklahoma City in 1963. Rother was sent to Oklahoma City's mission in Guatemala in 1968 after serving in several Oklahoma parishes. In Santiago Atitlan, Rother taught the natives how to improve their crops, helped build a hospital and repaired medical equipment. When danger grew in Guatemala, Rother returned to Oklahoma for a short visit. Though still in danger after death squads began killing priests and sisters, Rother chose to return to the people whom he loved and respected. On July 28, 1981, Rother, *the shepherd who would not run*, was shot in the head after struggling with his murderers in his rectory. His body was returned to Oklahoma, but with his parent's permission, his heart remains enshrined in his church with the people he loved and served. The cause for his canonization was opened in 2007. [from Vanderholt, p. 75; Dyer, Ray, "Sainthood cause opens for former Assumption seminarian", *Today's Catholic*, p. 6; Bird, Rev. Stephen and Shirley Kraft, "Rev. Stanley Rother: A Shepherd that Did Not Run . . .", *Assumption Seminary Bridge Builder*, Summer 2003, p. 10-11]

Kaam, CSSp and Doctor Susan Muto, spiritual writers, were presenters for the Archdiocesan annual Clergy Day.

o Rev. Richard McBrien (Priest of the Archdiocese of Hartford, CT), a professor at Notre Dame University, was on campus for a weekend presentation on "The Church: Past, Present, and Future."

In April 1979 Archbishop Furey died and in October 1979 Bishop Patricio Flores of El Paso was installed as the fourth Archbishop of the Archdiocese of San Antonio.

Father James Vanderholt returned to the Diocese of Beaumont in May 1981 and Father Lawrence Stuebben, appointed by Archbishop Flores, began his duties as rector on June 1, 1981.

The types of innovations begun under Fr. Roy Rihn in 1967 and continued under subsequent rectors had an advocate in Fr. Stuebben. Stuebben examined the "seminary world" of the US and lived in the seminary in the spring of 1981 in order to be oriented to seminary operations. A focus on developing bilingual priests continued and the relationship with MAAC was deepened (Interview with Stuebben, February 13, 2012).

Fourteen dioceses continued to send their men to Assumption and more than half of the students were Hispanic.

The spiritual direction staff at Assumption was augmented by the services of Father Michael Boulette who reorganized the spiritual formation program. His nationally-known program, *Words Made Flesh*, included a series of twelve sessions per year. Eventually the program was translated into Spanish by another San Antonio priest, Father Fernando Rubio-Boitel. Others who were added to the staff included Father José Lopez, recently returned from graduate studies in theology at Claremont University in California, who was named vice-rector and dean of students. Father David Garcia, secretary to the Archbishop, lived at the seminary assisting with field education and offering workshops in church management.

Assumption Mission Statement

The Assumption Seminary of the Archdiocese of San Antonio, Texas,
is a community of formation
which exists for the spiritual, academic and ministerial preparation of men
for the Roman Catholic priesthood, especially in the
Southwestern United States.

Our main goal is to
enable men to grow and develop as pastoral ministers committed to the service of the people of God.

This goal is distinguished by our special orientation toward Hispanic ministry.

[Probably 1982. Exact date of Statement not known]

Sister Madlyn Pape, CDP, was added to the staff to teach liturgical music, and Father James Janish continued as spiritual director (Vanderholt, p. 76-77).

Emphasis continued to be placed on preparing men for ministry with Hispanics. Recognizing the importance of on-going formation after ordination, seminarians were also introduced to various programs in spiritual growth that were popular with local priests. These included "Emmaus," a retreat plan loosely based on the Cursillo program. *Jesu Caritas*, a program designed around prayer and discussion with fellow priests, was introduced. Using the Blessed Sacrament as a centerpoint, *Jesu Caritas* provides support to priests who are increasingly called upon to live and minister alone. Seminarians were also introduced to journal-keeping and directed retreats.

Pastor-in-Residence, another new program, was aimed at bringing pastors who had been ordained from Assumption back to spend a significant amount of time with present seminarians. The first Pastor-in-Residence in 1982 was alumnus and former rector Bishop Sidney Metzger, retired Ordinary of El Paso. Among the participants in the Pastor-in-Residence program were Father Ramon Gaiton, OAR, Monsignor Joseph Schumacher, and Father Vicente Lopez of the USCC Hispanic Office.

> *Msgr. Lawrence Stuebben* (b. 1932), a native of San Antonio, grew up in downtown St. Joseph's Parish. He attended St. John's Seminary for four years and Assumption for three years and was ordained for the Archdiocese of San Antonio in 1955. Stuebben served as parochial vicar and pastor of four parishes in the archdiocese, chaplain at Incarnate Word High School, secretary for Bishop Stephen A. Leven, and Archdiocesan Vocation Director before he was named rector of Assumption by Archbishop Flores. In his last year as rector of Assumption, Monsignor was the coordinator of Pope John Paul II's visit to San Antonio in September 1987. After serving as rector, Stuebben was the Vicar General to Archbishop Flores, Head of Administration for the Archdiocese, Moderator of the Curia, and Associate Pastor at St. Margaret Mary Parish. He is now retired and lives at Casa de Padres. (From "Survey of Alumni", 2012)

Initial changes also included adding a fourth year to the theological studies and requiring seminarians to be on campus all the time. Community prayers and daily Mass became obligatory (Interview with Msgr. Stuebben, February 13, 2012).

In building the Christian community, priests are never to put themselves at the service of some human faction of ideology, but as heralds of the Gospel and Shepherds of the Church, they are to spend themselves for the spiritual growth of the Body of Christ.

--Decree on the Ministry and Life of Priests (De Presbyterorus Ministerio et Vita) Promulgated by His Holiness, Pope Paul VI on December 7, 1965, The Sixteen Documents of Vatican II, St. Paul Editions, p.426

By 1984, the student body at Assumption had nearly doubled. From twenty students representing nine dioceses in 1982, the enrollment in 1984 was nearly forty students representing seventeen dioceses.

Twenty-five years had passed since Saint Pope John XXIII called for "opening the windows" of the Church. Men who were answering the call to priesthood in the mid-1980's came to Assumption with professional careers, spiritual maturity, and personal focus on ministry. However, in the words of Father Stuebben, the men were not "saints, only real people struggling to respond to what they see and hear." They might be ordained only three or four years before they would be thrust into a pastorate. Therefore, Assumption expanded the programs that would prepare the men for the Church they would serve.

Candidates for the priesthood were required to do field work in hospitals, children's centers, or psychiatric institutes. Internships in parishes were designed to immerse the seminarians into the reality of parish life and Clinical Pastoral Education programs, housed in hospital environments, helped the future priests to encounter their personal inner world in a way that would strengthen them to assist those who would come for guidance and support (Ciarrocchi, Maura, "San Antonio's best kept secret," *Today's Catholic*, October 10, 1986, p. 10; Pruss, Teri, "Assumption Seminary: Offers the Whole Works," *Today's Catholic*, April 4, 1985).

A Bilingual-Bicultural Theologate

The relationship with the Mexican American Cultural Center was strengthened to better prepare Assumption seminarians for work in the Hispanic culture. At that time students took their first full year at Oblate and then spent nine weeks on the seminary campus while they took Spanish followed by a full Hispanic semester at MACC. The mini-pastoral at MACC included eight more weeks of Spanish and then a month at a Mexican-American parish in San Antonio followed by a week of theological reflection on the experience. The seminarian would then return to Oblate for his third year theology and re-immerse himself in his master's degree studies.

Only the Archdiocese of San Antonio utilized this program. Though the vocation directors of other dioceses had advocated for a bilingual-bicultural program, those dioceses continued with the academic program at Oblate but did not add the component that would have prepared their men for pastoral work with Latinos.

Fourteen dioceses continued to send their men to Assumption and more than half of the students were Hispanic.

Unfortunately, other dioceses did not take advantage of the bilingual-bicultural opportunities that MAAC offered at first.

"My soul gives thanks to the Lord; all my being, bless his holy name."

The September 1987 visit by Saint John Paul II began with Mass at a 144-acre site in Westover Hills, a development of Sea World even though the altar platform was left in disarray when the rising towers crashed three nights before the Mass during a forceful storm. After the Mass which drew between 300,000 and 350,000 people, the Pope was escorted to Assumption Seminary for lunch and a rest period in the Archbishop's quarters. The Pope's afternoon agenda included a motorcade route from Assumption to Municipal Auditorium lined with 700,000 San Antonians. At the Auditorium Saint Pope John Paul II gave his major talk to members of Catholic Charities and Catholic social ministry organization. Next, women and men in religious formation were addressed at the Cathedral. Hispanics, gathered at Our Lady of Guadalupe Plaza, greeted the Pope next and he spoke to them in Spanish; Polish Catholics then received him at the Assumption quadrangle. After spending the night at Assumption in the Archbishop's quarters, he left from Kelly Air Force Base the next morning (Vanderholt, p. 95-103).

But by the mid-1980's, "Assumption, Oblate, and MACC designed a one-year program for seminarians that were preparing for Hispanic ministry." Entitled "The *Servador* Program," it provided additional studies in pastoral Spanish, on-going spiritual formation at Assumption, and pastoral assignments in local Hispanic parishes (Vanderholt, p. 84).

As the tenure of Father Stuebben as rector was coming to an end in the spring of 1987, the bilingual-bicultural approach to preparing seminarians for ministry in the Archdiocese of San Antonio was mandated. Seminarians were informed upon entrance to Assumption that

> . . . Assumption Seminary requires that all incoming students understand and accept the full program of Assumption which includes preparation for bilingual-bicultural ministry.

The same leaflet noted that the staff at Assumption was bilingual, prayers would be in Spanish two days a week, and liturgy would be celebrated in Spanish two days a week. All seminarians were steeped in the Hispanic culture and

> all students are required to take the course in Homiletics to the Mexican-American. Each of the students is required to preach in Spanish in his last two semesters at the Seminary. The student is also asked to be Lector and lead morning prayer in Spanish from the first year onward . . . we desire that the student be prepared as much as possible to function in that capacity, especially if he is to serve in a Spanish-speaking parish (Vanderholt, p. 91-92).

In the six years that Father Stuebben served as rector, Assumption came to be nationally recognized as "the foremost theologate in the U.S. with an emphasis on Hispanic ministry" and a closer relationship with Oblate School of Theology was established. The enrollment had gone from twenty-one students in the first year to fifty-six students in Stuebben's last year—a 166% increase. The entry class in 1987 would be the "largest the seminary had had in eighteen years." Financial stability was solidified by an endowment fund begun by Father Stuebben which had already passed the $800,000 mark. Seminary burses had increased and the Friends of Assumption's annual festival had become more and more successful with each passing year (Interview with Father Stuebben published in *Today's Catholic*, May 22, 1987, Vanderholt, p. 89-90).

Father Stuebben joined the staff of Archbishop Flores, serving as the Texas coordinator of Saint John Paul II's visit which took place in September 1987.

Becoming a "Latino" Seminary

Rev. Gerald (Gerry) Barnes succeeded as rector of Assumption in the fall of 1987. The immediate goals of Father Barnes, himself Hispanic, for his tenure as rector were to 1) develop a seminary board which would help in planning for the future of the seminary; 2) diversify the seminary staff; 3) promote cultural diversity and appreciation; 4) improve facilities; 5) increase enrollment; and 6) collaborate with local Catholic universities and Oblate School of Theology (Interview with Bishop Gerald R. Barnes, Sept. 12, 2013).

Expanding the Faculty

The seminary staff that served the fifty seminarians with Father Barnes included Fathers Michael Boulette, Director of Spiritual Formation; José López, Director of Community Life; Fernando Rubio-Boitel, Director of Liturgical Formation. Fathers David Garcia, Don Curry, and Charles Schaub, CSSR also served on the faculty. In addition to a traditionally configured staff, Barnes added two women: Sisters Dorothea O'Meara, CSB, Director of Admissions and Director of Studies; and Sr. Jacinta Millán, CSC, Director of Cultural Formation and Director of

Las Hermanas Josefinas were the first in a long line of women who served as physicians, librarians, dietary managers, mother and grandmother-figures, music teachers, liturgists, spiritual directors, curriculum advisors, and directors of internships, at St. John's ≈ Assumption Seminaries.

Ms. Bernice M. Barnett
Sister Pat Casey, OP
Sister Mary Teresa Cullen, CSB
Sister Dianne Heinrich, CDP
Ms. Genevieve Huxoll
Ms. Anna Rose Kanning
Ms. Linda Krehmeier
Sister Carmen Therese Lazo, MCDP
Sister Jacinta Millán, CSC
Sister Mary Christine Morkovsky, CDP
Sister Dorothea O'Meara, CSB
Sister Madlyn Pape, CDP
Sister Guadalupe Ramirez, MCDP
Dr. Mary King Robbie
Ms. Edith Shumaker
Sister Jane Ann Slater, CDP
Ms. Frances Stortz
Sister Addie Loraine Walker, SSND [From *25 Years a Seminary*; Vanderholt; and various articles from *Today's Catholic*, et al.]

Bishop Gerald R. Barnes (b. 1945) a native of Phoenix, AZ, was raised in East Los Angeles where he and his siblings worked in their parents' grocery store. After graduating from Roosevelt High School in Los Angeles, Bishop Barnes earned a BA in Political Science from California State University in Los Angeles in 1967. Before entering Assumption Seminary for the Archdiocese of San Antonio, Barnes was in the formation program of the Holy Family priests and the Marianist Priests and Brothers, attending seminaries in St. Louis and Dayton, OH. After being ordained in 1975, Father Barnes served in St. Timothy Parish, St. Paul's Parish and on the Presbyteral Council, the Marriage Tribunal, the Personnel Board and other archdiocesan positions before being appointed the first Latino rector of Assumption in 1987. After serving as rector from 1987 until 1992, Barnes was appointed auxiliary bishop of San Bernardino. Pope John Paul II appointed him the second Ordinary for the Diocese of San Bernardino in 1995 when the former bishop of San Bernardino was transferred to the reconstituted Diocese of Reno. The Diocese of San Bernardino covers 27,000 miles and has over 1.2 million Catholics (Interview with Bishop Barnes, Sept. 12, 2013 and *sbdiocese. org/bishops/ barnes*)

Pre-Theology. Both women brought rich backgrounds.

Sister O'Meara, a Brigidine Sister, had been born in Ireland but had been in San Antonio for many years. In addition to teaching in and administering parochial schools, she had been a pastoral assistant at St. Brigid's Parish where the pastor, Rev. Thomas Flanagan (now Bishop Flanagan) appointed her "the first formally recognized non-clergy person to administer a parish in the Archdiocese of San Antonio". At Assumption, as Director of Pastoral Education, Sister O'Meara, affectionately known as "Sister Dot", supervised the field education program and assisted students in developing ministerial skills. "Gentlemen who learned from Sister Dot's pioneering presence on the seminary faculty considered themselves very fortunate indeed," notes Msgr. Jeff Pehl, the present-day rector.

Sister Millán, a daughter of Mexican immigrants who grew up in Ventura, CA, has a bachelor's degree from Stanford University. Having worked in inner city and suburban parochial schools, pastoral ministry, and with the United Farm Workers movement under César Chavez, Sister Millán brought a wealth of experience in bilingual-bicultural ministry to her position at Assumption. She was the director of the Spanish language and cultural program and also worked with Oblate School of Theology. Millán joined the seminary staff in 1988 (Vanderholt, p. 105-106; Young, Christine, "Sister Jacinta Millán retires, would do it all again," *Intermountain Catholic* [Diocese of Salt Lake City, UT], June 19, 2009).

Archbishop Patricio Fernandez Flores, born to migrant farm workers in Ganado, Texas, in 1929, was ordained a priest for the Diocese of Galveston-Houston in 1956. As a priest, Flores was active in guiding the Church's response to the needs of Hispanic Catholics. Before being named the Archbishop of San Antonio in 1979, Flores served as Auxiliary Bishop of San Antonio under Archbishop Francis J. Furey, and as Bishop of El Paso, TX, from 1978 to 1979. Flores retired as Archbishop in 2004, having served the archdiocese for 25 years. During his years as archbishop, Flores lived at Assumption Seminary. At the writing of this book, Archbishop Flores resides at Padua Place, an infirmary for retired priests and brothers in San Antonio (*en. wikipedia.org/ wiki/Patrick_Flores*).

Both women and the entire faculty were Spanish-speaking.

Melding the Cultures

As the third quarter-century of St. John's ≈ Assumption Seminary came to a close, the seminarians from Latino cultures increased. The Latino seminarians who were both US citizens and those who had been recruited from Latin America represented the following dioceses: Tuscon, AZ; Sacramento, Oakland, San Diego, CA; Peoria, IL; Lansing and Grand Rapids, MI; Jefferson

City and Kansas City, MO; Las Cruces, Santa Fe, NM; Toledo, OH; Oklahoma City, OK; and Amarillo, Brownsville, El Paso, Galveston-Houston, Austin, Fort Worth, Lubbock, San Angelo, Tyler, and San Antonio, TX.

Integrating them into the seminary world proved challenging. Due to language and cultural issues, the seminary community did not always perceive the seminarians from outside the US as "adults", thus melding these students into the larger seminary community required special attention (Interview with Bishop Gerald Barnes, Sept. 2013).

Issues with the Neighbors

When the seminary wanted the City of San Antonio to close West French Place so the campus could be more completely integrated, the administration learned that their relationship with their immediate neighbors was weak or nonexistent. Too little contact with the "neighborhood" had left the seminary isolated. Emphasis was put on building neighbors in a way that made the seminary one of the neighbors (Interview with Bishop Gerald R. Barnes, Sept. 12, 2013).

Celebrating Seventy-Five Years

In 1990, Assumption Seminary hosted the celebration of the St. John's ≈ Assumption Seminaries' diamond jubilee. Archbishops and bishops of ten of the dioceses whose seminarians were at Assumption concelebrated the jubilee Mass.

Of special note is the establishment of the Assumption Seminary Endowment Trust with major gifts from six families and three priests of the Archdiocese of San Antonio. In addition, Bishop Bernard Popp of San Antonio, Bishop Charles Grahmann of the Diocese of Dallas, Bishop John Morkovsky, of the Diocese of Galveston-Houston, and Bishop Michael Sheehan of the Diocese of Lubbock, all alumni of St. John's Seminary, established the Alumni Bishops' Endowment. Both endowments support the preparation of men for Roman Catholic priestly ministry at Assumption Seminary (Program for Jubilee Liturgy, October 18, 1990; copy held in Vincentian Archives, DePaul University, Chicago, IL).

Laborabo non mihi sed omnibus

"I will work not for myself but for others".

*[The motto of Most Reverend Patricio Flores,
Archbishop of San Antonio, TX]*

CHAPTER SEVEN

STRENGTHENING THE FOUNDATION FOR THE FUTURE

Concluding Seventy-five Years

In 1989-90 as Assumption Seminary prepared for its Diamond Jubilee, Msgr. Gerald R. Barnes, rector, reflected on the past and future of the 75 year-old seminary. In an article in *Today's Catholic*, Barnes noted that the central focus of Assumption was to prepare priests to serve a ***bi-lingual, bi-cultural*** Church with a ministry that would be ***collaborative and committed to the service of the People of God***. "Our focus," noted Barnes, "is on preparing collaborative, pastoral leaders to serve the church— not in isolation from the community but in collaboration with it and its leaders. Assumption students are invited to explore the collaborative model of priestly service through engaging in collaborative decision-making within the seminary structure itself" (Barnes, Msgr. Gerald, "75th Year for Assumption," *Today's Catholic*, Jan. 9, 1990, p. 1, 13).

In its seventy-fifth year Assumption provided a complete priestly formation program. The five-year academic program resulted in a Master of Divinity Degree from Oblate School of Theology.

Formation, as the Church understands it, is not equivalent to a secular sense of schooling or, even less, job training. Formation is first and foremost cooperation with the grace of God.
(From *Program of Priestly Formation* (fifth edition), approved by United States Conference of Catholic Bishops [USCCB] in 2005)

115

The Field Education Program gave seminarians the opportunity to serve in local pastoral settings for nine-months to one year. A three-month Clinical Pastoral Education program further honed a seminarian's sense of growth issues as well as helped him to be more self-aware in ministerial situations. Required languages courses, summer language emersion, and attending cultural seminars at the Mexican American Cultural Center assisted seminarians to be prepared for bi-lingual, bi-cultural ministry (Barnes, Msgr. Gerald, "75th Year for Assumption," *Today's Catholic*, Jan. 9, 1990, p. 1, 13).

Beginning with the early years of the pontificate of Pope John Paul II and including events like World Youth Day, vocations to the priesthood increased. Following these trends, enrollment had continued to increase at Assumption in the years immediately preceding the seminary's diamond jubilee and by its seventy-fifth year, the fifty-two seminarians at Assumption in 1989-90 represented sixteen Roman Catholic dioceses throughout the United States; fifty-three percent of the enrollment was Hispanic ("Enrollment Increases!", *Today's Catholic*, Oct. 11, 1985; *Assumption Seminary Newsletter*, Winter, Vol. I, 1990, p.1; Barnes, Msgr. Gerald, "75th Year for Assumption," *Today's Catholic*, Jan. 9, 1990, p.1; information from Msgr. Pehl, rector).

For the celebration of St. John's ≈ Assumption's seventy-fifth year, the Priests' Alumni Association published *Called to Serve: History of St. John's and Assumption Seminaries, San Antonio, Texas, 1915-1990* by Msgr. James Vanderholt, priest of the Diocese of

Msgr. David Garcia, a native of San Antonio, TX, and an alumnus of Assumption ('75), holds two master's degrees from Notre Dame University: one in theology and one in church administration. His B.S. from St. Mary's University in San Antonio is in history. He has served the Archdiocese as Secretary to the Archbishop, Director of Administrative Services, Vocation Director, interim Rector of the Seminary, Rector of San Fernando Cathedral, Director of the Old Spanish Missions. He has been a seminary faculty member and an adjunct faculty member at Oblate School of Theology. As rector of San Fernando Cathedral, Garcia produced a weekly televised bi-lingual Mass shown throughout North and South America. Presently, he is senior advisor for clergy outreach for Catholic Relief Services and in 2011 he received the Rev. John J. Cavanaugh, CSC Award from Notre Dame which is bestowed on an alumnus/alumna who has given outstanding service to his/her country or local community (crs.org/newsroom/expert.../profile-**garcia**; www.catholicidaho.org/; mynotredame.nd.edu).

Beaumont, who had served as rector of Assumption from 1975 to 1981. Vanderholt's book was the third of the histories of the seminary. The first two, *Twenty-five Years a Seminary* by the Seminary Staff and Seminarians and *Priest Forever*, written under the direction of Rev. Alois Goertz, chronicled the first twenty-five and the first fifty years.

In January 1992, eighteen months after the celebration of St. John's ≈ Assumption's 75th year, Msgr. Barnes was appointed the auxiliary bishop of San Bernardino, CA. After he became the Ordinary for the San Bernardino Diocese in 1995, the Diocese began sending more of its seminarians to Assumption for formation. Since 2000, twenty-two seminarians from San Bernardino have finished at Assumption and have been ordained to the priesthood.

Rev. David Garcia, the archdiocesan vocation director, served as rector pro-tem for Assumption upon Barnes' departure in February 1992.

Garcia had a good understanding of the seminarians and had had great success in recruiting as vocation director. He knew that it was "a terrifying decision to go into the seminary." He understood that young men were leaving family and friends to answer what might be experienced as a "vague call" from God.

Another source of anxiety for entering seminarians was that they had little understanding about seminary life. "A lot of people think they would walk into the seminary and see everybody on their knees (praying), but that's not the case. When they get in, they see seminarians are not weird; they actually have a sense of humor" (Reyes, Jr., Gilberto, "Future priests are flocking to local seminary," *San Antonio Light*, Aug. 17, 1991). As vocation director and during his short time as interim rector, Garcia recruited and influenced a great number of men who became priests including Arturo Cepeda, now Auxiliary Bishop of Detroit, and Msgr. Jeff Pehl, presently Assumption's rector. In addition, the Archdiocese benefits from the talents of many laymen who were impacted by Garcia, including Arturo Chavez, president of the Mexican American Catholic College.

In July 1992 Rev. Robert McGraw of the Diocese of Lansing, MI, began his tenure as rector. McGraw had been the Director of Seminarians in the Diocese of Lansing, MI, had served on two seminary boards, and attended various seminars on vocations and leadership development. But, most importantly, McGraw had been a pastor in various types of parishes.

When he began his duties, the newly-appointed rector inherited a seminary in which the seminarians were expected to be personally responsible for their daily decisions, use of their time, their personal prayer, study and work. Each seminarian had an assigned spiritual director and a formation team advisor who helped him "to discern areas of needed personal and professional growth, and to discuss current and future directions."

Classes in both English and Spanish assisted the seminarians to become proficient in both languages. Celebrations of Hispanic, Vietnamese, and Anglo-American cultures and liturgical rituals, begun under Msgr. Stuebben, Msgr. Barnes, and Msgr. Garcia, developed in the seminarians a reverence for the multi-cultural Church which they were preparing to serve.

Seminarians participated "in a full program of spiritual, cultural and pastoral formation at Assumption." The fifty-one Vietnamese, Hispanic, and Anglo men who were preparing to serve fifteen Roman Catholic dioceses in the United States attended Mass each day and began their day together with morning prayer. Common prayer and the Eucharistic Liturgy were in both English and Spanish.

Daily Eucharistic Liturgy was the centerpiece of the seminarians' life. Occasionally celebrating

Rev. Robert H. McGraw (b. 1950) of the Diocese of Lansing, Michigan, came to Assumption Seminary after serving in the Diocese of Lansing as a parochial vicar, pastor, and Chair of the Department of Pastoral Formation, and Director of Seminarians. After serving as rector of Assumption from 1992-1995, McGraw returned to the Diocese of Lansing where he has served as pastor of St. Michael's Parish (Grand Ledge, MI), and Queen of the Miraculous Medal Parish (Jackson, MI), and St. Agnes Parish (Fowlerville, MI). He was also a regional vicar, chair of the Presbyteral Council, and serves on the board at Catholic Charities and the Diocesan Pastoral Council. A parishioner at Queen of the Miraculous Medal experienced "Father Box [as] a great missionary. He thinks outside the box, how to best do things efficiently and he likes to work with all faiths because we are all here to help others (www.mlive. com/ news/...ssf/.../ the_rev_bob_ mcgraw_ of_queen_of)." At this writing, McGraw is the pastor of Ss. Charles and Helena Parish in Clio, Michigan and the canonical pastor of St. Francis Xavier Church in Otisville (dioceseoflansing. org/2012_ assignments; Interview with Sister Diane Langford, December 2013).

in small class groups or with the school community at Oblate School of Theology, and in local parishes, gave seminarians added exposure to varieties of ways to celebrate the Mass. Opportunities to participate in and prepare liturgical celebrations prepared the future priests well for their future Eucharistic ministries.

Seminarians continued to pursue the Master of Divinity degree at Oblate School of Theology and participated in various supervised field education experiences through Oblate as well ("Assumption Seminary changes with the times," *Today's Catholic*, October 1992).

Broadening Pastoral Experiences

Pastoral experiences begun under previous rectors were continued. Clinical Pastoral Education (CPE) helped seminarians to confront their own inner fears and uncertainties, giving them a firmer platform from which to minister to others. Three seminarians (including the present rector, Jeff Pehl of Fredericksburg) did missionary work with the Oblate Fathers in Zambia, immersing themselves into the basic life needs of that young African country. Two students worked at Holy Sepulcher Cemetery in Hayward, CA. Their experience allowed them to see first-hand how different Catholic cultures bid farewell to their deceased loved ones ("Assumption Seminary: A reflection of the universal church," *Today's Catholic*, Oct. 1, 1993).

By the mid-1990's Assumption Seminary had gained national recognition for its programs that emphasized ministry to the Hispanic population.

As McGraw began his tenure as rector, the Assumption Formation Staff consisted of Rev. Fernando Rubio, Rev. Norman Ermis, Sister Dorothea O'Meara, CSB, Sister Jacinta Millán, CSC, Rev. José Lopez. Sister Mary Teresa Cullen, CSB, joined the staff when Sister O'Meara was on sabbatical.

Goals under McGraw

The goals of Assumption while McGraw was rector, decided collaboratively with the faculty and other priests, were

- "To build a sense of the importance of priestly fraternity so that once a man was ordained he realized the importance of priestly support and identity back in his diocese.
- To encourage a strong development of a personal spirituality that would sustain the candidate. [Most of our men would be in rural, one-priest parishes, if not overseeing more than one.]
- To develop in our men strong pastoral skills.
- To improve the physical environment of the seminary" (McGraw Interview, December 2013).

McGraw improved his own ability to celebrate the Eucharist in Spanish and converse with students from other countries in their languages. He also invested himself in the interdependent relationship which Assumption had with Oblate School of theology. McGraw also expanded the relationship between the seminary and local artists. Through his liaison, Assumption engaged G. E. "Buddy" Mullen to paint a special image of Our Lady of the Assumption.

Being able to celebrate the Eucharist is incredible! I still find it hard to believe God has trusted me so much—I thank him every day for his leap of faith in me.
(Rev. Robert McGraw, November 2013)

Father McGraw's last year as rector (1994-95) began the 80th year of the San Antonio seminary's molding seminarians for the priesthood. His reflection on his time at Assumption was included in an article by Maura Ciarrochi in the April 28, 1995, issue of *Today's Catholic*. The drop in enrollment over the three years when he was rector was disappointing to McGraw but Assumption was experiencing the same challenges that all seminaries in the US experienced at the time. As his three-year term came to an end there were 33 seminarians, one-third of whom were preparing

Msgr. David R. Cruz (b. 1961), a native of LaMesa, TX, graduated from Lubbock High School and the College of Santa Fe. Cruz also studied at Immaculate Heart of Mary Seminary in Santa Fe and at the Louvain in Belgium before being ordained for the Diocese of Lubbock in 1986. Before serving a six-year appointment as rector at Assumption, Cruz, one of the youngest priests in the country to lead a seminary, served in several parishes in the Lubbock diocese, was director of the Cursillo Movement, director of the Christian Renewal Center, and director of a project in Lubbock to facilitate improving some of Lubbock's poorest neighborhoods. Msgr. Cruz presently serves as pastor to Our Lady of Grace Parish, a parish with 1500 families, and is involved with healthcare on the national level through the St. Joseph Health System. Cruz also has a weekly radio program, "Faith Matters," through Texas Tech University in Lubbock and he is the author of *The Human Face of God*. (from Interview with Sr. Diane Langford, May 2013; Parker, J Michael, "Flores names Hispanic priest rector of Assumption Seminary, *San Antonio Express News*, October 15, 1994)

for the Archdiocese of San Antonio. The other twenty-three men were from fourteen dioceses throughout the US.

However, his last reflection for the *Assumption Seminary Newsletter* (Vol. VII, Summer 1995, p. 1) captured the adage that "quality is more important than quantity."
McGraw wrote:

A priest who was concluding several weeks of study at the Mexican American Cultural Center made it a point to seek me out before he left . . . He shared with me that several years ago he had lost hope in the clergy being ordained. After living among our students for several months, he had gained new hope and a rekindled enthusiasm for ministry. He told me, 'if the students of Assumption are any indication of the caliber of tomorrow's priests, the church has a bright future.'

In 1994 the Seminary Board invited Rev. David R. Cruz of the Diocese of Lubbock, TX, to become the rector of Assumption Seminary. A native Hispanic Texan was a good match for the needs of the seminary. Cruz began his five year term in the fall of 1995.

A Diverse Faculty

The formation team that Cruz led included Rev. Norm Ermis, Rev. José Lopez, Rev. Gerald McBreaity, a Sulpician priest, and Rev. Aaron Arce, a Dominican priest. Cruz continued the practice of having women on his faculty and staff. Over the six years Cruz was the rector, Ms. Linda Krehmeier, a former Incarnate Word and Blessed Sacrament Sister, served as liturgist. Sister Mary Terese Cullen, CBS; Sister Jacinta Millán, CSC; Sister Guadalupe Ramirez, MCDP; Sister Addie Loraine Walker, SSND; and Sister Pat Casey, OP, were in various positions ranging from formation advisors and counselors to supervisors of field education. Sister Mary Terese Cullen recalls that Father Cruz was very intelligent, well-read and a very positive pastoral role model (Interview with Sister Terese Cullen, CSB, June 2012).

The women on the staff and faculty were conscious that the seminarians were going to be working with parish staffs that had a high percentage of women on them. They were aware that the young men needed to learn to collaborate with women. Sister Cullen recalls that the collaborative style of the diverse faculty (male, female, diocesan priests, religious, clerics, and laity) provided the seminarians with a model that would serve their ministerial lives in their future.

> The supreme good is like water, which nourishes all things without trying to. It is content with the low places that people disdain . . .
>
> In dwelling, live close to the ground. In thinking, keep to the simple. In conflict, be fair and generous. In governing, don't try to control. In work, do what you enjoy. In family life, be completely present. When you are content to be simply yourself, and don't compare or compete, everybody will respect you.
>
> (Fr. Cruz' prayer while rector . . . from Toa Te Ching, Loa-tzu; China, c. 604-531 BCE; in his book **The Human Face of God**, p. 16)

Goals of the Seminary under Cruz

At that time, the goals that Cruz had at Assumption emphasized strengthening the relationship with Oblate, reconnecting the seminary to the archdiocesan priests, and maintaining a strong working relationship with the faculty. Emphasis continued to be on cultural sensitivity (Cruz Interviews, May 2013; Cullen Interview, June 2012).

- Strengthening the Relationship with Oblate School of Theology

Cruz and Rev. Bill Morrell, OMI, the President of Oblate School of Theology, together visited all the bishops of the dioceses whose seminarians attended Assumption and Oblate. At that time Assumption's forty-five seminarians, representing seventeen dioceses, were all graduate students. Morrell and Cruz also attended national meetings together.

Both seminary leaders wanted to expand the number of Sulpician Fathers on the faculty at Assumption, but the Sulpicians hoped that the Archdiocese would make a more solid commitment to the future of the seminary. At the time, meetings[44] were in process which once again addressed joining Houston's St. Mary's Seminary with Assumption in San Antonio. Cruz recalls that from his point of view, the two seminaries did not need to be in competition: both could exist with different types of environments, different charisms (Interview with Msgr. Cruz, May 2013).

- Reconnecting with Archdiocesan Priests

In order to reconnect the archdiocesan priests with the seminary, local priests were invited to preside at liturgies at

---

[44] The meetings of this ad hoc committee of the Texas Catholic Conference of Bishops continued over a number of months. The committee actually recommended maintaining two seminaries in Texas: a college seminary and a major seminary. However, the Texas Catholic Conference was unable to come to agreement on this proposal. In 1986, however, Holy Trinity Seminary in Dallas and St. Mary's Seminary in Houston did reach an agreement. The two seminaries agreed Holy Trinity would be the college seminary; St. Mary's would be the theologate. Assumption was not involved in these plans (Correspondence of Ad Hoc Committee, Assumption Seminary Archives; St. Mary's Seminary website: www.sm**seminary**.com).

the seminary. Local pastors and associate pastors provided models for all the seminarians and established rapport with the seminarians who would serve in the San Antonio Archdiocese and their future confreres. Cruz's relationship with priests of the Archdiocese endures today. Frequently he is invited back to San Antonio to conduct missions and give presentations at parishes.

- Campus Development

Enhancing the campus continued to be a focus for Father Cruz into the new millennium. Archdiocesan architect, Robert E. Morkovsky, guided both the refurbishing of campus buildings as well as planning for new structures. He advised the Building Board to take down Mary-Catherine Hall. This seventy-plus year old building had been in service to Assumption since the Archdiocese acquired the campus in 1952 and in the last years of the twentieth century, the structure had served as part of the Mexican American Cultural Center. But it was no longer serviceable. Most of the permanent buildings, according to the San Antonio Historical Society, had historical value since they had been built during and prior to World War II for the Trinity University campus which had come to the Woodlawn property in 1941. Trinity and the University of San Antonio [formerly Westmoreland College], a Methodist-connected college located further west on Woodlawn merged in 1941 at the location that would become Assumption Seminary. Because of this background, the San

> **Msgr. Gerald Brown, SS** (b. 1938) entered the Sulpician Order the year he was ordained a priest for the Archdiocese of San Francisco in 1964. Brown worked at Catholic University in the early 1970's and completed his doctoral studies at Temple University in Philadelphia. Over his fifty years as a priest, Brown has served as rector for St. Joseph College in the Diocese of San Jose, a Sulpician ministry (1978-1985), and rector of St. Patrick's Seminary (2004-2009) in Menlo Park. In addition to his years in seminary work, Brown spent fifteen years in administration work with the Sulpicians, twelve of those years as Provincial Superior (1985-1997) in Baltimore, Maryland. While he was Provincial Superior he served as President of the Congregation of Major Superiors of Men.
>
> After leaving Assumption, Brown became the rector at his alma mater, St. Patrick's Seminary in Menlo Park. At this time, Father Brown is retired in Baltimore, MD, and serves Catholic communities as Eucharistic presider. (from Interview with Msgr. Jerry Brown, Dec. 5, 2013)

Antonio Historical Society challenged the decision to take the building down.

Cruz remembers that it was a "bad building." Negotiations and lawsuits eventually subsided and the Archdiocese received permission to raze the structure. Taking the building down was one of Cruz' last acts while he was rector.[45]

Into the New Millennium

Rev. David Cruz' five-year term as rector ended in July 2000 and he returned to pastoral work in the Diocese of Lubbock. The search committee for the next rector, supervised by Auxiliary Bishop Thomas Flanagan, did not have to look far.

After serving as Provincial Superior of the Sulpicians for twelve years, Rev. Gerald L. Brown, SS, had come to San Antonio in 1998 to assist in the Office of Continuing Education of Clergy. While he was Provincial Superior, the Sulpicians focused their efforts on missionary efforts in Zambia and with Latinos in US seminaries. In a fall 2013 interview with this author, Brown said that he had come to San Antonio to assist at Assumption Seminary and learn "how a Hispanic seminary worked." In the two years before he was named rector, Brown did field education supervision for Oblate School of Theology, spiritual direction at Assumption and Oblate, and organized developmental events for the priests of the Archdiocese. Brown had a reputation for identifying a community's gifts, reading the present, and offering guidance for the future. Among the Sulpicians, Brown was known for his visionary leadership.

Beginning as rector in 2000, Brown brought new energy and a focused vision to Assumption.

---

[45] More on the demolition of Mary-Catherine Hall is in Chapter Three: Building Up Sacred Grounds

The Sulpicians are "diocesan priests dedicated to priestly formation and seminary work." After having begun a seminary in Paris for diocesan priests in 1641, Father Jean-Jacques Olier was named pastor of St. Sulpice Parish. He asked several diocesan priests to join him and the Society of the Priests of the Seminary of St. Sulpice was established. This Society pioneered what would become the modern seminary we now know. In the 17th century, candidates for the priesthood were usually young boys who studied with their pastors in their home parish. St. Sulpice Seminary served adult candidates who came from all over France.

In 1790, Bishop John Carroll, the first bishop of the US, facing the burden of having only 35 priests to serve the 30,000 Catholics in the US at the time, asked Sulpicians to form a seminary in Baltimore, his see city. St. Mary's Seminary opened in 1791.

All diocesan priests, the Sulpicians are a society of apostolic life. To join the Sulpicians a priest must be ordained and functioning in a diocese. He never loses his diocesan status, though his home diocese releases him to the Sulpician community who can send him to any of their institutions.

The Sulpician Fathers were instrumental in assisting Elizabeth Seton to establish the Sisters of Charity and Mary Lange to establish the Oblate Sisters of Providence, the first religious congregation of women of African descent.

Though Sulpicians have served in many seminaries in the US, they presently direct St. Mary's Seminary and University in Baltimore; Theological College at the Catholic University of America; St. Patrick's Seminary in Menlo Park, CA, and serve in parishes and other diocesan institutions throughout the world. Several serve on the faculty of Assumption. (From en.wikipedia.org/wiki/Society-Saint-Sulpice; www. sulpicians.org; *Give Us This Day*, February 2014, p. 38)

The "Sulpician Ethos of Priestly Formation" guided his work: 1) a commitment to ministerial priesthood; 2) the cultivation of an apostolic spirit; 3) an emphasis on spiritual formation; 4) the creation of a formational community; and 5) the exercise of collegiality (www.sulpicians.org). And, his time in San Antonio prior to taking the position of rector, also committed him to the bilingual-bicultural environment which had already developed at Assumption. Brown was excited about the unique formational community he encountered at Assumption. The diversity built by the variety of ages and cultural backgrounds among the seminarians as well as different perspectives on the faculty formed a learning community that would benefit the seminary student.

Goals of the Seminary under Brown

Since 1996, the relationship between Assumption Seminary and the Sulpicians has grown stronger. The following Sulpicians have served at Assumption from 1996 through 2014.

Rev. Gerald Brown, SS
Rev. John C. Kemper, SS
Rev. Nam Kim, SS
Rev. Anthony Lobo, SS
Rev. Gerald D. McBrearity, SS
Rev. James E. Myers, SS
Rev. Hy K. Nguyen, SS
Rev. James P. Oberle, SS
Rev. Rafael M. Ramirez, SS
Rev. Jaime E. Robledo, SS

(Seminary records)

The goals which were established while Brown was rector were

- To increase the enrollment
- To develop a strategic plan
- To expand the vision to include other cultures in addition to Hispanics
- To expand and enhance the property and develop a plan for the campus.

Under Brown's leadership from 2000-2004 the enrollment at the seminary grew from thirty-two to seventy seminarians (Interview, Dec. 2013). With the influx of new vocations, space at the seminary was inadequate and outdated. The Seminary Board announced plans to raise $ 13 million to build a new dormitory, improve existing structures and operations, and create a facilities endowment. While Brown was rector the seminary purchased a house across the street from the convent on Ashby. Named Stuebben Residence for Msgr. Lawrence Stuebben, the house served as a residence for up to twenty seminarians. Today, Stuebben Residence is leased by the Claretians for postulants preparing for the priesthood and studying at Oblate School of Theology.

Msgr. Brown was focused on applying the tenets of *Pastores Dabo Vobis (I will give you shepherds)*, Pope St. John Paul II's 1992 apostolic exhortation on the priesthood, as it would impact the mission of Assumption. He wrote of the impact of *Pastores dabo vobis* on his own priesthood:

> Prior to the (Second Vatican) Council, I saw myself as radically changed, on the ontological

level, by the sacrament of ordination. [As a result of the emphasis of] the Council, my role seemed to be more defined by the functions I preformed, preaching, celebrating liturgy and the sacraments, and providing leadership after the mind and heart of the Good Shepherd, than by the symbolic witness of one consecrated by sacred ordination.

Pastores dabo vobis helped to clarify the distinct role of the priest in the Church in relation to other roles, as defined in the apostolic exhortation on the laity (1988) and then later in the document on consecrated life (1996). [Combining the functional and sacramental] . . . *Pastores dabo vobis* [calls] for a rich commitment to collaboration in the Church . . . applying the principles of shared team-work and subsidiarity in our parishes . . .

[This] is the first official Church document to situate human formation as the first building block in the shaping of a candidate for priesthood . . . **Pastores dabo vobis takes a mega-leap forward by saying that without solid human formation it will be impossible to develop the necessary spiritual, intellectual, and pastoral qualities and skills needed for priestly ministry in our times** (emphasis added) (from Brown, SS, Very Rev. Gerald L., "Impact of John Paul II on seminary formation," Assumption Seminary Bridge Builder, Fall 2003, p. 1, 9).

When asked about the types of men who were preparing for the priesthood when he was rector, Brown noted: "There were Hispanics, more Anglos, some Asians; they came from poorer families, were open to the Church and were older candidates. They were very pastoral in their approach to their future and very collaborative. We were trying to train a priest who 'stands in the middle' and reaches out to all people . . . to all needs. He needs to be a well-put-together person who identifies with people's needs, especially their struggles and failings, and sees himself as growth-oriented. We wanted to mold collaborating persons who are not gender-biased" (Brown Interview, Dec. 2013).

In 2004, the Sulpicians called Brown to serve as rector of his alma mater, St. Patrick's Seminary in Menlo Park, CA.

Rev. Lawrence J. Christian who had served as vice-rector at Assumption under Brown was named the rector by Archbishop Patricio Flores in March 2004 and began his five year term in June 2004. Christian had come to San Antonio as a Claretian[46] priest, working with their men in formation. However, he became a priest of the Archdiocese of San Antonio before he was asked to serve as rector from 2004 until 2009.

Rev. Lawrence J. Christian, a native of southern California, entered the seminary in 1975. He was ordained in 1983. He holds a MA in Counseling from Holy Names College and an MDiv from the Jesuit School of Theology, both in Berkeley, CA. With his appointment as rector of Assumption Seminary in 2004, Father Christian began his 17th year in the work of priestly formation. Prior to serving as rector, Christian had been a member of the Congregation of the Immaculate Heart of Mary (Claretians) and had been accepted into the Archdiocese of San Antonio. As a priest of the Archdiocese, Christian was the pastor of St. Matthew Church in Jourdanton before being appointed the vice-rector of Assumption in 2001. Christian is also involved in the Right to Life Movement in San Antonio; he is a Fourth Degree Knight of Columbus; and active in ecumenical events. At this writing, Christian is the pastor of St. Francis of Assisi Catholic Church in San Antonio, TX ("Seminary installs new rector-president," *Today's Catholic*, Oct. 29, 2004, p. 4; Interview, June, 2013).

As Christian assumed the position of rector, questions about the future of the seminary continued, but Archbishop Flores remained committed to the mission of Assumption. Flores and Msgr. Lawrence Stuebben, the

---

[46] The Congregation of Sons of the Immaculate Heart of Mary (Claretians) was founded by St. Anthony Maria Claret in Vich, Spain in 1849. The Claretians have served in the Diocese/Archdiocese of San Antonio since the episcopate of Bishop John A. Forest who invited them to serve parishes that were predominately Hispanic in the early part of the 20th century. They still serve Immaculate Heart of Mary Parish and have men at other places in San Antonio (Langford, CDP, Mary Diane, et al., *God Has Been God for Us*, Chap.1; and *Archdiocesan Directory, 2011*, p. 245).

Vicar General for the Archdiocese, saw in Christian a stabilizing force for the seminary's future.

Some things were already in process when Christian began his tenure. Ms. Barbara Spinner, a well-known local development expert, was the development officer who was working on raising the millions for the capital campaign that had been begun under Brown. Robert Morkovsky, the Archdiocesan architect, was working on Flores Hall, which was scheduled to open for the fall term of 2007. And the retirement of Archbishop Patricio Flores who had served as Archbishop for twenty-five years (1979-2004) was imminent.

2004-2010: Archbishop José H. Gomez

The quarter-century episcopate of Archbishop Patricio Flores in San Antonio, TX, came to an end with the conclusion of the year 2004. He was succeeded by Most Rev. José H. Gomez, Auxiliary Bishop of Denver, CO, for whom San Antonio and south Texas were familiar territories. Gomez, as a priest of Opus Dei Prelature, had lived in San Antonio at Our Lady of Grace Parish for a period of time in the late 1980's and early 1990's while working in various capacities with the National Association of Hispanic Priests. In addition to working with the spirituality of the laity, during these years Gomez was also active in

Archbishop José Horacio Gomez (b. 1951), a native of Monterrey, Mexico, was ordained a priest of Opus Dei in 1978 in Spain. Before being named Auxiliary Bishop of Denver, CO, in 2001 Gomez had served in various pastoral capacities in Texas, as a regional representative of the National Association of Hispanic Priests, and later its director. Gomez came to San Antonio, TX, as Archbishop from 2004 to 2010, and here he was known for his orthodox positions. He was appointed Co-adjutor Archbishop of the Archdiocese of Los Angeles in 2010, serving there with Cardinal Roger Mahoney until 2011 when he succeeded Mahoney upon his retirement (en.wikipedia. org/wiki/ José_Horacio_Gomez).

the National Catholic Council of Hispanic Ministry, being elected treasurer in 1999.

Archbishop Gomez sometimes took a conservative posture in opposition to controversial individuals who were invited by Catholic entities in San Antonio to speak or teach, but he is also remembered for being a "moderate." In an April 9, 2012 article in the *National Catholic Reporter*, John L. Allen, Jr. noted that some believed that Gomez would unravel Flores' more liberal legacy in social justice and especially in immigrant rights. Msgr. David Garcia said, "He didn't come in and squash anything."

Allen wrote, "In fact, Gomez became a staunch supporter of immigrant rights. Garcia said he remembers marching with Gomez down the streets of San Antonio during his second year in a pro-immigrant rally" (en.wikipedia.org/wiki/ José_ Horacio_Gomez; Allen, Jr., John L, "Four points to make about Gomez and L.A.," *The National Catholic Reporter*, April 9, 2010, online issue).

Gomez' unique experience of the US Catholic Church, his perspective as a citizen of the US yet a native of Mexico, and his intellectual talents became immediate assets for the Archdiocese and for the seminary.

According to Christian, Gomez was very supportive of the seminary and really had a vision for its future. He worked well with Development Director Barbara Spinner who was organizing the expansion campaign for Flores Hall, operations, and endowment. He was very good at helping the seminary acquire resources for

> *Rev. Alex Pereida*, the Archdiocesan Vocation Director since 2010, prepared for the priesthood at Assumption between 2003 and 2008 and recalls being at Assumption a wonderful experience. Though a native San Antonian, he was not bi-lingual and had grown up in the Church of Christ. He appreciates the bilingual formation received at Assumption. "The women at Oblate helped me a lot. We had a different kind of community—non-clerical; now seminarians seemed to be drawn to clericalism. But Assumption forms students as effective pastors and collaborators who want to work with 'wounded souls'." (Perieda Interview, Summer 2013).

To be a priest is the privilege of being with people in all types of circumstances. It requires being a bridge-builder, creating, fostering and sustaining relationships.

(Rev. Lawrence Christian Interview, June 2013).

the future (Christian Interview, June 2013).

From his unique point of observation as vice-rector and rector of Assumption from 1998 through 2009, Father Christian saw a shift in the types of men who entered the seminary. The seminarians of the latter part of the twentieth century often had come from social outreach experiences which had inspired them to listen to God's call. Men coming in the new millennium, on the other hand, were more often traditionalists who were more interested in doctrine and ritual. However, they did not have solid backgrounds in theology and philosophy. Christian's observations were corroborated by other faculty and staff members including Sister Addie Loraine Walker, SSND, and Sister Mary Christine Morkovsky, CDP. Though coming with a "willingness of spirit," the seminarians who came to Assumption after 2000 were often from broken homes and blended families. Their preparation for ministry required more attention to their human formation issues (Christian Interview, June 2013; Walker Interview, June 2013; Sr. Mary Christine Morkovsky Interview, June 2013).

The Apostolic Visitation of Seminaries

During Christian's tenure, all US seminaries, schools of theology, houses of formation, and college-level seminaries, including Assumption, were notified that there would be an apostolic visitation during the 2005-2006 school year. The process involved 229 institutions. These had occurred in the past, but this one took on significant meaning after the US Bishops adopted the *Charter for the Protection of Children and Young People* in June 2002. Christian welcomed the visitation in February 2005 and Assumption was noted for its compliance with national regulations.

Growth in Vocations

Under Brown and Christian, Assumption entered a growth mode. In his interview Christian noted, "Until 2004 we were averaging thirty-six seminarians a year; by 2008 we had over

109 seminarians and, including the twenty Oblate seminarians, we were the sixth largest seminary in the US. Before Flores Hall was opened (2007), it was filled." Christian attributed the upsurge in enrollment to the "special type of priestly formation with a bilingual, bicultural ambience . . . [which] the whole Catholic Church in the US urgently needs . . . [with] the personal accompaniment by faculty members from both Oblate and Assumption in the continuing formation process." Of equal importance is, in Christian's own words, "We haven't had a single ordinand (newly-ordained priest) leave [the priesthood] in the past eight years . . . our retention was four times better than the norm" (Christian Interview, June 2013; Parker, J. Michael, Oblate, Assumption have sixth largest seminary enrollment, Today's Catholic, Aug. 29, 2008, p. 22).

Part of the growth was certainly influenced by Oblate School of Theology's ability to sustain and improve the fine academic program it had offered for years. Through an affiliation with another Oblate of Mary Immaculate School, St. Paul University in Ottawa, Canada, OST offers an ecclesiastical degree, the STB or Baccalaureate in Sacred Theology.

Opening of the Mexican American Catholic College

During the early part of the 21st century, college-aged men prepared for their studies at Assumption at St. John's (Vincentian) Seminary, Camarrillo, CA. With the opening of Flores Hall, Stuebben Residence was reserved for men of college age who were "discerners" (Christian Interview, June 2013).

In 2008, with an increase of younger vocations and following the vision of Archbishop Gomez, the Mexican American Cultural Center begun in 1972[47] under Archbishop Furey, in collaboration with the Archdiocese and Assumption, was reorganized into the

---

[47] Raul Garcia, "Mexican American Cultural Center," Handbook of Texas Online (http://www.tshaonline.org/handbook/ online/ articles/lbm10) accessed February 6, 2014. Published by the Texas State Historical Association. See more on MACC in Chapter 6: Refounding a Seminary.

Mexican American Catholic College (MACC). Gomez believed that younger vocations to the priesthood needed to be supported by having a college in the archdiocese which could focus on the spirituality and academic foundation needed by major seminarians. The Mexican American Catholic College, under its own board,[48] holds membership in several national accrediting organizations including The Association of Catholic Colleges and Universities and Federation of Pastoral Institutes. The college collaborates with the University of the Incarnate Word in San Antonio to provide a college curriculum toward a Bachelor's degree. In addition, MACC collaborates with Oblate School of Theology, Our Lady of the Lake University, and St. Mary's University in order to enhance its degree programs.

In addition to offering degrees to men and seminarians, religious and lay persons from around the country, MACC provides a bilingual-bicultural academic environment for those collegians who will do their future studies for the priesthood at Assumption Seminary (2013-2014 Academic Catalog, Vol. 5.1., Aug. 2013, Mexican American Catholic College, www.maccsa. org).

After serving nine years in the administration of Assumption Seminary, Christian asked for a sabbatical and left the position of rector in the spring of 2010. Rev. Arturo Cepeda, vice-rector of Assumption and the archdiocesan vocation director, was appointed as rector in 2010 by Archbishop Gomez.

---

[48] The Rector of Assumption is an ex-officio member of the College Board and the faculty of Assumption may also serve as adjunct faculty of MACC.

> **Most Rev. José Arturo Cepeda** (b. 1969 in San Luis Potosi, MX), came to the US with his family after completing a year of spiritual formation and philosophy studies at Seminario Arquidiocesano Guadalupano Josefino in San Luis Potosi. He continued his college studies at Our Lady of the Lake University and earned a BA degree in religious studies from the College Seminary of Immaculate Heart of Mary in Santa Fe, NM before returning to Assumption to study for the priesthood. Cepeda was ordained to the priesthood by Archbishop Flores in 1996. His higher degrees are from St. Mary's University in San Antonio and St. Thomas Aquinas "Angelicum," Pontifical University in Rome. Before his short tenure as rector of Assumption, Cepeda taught at Assumption Seminary and Oblate School of Theology, and served as vocation director and vice-rector of Assumption. He was ordained Auxiliary Bishop of Detroit on May 5, 2011 (en.wikipedia. org/wiki/José_Cepeda)

Cepeda, born in San Luis Potosi, Mexico, and educated through high school by the Hermanas and Hermanos Josefinos, moved to San Antonio with his family before finishing his college education. As a seminarian at Assumption and when he became rector, the young priest had the countenance of a bilingual-bicultural seminarian.

While in charge of one of the nation's largest seminaries, Cepeda was the youngest seminary rector in the US. Having been the Archdiocesan vocation director for several years, he was associated with the vocation directors through Texas and the nation.

Archbishop Gustavo Garcia-Siller, MSpS

In the fall of 2010, the Archdiocese welcomed Most Rev. Gustavo Garcia-Siller, MSpS, the Auxiliary Bishop of Chicago who had been named to replace Archbishop Gomez who was assigned to the Archdiocese of Los Angeles.

In 2011, Cepeda was appointed the Auxiliary Bishop of Detroit. He left behind a thriving seminary. His intellect and his experience were a good foundation for his tenure during which Assumption climbed to its highest enrollment in years—104

seminarians in the fall of 2010. Nine seminarians resided in parishes for internships; 75 theologians and pre-theologians resided in Flores Hall; 20 collegians resided at MACC.

Assumption Seminary Today

Archbishop Gustavo installed Rev. Jeffrey Pehl to serve as rector on August 15, 2011, after a short period as interim rector. Pehl, an alumnus of Assumption, had been appointed to the Assumption formation faculty in 2007 where he served as a formation advisor, dean of men, and vice-rector. Before beginning his seminary studies at Assumption, Pehl acquired a degree in Speech Communication from Texas A & M University. He was

> **Most Rev. Gustavo Garcia-Siller, MSpS,** born in San Luis Potosi Mexico in 1956, is the oldest of fifteen children. He entered the Missionaries of the Holy Spirit in Mexico City in 1973 and was sent to the US in 1980 to minister to migrant workers in California. He obtained two Master's degrees (MDiv and Master's in Theology) from St. John's Seminary in Camarillo, CA. In 1998, Garcia-Siller became a citizen of the US. Before being named Auxiliary bishop of Chicago in 2003, Garcia-Siller served in his order's theologate in California and in three parishes in the Archdiocese of Los Angeles. Garcia-Siller, known affectionately as Archbishop Gustavo, was named the Archbishop of San Antonio in October 2010. (From http://en.wikipedia. org/wiki/ Gustavo_Garc%C3%ADa-Siller)

ordained in September 1995. As a seminarian, Pehl experienced Assumption as "a home." He became acquainted with local priests and with Archbishop Flores. He remembers that the seminarians with whom he studied were "middle of the road" Catholics, heavily Hispanic, and that two languages were spoken all the time.

From his experience at a state university Pehl offers Assumption the perspective that many present-day seminarians bring to their personal journey to the priesthood at this time.

Goals of the Seminary under Pehl

As Pehl leads Assumption into its second century, his goals mirror those of his recent predecessors: 1) to assemble a good formation faculty and staff; 2) to build relationships with the partner institutions; 3) to care for the community and the campus; and 4) to collaborate with the Archbishop. However, Pehl adds a fifth goal that no other rector noted explicitly: to work hard.

The 2013-2014 Faculty

Msgr. Pehl collaborates with a faculty of eleven very qualified and diverse people, including

* Rev. John Collet, OMI (Oblate of Mary Immaculate), Instructor at Mexican American Catholic College and a spiritual director at Assumption;
* Rev. Virgil Elizondo, Arch. of San Antonio, Vice-Rector, Director of Pastoral Formation at Assumption; Professor of Pastoral and Hispanic Theology at University of Notre Dame;
* Rev. Martin Elsner, SJ (Jesuit), parochial vicar at Our Lady of Guadalupe Parish; spiritual director at Assumption;
* Rev. Agustín Estrada, Arch. of San Antonio; director of liturgical formation; director of the college program at Assumption;
* Deacon Robert M. Garza, Archdiocese of San Antonio, administrator of the Pastoral Formation Program;
* Sister Dianne Heinrich, CDP (Congregation of Divine Providence), Director of Academic Studies;
* Rev. Arnold Ibarra, a priest for the Diocese of Tarlac, Philippines; Vice-Rector and Dean of Men for Theology, instructor at MACC and Oblate;
* Martín de Jesús Martínez, instructor at MACC and Our Lady of the Lake University;

> *Msgr. Jeffrey Pehl* (b. 1966), a native of Fredericksburg, TX, and St. Mary's Parish, finished a BA in Speech Communication at Texas A & M University in 1989. At A & M, Pehl was an officer in the ROTC Corps of Cadets, a drummer in the Texas Aggie Band, and a participant in the St. Mary's Catholic Student Assn. at College Station. After studying at Assumption Seminary and receiving a Master's in Divinity from Oblate School of Theology, Pehl was ordained for the Archdiocese of San Antonio in 1995. His pastoral assignments include parochial vicar at St. Leo the Great Church and St. Matthew Church in San Antonio and pastor of St. John the Evangelist Church in Hondo for eight years. He was appointed to the formation faculty of Assumption in 2007 (Pehl Interview, June 27, 2012).

- Rev. Jim Myers, SS, Diocese of Peoria, (Sulpician); Director of Spiritual Formation;
- Rev. Hy K. Nguyen, SS (Sulpician); member of the formation team, instructor at Oblate;
- Chris Stravitsch, Associate Director of College Formation, Chair of Admissions; formation faculty at Assumption and adjunct faculty for the Institute for Priestly Formation in Omaha (www.asumptionseminary.org).

Pehl intends to maintain a faculty and staff that mirrors the diversity of the Catholic Church. The present faculty shares Pehl's goal to care for the community at Assumption so that the men can best grow toward a spiritual maturity which will serve as the bedrock of their priesthood.

Care of the Campus

Msgr. José Lopez Hall

With the guidance of the Seminary Board and Mr. Robert E. Morkovsky, the vision of Archbishop Gustavo has included renovating St. Alice Hall to bring it up to 21st century standards for housing seminarians and remodeling Assumption Chapel.

> It is an honor and a privilege to serve as the rector of Assumption Seminary. I look up to the men who have served in this role in San Antonio, and I want to be equally faithful in the task of caring for the seminary community before I pass it on to the next leader. My work as rector is leading the seminary in carefully forming and training men for priestly service . . . and providing pastoral care with my brother priests, faculty, and staff, as we build up our seminarians into good disciples of Christ.
>
> --Msgr. Jeff Pehl, Feb. 2014

This major renovation became Msgr. Pehl's first project, now Msgr. José Lopez Hall, the building, erected in 1955-1956, was completely re-worked: double-bedrooms were reframed for single use with each bedroom having its own bath. Other amenities provided a simple, yet usable residence for theologians. (See more on this building in Chapter Three.)

Our Lady's Chapel

In 2014, Assumption's chapel was renovated and rededicated as Our Lady's Chapel at March 25, 2014 ceremonies. (More information on improvements is in Chapter Three.)

Projects to Continue

The Seminary Board wants to continue to improve the campus into its second century. In recognition of the centennial, the Alumni Assocation (Priests and Laymen) has started a campaign to raise one million dollars for the Assumption Seminary Endowment Fund. The Seminary and the Board, following the lead of the Alumni Association, have pledged to raise an additional two million dollars.

Into the Future

In the last year of its first century, Assumption Seminary has eighty seminarians—all theologians—who represent the archdioceses of San Antonio, Omaha, and San Salvador, as well as the dioceses of Amarillo, Brownsville, El Paso, Fort Worth, Laredo, San Angelo, Nashville, Salt Lake City, and San Bernadino.

"Building Faith ▲ Preparing Leaders"

There is both a rhythm and stability to Assumption Seminary in its 100th year. Standing on the broad shoulders of St. John's, the mother seminary, Assumption's bi-lingual, bi-cultural character is firmly implanted and is obvious from the vitae of the present faculty and staff as well as the visage of the seminarians who call the historical campus "home".

Assumption Seminary has established itself in an international leadership role in the formation of future priests who are called to minister in the multicultural reality that requires a special understanding and respect for the diversity that will continue to be the Church of the future. I pledge my dedication to nurturing the vocations of those who have been called by God to embrace the great mystery that is the priesthood.

--Archbishop Gustavo Garcia-Siller, MSpS, 2013, AssumptionSeminary.org

Prayer brings the faculty and seminarians together, allowing them to build their relationships through their common quest to encounter our loving God.

Inter-cultural celebrations underscore respect for a Church that is a multi-faceted gem reflecting the beauties of the mysteries of God.

Dedication to forming whole and healthy priests focuses the faculty on the particular needs of each seminarian, crafting the programs of spiritual and human development for their unique background and characteristics.

In concert with Oblate School of Theology, Assumption imparts the dogma of the Catholic Church which is built on centuries of philosophical and theological study by thousands of monks, priests, nuns, and lay theologians from every continent where the Church lives.

Ever old and yet ever new, Assumption Seminary, rooted in the history and legacy of St. John's Seminary, emits all that is splendid in the Catholic Church of the 21ˢᵗ century.

APPENDIX I

THE NOTABLES

The Bishops

Most Rev. Gerald R. Barnes, a native of Phoenix, AZ, was raised in East Los Angeles, CA where his family owned a grocery store.

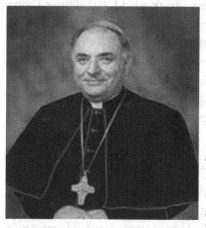 One of seven children, Barnes was educated in the Los Angeles public school system with his religious education provided by Our Lady of Victory Missionary Sisters at San Basilio Center. After high school graduation, Barnes went on to California State University, Los Angeles where he earned a Bachelor's Degree in Political Science in 1967. He attended seminaries in St. Louis, MO and Dayton, OH before finishing his studies at St. John's Assumption Seminary and being ordained by Archbishop Furey in 1975. After serving in several parishes in San Antonio and as rector of Assumption Seminary, Msgr. Barnes was appointed Auxiliary Bishop of San Bernardino in 1992. He was installed as the second bishop of San Bernardino, a diocese with 1.2 million Catholics, in 1996. Bishop Barnes is also active in the United States Bishops' Conference and served on the subcommittee on Hispanic Affairs and on the Committee on Cultural Diversity in the US. (Photo and information from www.sbdiocese.org)

Most Rev. Stephen J. Berg, born in Miles City, Montana, is the oldest of ten children. Berg, a product of Catholic schools, graduated from Gonzaga University in 1970. In 1973 he completed

a Bachelor of Music in Piano performance at the University of Colorado at Boulder; in 1975, a Masters of Music in Piano Performance at Eastern New Mexico University in Portales, New Mexico. Before entering Assumption Seminary in 1993, Berg was employed by Wolfe Nursery in Fort Worth, TX; was a piano instructor at Tarrant County College in Fort Worth; and was in independent sales, brokering nursery stock and Christmas trees in Fort Worth. He was ordained for the Diocese of Fort Worth in 1999. His assignments in the Diocese of Fort Worth included pastoring several parishes and serving as Vicar General of the Diocese and Moderator of the Curia. In 2005, Berg completed the three-year program of the Institute for Priestly Formation at Creighton University. He was installed at the Bishop of Pueblo, CO, on February 27, 2014. (Photo and information from www. dioceseofpueblo.com)

Most Rev. José Arturo Cepeda was born in San Luis Potosi, Mexico in 1969. He was educated in Catholic schools in San Luis Potosi under the direction of the Hermanas and Hermanos

Josefinos. After finishing the equivalency of high school, Cepeda completed a year of spiritual formation at Seminario Arquidiocesano Guadalupano Josefino in San Luis Potosi. His family moved to San Antonio where he entered Assumption Seminary. Cepeda also studied at the College Seminary of the Immaculate heart of Mary in Santa Fe, NM, but finished his seminary studies at Assumption, receiving an MDiv from Oblate School of Theology. He was ordained to the priesthood by Archbishop Flores in June of 1996. He was awarded a Licentiate in Sacred Theology (STL) and a Doctorate in Theology (STD) from St. Thomas Aquinas Pontifical University in Rome and taught on the faculty at Oblate while serving at Assumption. In 2010, Cepeda was installed as rector of Assumption and was appointed Auxiliary Bishop of Detroit in 2011. (Information and photo: www.aod.org)

Most Rev. Laurence J. FitzSimon, born in 1895 in San Antonio, grew up in Castroville, TX. He attended St. Anthony's

College (the Oblate Seminary) from 1907 until 1911 and then did further studies at the Pontifical North American College in Rome. After returning to Texas because of poor health in 1916, FitzSimon served in the US Navy during World War I. Upon discharge, he resumed his theological studies at St. Meinrad's Seminary in Indiana. After ordination in 1921, FitzSimon taught at St. John's Seminary. He served several parishes as pastor from 1925 through 1932 when he was appointed chancellor under Archbishop Drossaerts. FitzSimon was appointed the third Bishop of Amarillo by Pope Pius XII in 1941. He served as the Ordinary of Amarillo for seventeen years. FitzSimon died in Amarillo at age 63 in 1958. (Information from en.wikipedia.org/wiki/Laurence_Julius_FitzSimon; photo from *Archdiocese of San Antonio, 1874-1974,* p. 279)

Most Rev. Hugo M. Gerbermann, MM, was born in Nada, TX in 1913. After attending St. John's Seminary for seven years, Gerbermann entered the Maryknoll Novitiate in Bedford, MS in 1939; he was ordained at the Maryknoll Seminary in New York in 1943. Between 1943 and 1975 Gerbermann served in Maryknoll missions throughout Central and South America. In 1962, while serving at the Huehuetenango Mission in Guatemala, he was named the Bishop of Huehuetenango and served that diocese

until, with failing health, he asked to be reassigned. He accepted the appointment as Auxiliary Bishop in the Archdiocese of San Antonio in 1975, serving in the Archdiocese until he retired in Nada in 1982. Gerbermann died at the Czech Catholic Home in Hilge in 1996 at 83. He had served as a Maryknoll priest for 53 years. (Information and photo: internet)

Most Rev. Charles V. Grahmann, DD, was born in Halletsville, TX in 1931, and entered St. John's Seminary in 1945. In 1956 he was ordained for the San Antonio Archdiocese

in 1956. After serving in several parishes in the Archdiocese, he was appointed secretary to Archbishop Lucey in 1964. Grahmann continued this position under Archbishop Furey. In 1970 he was assigned as the pastor of St. Gregory's Parish in San Antonio while continuing as the Archbishop's secretary. During his ten years at St. Gregory's, Grahmann began an alternative seminary, allowing students to live at the parish while attending classes at Oblate School of Theology. Five priests were ordained through this program. In 1981, he was appointed Auxiliary Bishop of San Antonio and in 1982 was installed as the first bishop of Victoria, TX, a new diocese. In 1989, Grahmann was appointed Coadjutor Bishop of Dallas and became the Ordinary of the Diocese of Dallas in

1990. After his retirement in 2007, Bishop Grahmann continued his involvement in the Focolare Movement and assisted with ministries in Dallas. At the writing of this book, Bishop Grahmann lives in retirement at Casa de Padres in San Antonio. (Information from Bishop Grahmann's memoir-notes; photo: web image)

Most Rev. Charles Edwin Herzig, DD, a native San Antonian, was born in 1929. Herzig was ordained to the priesthood for

the Archdiocese of San Antonio in 1955 after finishing his studies at Assumption Seminary. After serving at various pastoral assignments and in the administration of Assumption Seminary as Vice-President, Herzig was installed as the first bishop of Tyler, TX in 1987. In the fifth year of his tenure as the Bishop of Tyler, Herzig died after a long battle with cancer. He is buried at Rose Hill Cemetery in Tyler. In his memory the Diocese of Tyler established the Bishop Charles E. Herzig Humanitarian Award which is presented annually to persons of the Diocese of Tyler who "demonstrate great love for the human person and whose life in the Catholic Church has been marked by actions that have enabled families or individuals to receive basic care." (From www.dioceseoftyler.org; photo: Photo of a painting of Bishop Herzig by Michael Lawrence of Tyler, TX, used with permission of the artist)

Most Rev. Sidney M. Metzger, STD, was born in Fredericksburg, TX. He was a member of the first class of seminarians of St. John's Seminary, entering in the fall of 1915. He finished his seminary studies at the Pontifical North American College in Room, obtaining a doctorate in Sacred Theology and Canon Law.

After being ordained in 1926, Metzger worked at St. John's Seminary, eventually serving as Rector. In 1940 he was appointed Auxiliary bishop of Santa Fe, NM, by Pope Pius XII. In 1941,

Metzger was named Coadjutor Bishop of El Paso and was installed as the Bishop of El Paso in 1942. After 35 years as Bishop of El Paso, Metzger resigned in 1978. He died at Hotel Dieu Hospital in New Orleans at age 83. (From www.en.wikipedia.org/wiki/Sidney_Matthew_Metzger; photo from Archdiocese of San Antonio, 1874-1974, p. 278)

Most Rev. John L. Morkovsky, born in 1909 in Praha, TX, studied at St. John's Seminary from 1924 until 1930. He completed his theological studies at the College of the Propaganda and the

Pontifical Gregorian University in Rome and was ordained in Rome in 1933. After returning to San Antonio, he served at several parishes in San Antonio and taught at St. John's Seminary. Before being appointed Auxiliary Bishop of Amarillo in 1955, Morkovsky was the Superintendent of Catholic Schools in the Archdiocese of San Antonio. In 1956 he was installed as Bishop of Amarillo and served that diocese for four years. In 1963 he was appointed Coadjutor bishop of Galveston-Houston by St. Pope John XXIII. While the Coadjutor, Morkovsky established the first diocesan mission in Guatemala City, founded the diocesan newspaper *The Texas Catholic Herald*, and was the first Catholic bishop to preside over the Texas Conference of Churches. In 1975, Morkovsky became the sixth

Bishop of Galveston-Houston. He resigned in August of 1984 at age 75. Bishop Morkovsky died from a stroke in Tacoma, WA, in 1989 at age 80. (From en.wikipedia.org/wiki/John_ Louis_Morkovsky)

Most Rev. Raymundo Joseph Peña, born in Corpus Christi, TX, in 1934, attended both public and parochial schools in Robstown, TX, where he was raised. He attended both St. John's

and Assumption Seminaries. He was ordained at Corpus Christi Cathedral in 1957 by Bishop Mariano S. Garriga, DD, one of the first faculty members at St. John's Seminary. During his priesthood in the Diocese of Corpus Christi, Peña pastured Our Lady of Guadalupe Church in Corpus Christi, was Diocesan Youth Director, Editor of the Texas Gulf Coast Catholic, and Vice-President of the Priests' Senate. Peña was ordained the Auxiliary Bishop of San Antonio in 1976 and served as archdiocesan administrator at the death of Archbishop Furey in 1979. Bishop Pena was appointed the Bishop of El Paso in 1980 and served there until 1995 when he was appointed the fifth Bishop of Brownsville, TX. At age 75 Bishop Peña resigned as Ordinary of Brownsville. He continues pastoral work in the Diocese of Brownsville. (From en.wikipedia.org/wiki/Raymundo_ Joseph_; www.cdbob.org; Photo: www.cdbob.org)

Most Rev. Bernard Popp, DD, was born in 1917 and ordained in 1943 after his studies at St. John's Seminary. After ordination, Popp served as associate pastor at St. Agnes Church in San Antonio and was then appointed priest-secretary to Archbishop Lucey, a position he held for 22 years. During these years, Popp served as associate pastor at St. Joseph's (downtown), St. Patrick's, and St. Mary Magdalene, all in San Antonio. He served as pastor at St. Mary Magdalene (1956-1964), and is the founding pastor of Holy Spirit Parish. Other pastoral assignments before he was ordained a bishop were in Victoria and again in San Antonio.

Popp was ordained a bishop at San Fernando Cathedral in July 1983 and served as an Auxiliary Bishop of San Antonio until his retirement at age 75 in 1993. Bishop Popp resides at Padua Place at this writing and celebrated 70 years of priesthood in March 2013. (From www.satodayscatholic.com/ Poppanniv; www.adore24.org/ adore24/BishopPopp; Photo from the internet)

Most Rev. Michael Sheehan, born in 1939 in Wichita, KS, attended St. John's High School Seminary and Assumption Seminary. He then did further studies in Rome at the Pontifical

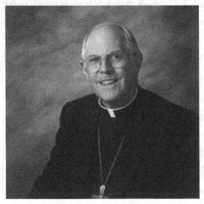

Gregorian University where he obtained a Licentiate of Sacred Theology in 1965. He was ordained for the Diocese of Dallas in Rome in 1964. In the Diocese of Dallas, Sheehan served as a parochial vicar before returning to Rome to earn a doctorate in canon law from the Pontifical Lateran University in 1971. He served as Assistant General Secretary of the National Conference of Catholic Bishops/ United States Catholic Conference from 1971-1976; rector of Holy Trinity Seminary in Dallas from 1976 to 1982; and pastor of Immaculate Conception Parish in Grand Prairie, TX. Sheehan was appointed the founding Bishop of Lubbock in 1983; he became the eleventh Archbishop of Santa Fe in 1993 where he continues to serve. In 2003, Sheehan served for a short time as the Apostolic Administrator of the Diocese of Phoenix after Bishop Thomas J.

O'Brien resigned. (From enwikipedia.org/wiki/Michael_Sheehan; photo: internet)

Most Rev. John Yanta, a native of Runge, TX, was born in 1931. Yanta went to St. John's ≈ Assumption Seminary, finishing in 1956 when he was ordained a priest for the Archdiocese of San

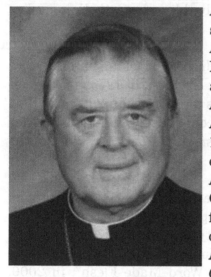

Antonio by Archbishop Lucey. He served in pastoral positions at St. Ann's, Our Lady of Grace, Holy Name, St. Pius X, Sacred Heart and St. James Parishes in San Antonio before he was ordained Auxiliary Bishop of San Antonio in 1994. Yanta was founder and executive director of the San Antonio Neighborhood Youth Organization from 1965-1971; co-founder and first executive director of Catholic Television of San Antonio; and editor of *Today's Catholic* from 1981-83. Bishop Yanta is very proud of his Polish heritage and has served in various leadership capacities for Polish Texans. During his pastorates, Yanta was very involved in starting Sacred Heart Apartments and El Jardin de St. James, both housing projects for the elderly. After serving as Auxiliary Bishop of San Antonio, Yanta was installed as Bishop of Amarillo in 2008. He retired from that position in 2012 and now resides in San Antonio where he is "trying to lead a balanced life of prayer, work, exercise, recreation, etc." in his monastery-home. (From Bishop Yanta's vitae; photo from internet)

The Innovators and Newsmakers[49]

Rev. Conley Bertrand of the Diocese of Lafayette, LA: alumnus of St. John's Seminary and Notre Dame of New Orleans; ordained in 1959; author of the "Come, Lord Jesus" program for spiritual growth and community building in Catholic parishes (ComeLordJesus.com)

Rev. Stephen Bird of the Archdiocese of Oklahoma City: an alumnus of Assumption Seminary; ordained in 1976; as member of the National Pastoral Musicians for more than 25 years, Bird edited *The Book of the Elect*; has contributed numerous articles to journals including *Pastoral Musician*; is past president of the Southwest Liturgical Conference.

Msgr. Michael J. Boulette of the Archdiocese of San Antonio: an alumnus of St. John's ≈ Assumption Seminary, finishing his training at Notre Dame University (ordained 1976); served as Director of Formation at Assumption Seminary, writing a three-year formation program entitled "Word Made Flesh"; in 2006, founding the archdiocesan ministry, St. Peter Upon the Water: a Center for Spiritual Direction and Formation in Ingram, TX.

Rev. Virgilio Elizondo of the Archdiocese of San Antonio: an alumnus of Assumption Seminary (ordained 1963); STD/PhD from Institut Catholique, Paris; known as the father of US Latino religious thought; author of numerous books and articles on the interplay between culture and religion, including *The Future is Mestizo: Life Where Cultures Meet, Guadalupe: Mother of the*

---

[49] The author is very grateful to Msgr. James Vanderholt for the information from his book, *Called to Serve*, and the priests who identified notable experiences in their initial survey. She regrets any oversight or misinformation. In addition, due to her experience with a number of the priests and laymen who are alumni of St. John's ≈ Assumption, this list is *far from complete*. Sources for the information in this section include: the internet, survey material, *Called to Serve*, memoirs, and interviews.

New Creation; *Mestizo Worship;* faculty, Assumption Seminary; Endowed Professor of Pastoral and Hispanic Theology, University of Notre Dame.

Msgr. Alois Goertz of the Archdiocese of San Antonio: an alumnus of St. John's (ordained in 1948); collaborated on the writing of *25 Years a Seminary* and *Priest Forever*; author *Rockne, Sacred Heart Parish, Bastrop County, Texas, 1876-1976* (updated 1996); first director of Campus Ministry at San Antonio College and the Archdiocese (1965-1968); pioneered the "New-Cor" (New Heart) retreats for collegians

Rev. Samuel Heitkamp of the Archdiocese of San Antonio: an alumnus of St. John's ≈ Assumption (ordained 1967); began campus ministry for Catholics on campus at Texas Lutheran College in Seguin; Rural Life Director for the Archdiocese with a column in *Today's Catholic*; Texas Rural Minister of the Year in 1978 (a non-denominational award); elected to the National Catholic Rural Life Conference Board of Directors in 1982; co-founder, Texas Catholic Conference Committee on Rural Life and Ministry; in 1987, Roman Catholic representative on the design team of Rural Social Science by Extension; worked with US Department of Agriculture in a special project for the US Foreign Aid Program; worked on projects to bring water to third world countries; 1989, named Wilson County's Business/Professional Man of the Year; in 2000 (with the approval of Archbishop Flores) became the legal guardian of a nine year old orphaned girl and raised her to adulthood.

Rev. Joseph Montalbano of the Diocese of Alexandria, LA: an alumnus of Assumption (ordained 1955); appointed by Louisiana Governors Edwin Edwards and David C. Treen to serve on the Louisiana Governor's Advisory Board for Juvenile Justice and Delinquency Prevention; served for 12 years; founded a home, Vernon House, located in Leesville, LA, that provided shelter and care for "runaways" and statute offenders between the ages of 9 and 16 years; over a period of 20 years, fostered 12 children.

Msgr. Roy Rihn of the Archdiocese of San Antonio: an alumnus of St. John's Seminary (ordained 1942); author of *The Priestly Amen*; *Our Stories* (published in 1999); contributor to *The Parish in a Time of Change*

Rev. Stanley Rother of the Archdiocese of Oklahoma City: an alumnus of St. John's ≈ Assumption Seminary (ordained in 1962); served at Catholic Mission of Oklahoma in Santiago Atitlan, Guatemala (Diocese of Solola) from 1968 until he was martyred at St. James the Apostle Church in Santiago Atitlan in 1981; the cause for his canonization is under the direction of the Archdiocese of Oklahoma City.

Msgr. Sherrill Smith of the Archdiocese of San Antonio (deceased 2013): an alumnus of Assumption Seminary (ordained 1955); from Chicago; invited by Archbishop Lucey to serve the Archdiocese of San Antonio; a champion of the poor, the unborn, civil rights, labor and racial justice, serving a number of jail sentences for his actions; marched in Selma with Martin Luther King; poet.

Msgr. James Tucek of the Diocese of Dallas (deceased): alumnus of St. John's (Ordained in 1947); head of the Rome Bureau of the National Catholic Welfare Conference News Service, now Catholic News Service during the first session of the Second Vatican Council; author of numerous articles in newspapers and magazines about the Council; collaborating author of a number of books including *The Biography of Pope John XXIII*.

Msgr. John Wagner of the Archdiocese of San Antonio: an alumnus of St. John's Seminary (ordained 1949); pioneered Hispanic ministry beginning with his work at Cementville while parochial vicar at St. Peter, Prince of the Apostles Church and as priest-in-charge of St. Anthony Shrine; served as executive secretary for the US Bishops Committee for the Spanish Speaking that began preparations of US dioceses for ministering to the growing Hispanic population in the US; worked with Sen. Ted Kennedy on establishing the Peace Corps and Vista Volunteers;

worked with Sen. Robert Kennedy on issues regarding migrant farm workers; worked with Martin Luther King in the Civil Rights Movement; involved with the War on Poverty and Barcero Program; first pastor of Holy Redeemer Church, the African-American parish in East San Antonio;

Rev. James D. White of the Diocese of Tulsa: an alumnus of Assumption (ordained 1969); while a seminarian, influential in the design and building of St. Edith and St. Florence Chapel; author of *The Souls of the Just: A Necrology of the Catholic Church of Oklahoma* (1976); *A History of Immaculate Conception Parish, Poteau, Oklahoma* (1978); *This Far by Faith—1875-2000, The History of the Diocese of Tulsa, OK; Roman and Oklahoman, A Centennial History of the Archdiocese of Oklahoma City.*

ALUMNI ASSOCIATION OF ST. JOHN'S AND ASSUMPTION SEMINARIES

Organized in August 1932 at a priests' retreat, the Alumni Association aims "to strengthen the spiritual and fraternal bond among the Alumni of St. John's ≈ [Assumption] Seminary and to foster their filial devotion to their Alma Mater" (*25 Years*, p. 25). The newly-written constitution, which was approved by Archbishop Drossaerts, noted that "any priest who has made any part of his studies in St. John's Seminary" is eligible for membership. At the writing of *25 Years a Seminary*, Father Joseph A. Pustka[50] was the president; Father Paul Ehlinger ('37), vice-president; Fr. Edward J.Jansky ('30), secretary-treasurer (*25 Years*, p. 25; Vanderholt, p. 157).

The Association met annually from 1932 until 1941. Due to "la guerre", no meetings were held in 1942 or 1943. Forty-three alumni (of the 101 members) attended the 1944 meeting. Two more years passed with no meetings (also because of "la guerre"),

---

[50] Msgr. Joseph Aloysius Pustka entered St. Benedict Seminary in Louisiana (then commonly used by the Diocese of San Antonio) in 1911 and then transferred to St. John's Seminary in 1915 when it opened. He completed his studies as St. Mary's Seminary (Sulpician) in Baltimore in 1922 and was ordained May 1, 1922 at St. Mary's Church in Halletsville, TX [Source: Gilbert, M.J. (ed.) & Archdiocese of San Antonio, Archdiocese of San Antonio, 1874-1949, pages 149-151; and *groups.yahoo.com/group/ TexasCzechs/ message/35052*].

but the Association again gathered in May 1947 when a regular meeting date was established: the second Tuesday of October.

However lofty the intention to meet annually had been at the May 1947 meeting, the next meeting did not occur until October 1951. By then the Priest-Alumni Association numbered 157 members. At the 1951 meeting, the alumni were determined to begin anew, and "the old Association got its 'second wind' and from this point on the annual meetings have been held annually. The 1951 meeting drew sixty-one alumni to the first meeting held away from St. John's Seminary in St. James Parish in Seguin, TX "indicating perhaps that we had grown up sufficiently to get away from Alma Mater's apron strings" ("A Report to the Alumni Association of St. John's and Assumption Seminaries, Seventeenth Annual Reunion and Meeting, San Antonio, Texas, October 10-11, 1955, p. 3-7 [Original copy held at Vincentian Archives, DePaul University, Chicago]).

The year that Assumption opened (1952), Father Vincent Wolf ('38), Diocese of Dallas, was the president of the Association. He hosted a re-organizational meeting in Tyler, TX, at which the Association acquired new energy and changed the name of the Association to "Alumni Association of St. John's and Assumption Seminaries".

The October 1953 meeting was expanded to a two-day meeting in order to provide recreational time and an opportunity to "relax and share information with old friends from far-away places" ("A Report to Alumni Association, 1955", p. 8)

"The 1955 Directory of the Priest-alumni of St. John's and Assumption Seminaries", listed 201 alumni from sixteen archdiocese and dioceses and five religious orders. These priests were serving in the Dioceses of Alexandria, LA; Amarillo, TX; Austin, TX; Corpus Christi, TX; Dallas-Ft. Worth, TX; El Paso, TX; Galveston, TX; Grand Rapids, MI; Guatemala City, Guatemala; Kansas City, MO: Lafayette, LA; Oklahoma City-Tulsa; Ontario, Canada; Peoria, IL; St. Augustine, FL; and San Antonio, TX.

Since 1944, the Alumni Association has enlarged its vision beyond being a fraternal organization of alumni from St. John's and Assumption Seminaries. Beginning in 1944, the Alumni

Association have made many significant monetary gifts to their Alma Mater including

- A gift of $150 donated in 1944 for the "vocation issue" of "The Bulletin", the students' publication of St. John's ("A Report to the Association," p. 7);
- In 1960 "more than $40,000 pledged to the St. John's Chapel" (Vanderholt, p. 157);
- In 1968, the establishment of a chair of theology with a goal of $200,000 (Vanderholt, p. 158);
- In 2013, the publication of the centennial history;
- In 2014-15 the creation of a Centennial Endowment in order to assure quality faculty, the establishment of a lecture and conference series, scholarships and grants-in-aid for college or graduate theology seminarians, a fund for the Rector for emergency special needs, resources that will promote collaboration between faculty and staff and the vocation office in the promotion of vocations for the rural areas of the Archdiocese, funds reserved for the upkeep of Archbishop Flores Hall, St. John's Hall, and the Chapel; and funds to address other concerns.

Since 1954, the following alumni have served the Association as president:

1954	*Rev. John Wiewell ('37**)	Diocese of Fort Worth***
1955	Rev. Roy Rihn ('41)	Arch. of San Antonio
1956	Rev. John Basso	Diocese of Corpus Christi
1957	Rev. Henry Buchanan ('21)	Diocese of El Paso
1958	Rev. Charles Drees	Arch. of San Antonio
1959	Rev. Thomas Weinzapfel ('45)	Diocese of Dallas
1960	Rev. Albert Maneth ('37)	Arch. of San Antonio
1961	Rev. Victor Goertz ('52)	Diocese of Austin
1962	Rev. Robert Schmidt ('44)	Arch. of San Antonio
1963	Rev. William Botik ('44)	Diocese of Dallas
1964	Rev. Alois Goertz ('48)	Arch. of San Antonio
1965	Rev. Balthasar Janacek ('50)	Arch. of San Antonio
1966	Msgr. William Thompson ('54)	Diocese of Corpus Christi

1967	Rev. Robert Wilson ('57)	Diocese of Fort Worth
1968	Rev. Lawrence Stuebben ('55)	Arch. of San Antonio
1969	Rev. Lawrence Stuebben	Arch. of San Antonio
1970	Rev. Edward Bily ('51)	Arch. of San Antonio
1971	Rev. Albert Tyl ('54)	Diocese of Ft. Worth
1972	Rev. Louis Fritz	Arch. of San Antonio
1973	Rev. Joseph Montalbano ('55)	Diocese of Alexandria, LA
1974	Rev. Arnold Anders	Diocese of Victoria, TX
1975	Msgr. Harold Palmer	Diocese of Corpus Christi
1976	Rev. Benton Thurmond ('46)	Arch. of San Antonio
1977	Rev. Raphael Kamel	Diocese of Dallas
1978	Msgr. Rafael Kamel ('54)	Diocese of Dallas
1979	Rev. John Yanta ('56)	Arch. of San Antonio
1980	Rev. George Harris ('65)	Diocese of Brownsville
1981	Rev. Joseph Hybner ('63)	Diocese of Victoria
1982	Rev. Philip Johnson ('64)	Diocese of Fort Worth
1983	Rev. Thomas Lyssy ('52)	Arch. of San Antonio
1984	Rev. Michael O'Shaugnessey ('50)	Diocese of Victoria
1985	Rev. Gerald Hubertus ('64)	Arch. of San Antonio
1986	Rev. Stephen Bird ('76)	Arch. of Oklahoma City
1987	Rev. Charles Pugh ('60)	Arch. of San Antonio
1988	Rev. Louis Joseph ('55)	Diocese of Corpus Christi
1989	Rev. John Peters ('74)	Diocese of Victoria
1990	Rev. Lawrence Stuebben ('55)	Arch. of San Antonio
1991	Rev. Bernard Gully ('62)	Diocese of San Angelo
1992	Rev. David Garcia ('75)	Arch. of San Antonio
1993	Rev. Gonzalo Morales ('52)	Diocese of Fort Worth
1994	Rev. George Stuebben ('85)	Arch. of San Antonio
1995	Rev. Pat Seitz ('92)	Diocese of Brownsville
1996	Rev. Raymond Schuster ('93)	Arch. of San Antonio
1997	Rev. Fernando Rubio Boitel ('75)	Diocese of Santa Fe
1998	Rev. Eduardo Morales ('96)	Arch. of San Antonio
1999	Rev. Joe Baker ('86)	Diocese of Tucson
2000	Rev. Toribio Guerrero ('96)	Diocese of Laredo
2001	Rev. George Harris ('65)	Diocese of Brownsville

2002	Msgr. Jeff Pehl ('95)	Arch. of San Antonio
2003	Rev. Stephen Duyka ('97)	Diocese of Tyler
2004	Rev. Jimmy Drennan ('96)	Arch. of San Antonio
2005	Rev. Daniel Kelley ('95)	Diocese of Fort Worth
2006	Most Rev. José Arturo Cepeda ('96)	Arch. of San Antonio [now Aux. Bishop of Detroit]
2007	Rev. Charles Brown ('93)	Diocese of Grand Rapids
2008	Rev. José Francisco Puente ('00)	Arch. of San Antonio
2009	Rev. John Gunningham ('07)	Diocese of San Bernardino
2010	Rev. Jonathan Felux ('09)	Arch. of San Antonio
2011	Rev. M. Rene Perez ('03)	Diocese of Lubbock
2012	Rev. Eric Ritter ('03)	Arch. of San Antonio
2013	Rev. Pat Seitz ('92)	Diocese of Brownsville
2014	Rev. Jimmy Drennan ('96)	Arch. of San Antonio

In their one hundred years, the alumni of St. John's and Assumption Seminaries have served in 58 archdioceses/dioceses throughout the US, Canada, and Puerto Rico and five congregations of men religious.

Notes:

*The priest-presidents up through 1990 are titled as they were in 1990 when Vanderholt wrote *Called to Serve*. The names of these presidents in the first seventy-five appear on pages 157-160 in his book. The priest-presidents since 1990 are titled with their current title.

**The year designated is the year of ordination; priests would thus say they were in the Class of ___, meaning that class of Ordinands.

***The diocese named in this listing is the diocese in which he served at the time he was president.

LIVING ALUMNI (ACTIVE AND INACTIVE)

Aguilar, Ricardo (Inactive)
Year of Ordination: 1995
Arch/Diocese of Austin

Aguilera, Salvador Rev.
Year of Ordination:
1985
Arch/Diocese of El Paso

Akpanobong, Patrick Rev.
Year of Ordination: 2011
Arch/Diocese of San
Angelo

Alaka, Allan Oluoch Rev.
Year of Ordination: 2013
Arch/Diocese of El Paso

Alvarado, Roberto Rev.
Year of Ordination:
1989
Arch/Diocese of El Paso

Anders, Arnold Rev.
Year of Ordination: 1950
Arch/Diocese of Victoria

Anderson, Ronald C.
(Inactive)
Year of Ordination: 1966
Arch/Diocese of Brownsville

Anguiano Rivera, Jesus
Rev.
Year of Ordination:
2009
Arch/Diocese of San
Antonio

Aramburo Garcia,
Eugenio Rev.
Year of Ordination: 1988
Arch/Diocese of Monterey

Arechiga, Dennis D. Rev.
Year of Ordination: 2000
Arch/Diocese of San Antonio

Ausberger, Charles P.
Rev.
Year of Ordination:
1961
Arch/Diocese of Grand
Rapids

Ayala, III, Ricardo
(Inactive)
Year of Ordination: 1994
Arch/Diocese of
Brownsville

Barley, Thomas Rev.
Year of Ordination: 1991
Arch/Diocese of San Angelo

Barlow, James P. Rev.
Year of Ordination:
1973
Arch/Diocese of San
Antonio

Barnes, Gerald R. Most
Rev.
Year of Ordination: 1975
Arch/Diocese of San
Bernardino

Barnum, Matthew J. Rev.
Year of Ordination: 2007
Arch/Diocese of Grand
Rapids

Barragan, Juan Carlos
Rev.
Year of Ordination:
1997
Arch/Diocese of
Amarillo

Barran, Joseph (Inactive)
Year of Ordination: 1972
Arch/Diocese of San
Antonio

Barrera Campos, Filiberto
Rev.
Year of Ordination: 1998
Arch/Diocese of Oakland

Barton, Leslie
(Inactive)
Year of Ordination:
1960
Arch/Diocese of
Oklahoma City

Bednorz, Jr., Alfred S.
(Inactive)
Year of Ordination: 1976
Arch/Diocese of Amarillo

Bedoya, Ferley De Jesus
(Inactive)
Year of Ordination: 2001
Arch/Diocese of
Galveston-Houston

Bell, John P. Rev.
Year of Ordination:
1975
Arch/Diocese of Dallas

Berg, Stephen J. Most Rev.
Year of Ordination: 1999
Arch/Diocese of Pueblo

Bernal, Edward M. Rev.
Year of Ordination: 1987
Arch/Diocese of San Antonio

Bertini, Angelo Rev.
Year of Ordination:
1973
Arch/Diocese of Austin

Bertrand, Charles Conley
Rev.
Year of Ordination: 1959
Arch/Diocese of Lafayette

Betancourt, Cesar Rev.
Year of Ordination: 2009
Arch/Diocese of San Antonio

Bilski, Harry S. Rev.
Year of Ordination:
1958
Arch/Diocese of Austin

Bily, Lambert S. Rev.
Msgr.
Year of Ordination: 1963
Arch/Diocese of San
Antonio

Bily, John C. Rev. Msgr.
Year of Ordination: 1958
Arch/Diocese of Victoria

Bird, Stephen J. Rev.
Year of Ordination:
1976
Arch/Diocese of
Oklahoma City

Bland, Thomas A. Rev.
Year of Ordination: 1974
Arch/Diocese of
Sacramento

Bonazza, Benjamin
(Inactive)
Year of Ordination: 1954
Arch/Diocese of San Antonio

Bone, Patrick (Inactive)
Year of Ordination:
1968
Arch/Diocese of San
Antonio

Bonfanti, Samuel E.
(Inactive)
Year of Ordination: 1970
Arch/Diocese of
Alexandria

Bordeaux, OCD, Henry
Gratian Rev.
Year of Ordination: 1962
Order of Carmelites

Boulette, Michael J.
Rev. Msgr.
Year of Ordination:
1976
Arch/Diocese of San
Antonio

Bozung, James M. Rev.
Year of Ordination: 1961
Arch/Diocese of Grand
Rapids

Brasher, John C. Rev.
Year of Ordination: 1975
Arch/Diocese of Santa Fe

Brenon, Terence Rev.
Year of Ordination:
1991
Arch/Diocese of San
Angelo

Brown, Timothy (Inactive)
Year of Ordination: 1966
Arch/Diocese of San
Antonio

Brown, Charles Rev.
Year of Ordination: 1993
Arch/Diocese of Grand
Rapids

Bueno, Julian (Inactive)
Year of Ordination:
1970
Arch/Diocese of
Brownsville

Bui, Anthony Rev.
Year of Ordination: 2011
Arch/Diocese of San
Bernardino

Buxkemper, Roland Rev.
Year of Ordination: 1965
Arch/Diocese of Lubbock

Cade, OCD, John Mary
(Inactive)
Year of Ordination:
1961
Order of Carmelites

Camacho, Jesus Rev.
Year of Ordination: 2006
Arch/Diocese of San
Antonio

Camacho, Enrique Rev.
Year of Ordination: 1981
Arch/Diocese of Yakima

Canney, Michael
(Inactive)
Year of Ordination:
1955
Arch/Diocese of San
Antonio

Cardenas, OCD, Daniel
(Inactive)
Year of Ordination: 1965
Order of Carmelites

Cardoza, Manuel C. Rev.
Year of Ordination: 2009
Arch/Diocese of San
Bernardino

Carrola, Jr., Rudy T.
Rev.
Year of Ordination:
1988
Arch/Diocese of San
Antonio

Carroll, Gregory G. Rev.
Year of Ordination: 1974
Arch/Diocese of Santa Fe

Casares, Angel Diaz Rev.
Year of Ordination: 1976
Arch/Diocese of Arecibo
Puerto Rico

Catanach, Richard A.
Rev.
Year of Ordination:
1988
Arch/Diocese of Las
Cruces

Celino, Juventino
(Inactive)
Year of Ordination: 1982
Arch/Diocese of El Paso

Cepeda, Jose Arturo Most
Rev.
Year of Ordination: 1996
Arch/Diocese of Detroit

Cernoch, Gerard Rev.
Year of Ordination:
1964
Arch/Diocese of
Victoria

Chamberlin, Mark Rev.
Year of Ordination: 1968
Arch/Diocese of Corpus
Christi

Chaumont, James Rev.
(Inactive)
Year of Ordination: 1977
Arch/Diocese of San Angelo

Chavez, Frank Rev.
Year of Ordination:
1976
Arch/Diocese of San
Angelo

Chavez, Patrick J. Rev.
Year of Ordination: 1968
Arch/Diocese of Santa Fe

Chavez, Carlos Rev.
Year of Ordination: 1984
Arch/Diocese of Santa Fe

Chengazacheril, George
Rev.
Year of Ordination:
1980
Arch/Diocese of San
Antonio

Chilen, Michael D. Rev.
Year of Ordination: 1969
Arch/Diocese of Corpus
Christi

Choong, Kai Norbert Rev.
Year of Ordination: 1984
Arch/Diocese of Amarillo

Chrusciel, Andrew Rev.
Year of Ordination:
1963
Arch/Diocese of Grand
Rapids

Colin Marin, Alberto G.
Rev.
Year of Ordination: 2008
Arch/Diocese of San
Antonio

Collins, Richard M. Rev.
Year of Ordination: 2004
Arch/Diocese of Fort Worth

Colwell, Michael Rev.
Year of Ordination:
1994
Arch/Diocese of
Amarillo

Combs, BBD, Will H. Rev.
Year of Ordination: 2004
Arch/Diocese of San
Antonio

Comparan, Jose Luis Rev.
Year of Ordination: 2003
Arch/Diocese of Dubuque

Conroy, Francis Rev.
(Inactive)
Year of Ordination:
1972
Arch/Diocese of
Beaumont

Contreras, David Rev.
Year of Ordination: 1993
Arch/Diocese of Amarillo

Conway, John R. Rev.
Year of Ordination: 1969
Arch/Diocese of Santa Fe

Cordero, Martin Rev.
Year of Ordination:
1999
Arch/Diocese of Las
Cruces

Correa, Adrian Rev.
Year of Ordination:
Arch/Diocese of
Brownsville

Cosgrove, James (Inactive)
Year of Ordination: 1969
Arch/Diocese of San Antonio

Courtwright, Lawrence
P. Rev.
Year of Ordination:
1961
Arch/Diocese of Tulsa

Covos, Ruben G. Rev.
Year of Ordination: 2006
Arch/Diocese of San
Angelo

Cowan, Anthony (Inactive)
Year of Ordination: 1995
Arch/Diocese of San Antonio

Crane, Jeffrey J.
(Inactive)
Year of Ordination:
1989
Arch/Diocese of San
Antonio

Crisp, Robert R. Rev.
Year of Ordination: 1975
Arch/Diocese of Dallas

Cruz, Gilbert (Inactive)
Year of Ordination: 1955
Arch/Diocese of San Antonio

Currie, Donald S.
(Inactive)
Year of Ordination:
1979
Arch/Diocese of San
Antonio

Dakin, Kenneth M. Rev.
Year of Ordination: 1988
Arch/Diocese of San
Antonio

Darilek, Dennis Rev. Msgr.
Year of Ordination: 1973
Arch/Diocese of San Antonio

Davila, Johnny G.
(Inactive)
Year of Ordination:
1984
Arch/Diocese of San
Antonio

De La Rosa, Jose Luis
Rev.
Year of Ordination: 1984
Arch/Diocese of San
Antonio

Deaconson, James Rev.
Year of Ordination: 1985
Arch/Diocese of Austin

DeGeralomi, Michael
Rev.
Year of Ordination:
1974
Arch/Diocese of San
Antonio

Dehetre, Mark (Inactive)
Year of Ordination: 1993
Arch/Diocese of Lansing

Delgado, Ruben Rev.
Year of Ordination: 1990
Arch/Diocese of Brownsville

Diaz, Nelson De Jesus
Rev.
Year of Ordination:
2001
Arch/Diocese of
Lubbock

Diegel, Ronald Rev.
Year of Ordination: 1975
Arch/Diocese of Tyler

Do, Timothy Truong Rev.
Year of Ordination: 2010
Arch/Diocese of San
Bernardino

Dolin, John E.
(Inactive)
Year of Ordination:
1958
Arch/Diocese of
Oklahoma City

Dominguez, Jesus A.
(Inactive)
Year of Ordination: 1983
Arch/Diocese of San
Bernardino

Dornak, Melvin Rev.
Year of Ordination: 1992
Arch/Diocese of Austin

Dowdell, Thomas R.
Rev.
Year of Ordination:
1971
Arch/Diocese of
Oklahoma City

Drennan, Jimmy D. Rev.
Year of Ordination: 1996
Arch/Diocese of San
Antonio

Droll, Larry Rev. Msgr.
Year of Ordination: 1973
Arch/Diocese of San Angelo

Drozd, Henry J. Rev.
Year of Ordination:
1962
Arch/Diocese of Dallas

Duesman, Jerome Rev.
Year of Ordination: 1968
Arch/Diocese of Dallas

Duet, Jerod J. (Inactive)
Year of Ordination: 2008
Arch/Diocese of
Houma-Thibodaux

Duyka, Stephen J. Rev.
Year of Ordination:
1997
Arch/Diocese of Tyler

Dybala, Robert E.
(Inactive)
Year of Ordination: 1971
Arch/Diocese of San
Antonio

Eichhoff, Paul E. Rev.
Year of Ordination: 1970
Arch/Diocese of Tulsa

Eke, Raphael Rev.
Year of Ordination: 2001
Arch/Diocese of San Antonio

Elizondo, Ernesto Rev.
Year of Ordination: 2000
Arch/Diocese of Austin

Elizondo, Virgil Rev.
Year of Ordination: 1963
Arch/Diocese of San Antonio

Ermis, Norman A. Rev.
Year of Ordination: 1983
Arch/Diocese of San Antonio

Ernst, Robbi W. (Inactive)
Year of Ordination: 1974
Arch/Diocese of Austin

Escobedo, Armando Rev.
Year of Ordination: 1964
Arch/Diocese of Brownsville

Esparza, Erik L. Rev.
Year of Ordination: 2008
Arch/Diocese of San Bernardino

Eustice, Richard (Inactive)
Year of Ordination: 1963
Arch/Diocese of Brownsville

Eziefule, Innocent Rev.
Year of Ordination: 2013
Arch/Diocese of San Angelo

Faylona, Joey Rev.
Year of Ordination: 2003
Arch/Diocese of San Angelo

Feehily, John W. Rev.
Year of Ordination: 1973
Arch/Diocese of Oklahoma City

Felux, Jonathan W. Rev.
Year of Ordination: 2009
Arch/Diocese of San Antonio

Ferrer, TOR, Gonzalo
Rev. (Inactive)
Year of Ordination:
1981
Arch/Diocese of Austin

Fey, Everett A. (Inactive)
Year of Ordination: 1962
Arch/Diocese of San
Antonio

Flores Alvarez, Ramiro Rev.
Year of Ordination: 1995
Arch/Diocese of Oakland

Flynn, James S. Rev.
Year of Ordination:
2006
Arch/Diocese of Fort
Worth

Fowler, John W. Rev.
Year of Ordination: 1953
Arch/Diocese of Dallas

Frank, Gerald W. Rev.
Year of Ordination: 1970
Arch/Diocese of Brownsville

Gallegos, Jr., Valentine
Rev.
Year of Ordination:
2009
Arch/Diocese of San
Antonio

Gamez, Steven A. Rev.
Year of Ordination: 2008
Arch/Diocese of San
Antonio

Gamino, Jr., Alexander Rev.
Year of Ordination: 2010
Arch/Diocese of San
Bernardino

Garcia, Eugenio
Aramburo Rev.
Year of Ordination:
1988
Arch/Diocese of
Monterey

Garcia, David H. Rev.
Year of Ordination: 1975
Arch/Diocese of San
Antonio

Garcia Avila, Martin Rev.
Year of Ordination: 2009
Arch/Diocese of San Antonio

Garcia Ayala, Jorge
Rev.
Year of Ordination:
2008
Arch/Diocese of San
Bernardino

Garcia Chavez, Luis
Alfredo Rev.
Year of Ordination: 2002
Arch/Diocese of Colorado
Springs

Garcia Ramirez, Pedro Rev.
Year of Ordination: 1992
Arch/Diocese of Austin

Garza, Jose Rev.
Year of Ordination:
2014
Arch/Diocese of
Brownsville

Gerber, Nicholas J. Rev.
Year of Ordination: 2008
Arch/Diocese of Amarillo

Goertz, Benedict E.
(Inactive)
Year of Ordination: 1958
Arch/Diocese of Austin

Goertz, Victor M. Rev.
Year of Ordination:
1952
Arch/Diocese of Austin

Goertz, Howard H. Rev.
Year of Ordination: 1977
Arch/Diocese of Austin

Goertz, Alois J. Rev. Msgr.
Year of Ordination: 1948
Arch/Diocese of San Antonio

Gollob, Timothy Rev.
Year of Ordination:
1958
Arch/Diocese of Dallas

Gomez, Frank J. Rev.
Year of Ordination: 1961
Arch/Diocese of
Brownsville

Gomez, Humberto Rev.
Year of Ordination: 1988
Arch/Diocese of Sacramento

Gomez Duran, Jorge
Jaime Rev. (Inactive)
Year of Ordination:
1975
Arch/Diocese of San
Antonio

Gomez Medina, Oscar
Rev.
Year of Ordination: 2002
Arch/Diocese of
Sacramento

Gomez Vazquez, Jose E. Rev.
Year of Ordination: 1995
Arch/Diocese of Amarillo

Gonzalez, Rogelio Rev.
Year of Ordination:
2011
Arch/Diocese of San
Bernardino

Gonzalez Hernandez,
Marco Antonio Rev.
Year of Ordination: 2007
Arch/Diocese of Raliegh

Gonzalez P., Antonio Rev.
Year of Ordination: 2013
Arch/Diocese of San Antonio

Gonzalez-Cabrera,
Javier Rev.
Year of Ordination:
2008
Arch/Diocese of San
Bernardino

Grahmann, Charles Most
Rev.
Year of Ordination: 1956
Arch/Diocese of Dallas

Greiner, James A. Rev.
Year of Ordination: 1964
Arch/Diocese of Oklahoma
City

Guerrero, Toribio Rev.
Year of Ordination:
1996
Arch/Diocese of Laredo

Guerrero Ponce, Servando
Rev.
Year of Ordination: 2014
Arch/Diocese of San
Antonio

Guevara, Alfonso M. Rev.
Year of Ordination: 1977
Arch/Diocese of Brownsville

Guido, Luis A. Rev.
Year of Ordination:
2008
Arch/Diocese of San
Bernardino

Gully, Bernard L. Rev.
Msgr.
Year of Ordination: 1962
Arch/Diocese of San
Angelo

Gunningham, John R. Rev.
Year of Ordination: 2007
Arch/Diocese of San
Bernardino

Guste, OCD, Placid
Rev.
Year of Ordination:
1961
Order of Carmelites

Gutierrez, Juan Rogelio
Rev.
Year of Ordination: 2007
Arch/Diocese of
Brownsville

Gutierrez Jauregui, Ismael
Rev.
Year of Ordination: 2004
Arch/Diocese of Oakland

Hall, James W. Rev.
Year of Ordination:
1970
Arch/Diocese of El Paso

Hanus, Thomas Rev.
Year of Ordination: 1966
Arch/Diocese of Austin

Harrold, Michael Rev.
Year of Ordination: 1950
Arch/Diocese of Victoria

Hatch, Lorenzo Rev.
Year of Ordination:
2013
Arch/Diocese of San
Angelo

Hazel, John P. (Inactive)
Year of Ordination: 1960
Arch/Diocese of Dallas

Heathcote, Howard Rev.
Year of Ordination: 1981
Arch/Diocese of Austin

Heitkamp, Samuel Rev.
Year of Ordination:
1967
Arch/Diocese of San
Antonio

Henke, James Rev. Msgr.
Year of Ordination: 1966
Arch/Diocese of San
Antonio

Henning, Philip Rev.
Year of Ordination: 1993
Arch/Diocese of San Antonio

Henseler, Jr., Philip
Rev.
Year of Ordination:
1996
Arch/Diocese of
Chicago

Hermes, Eustace A. Rev.
Year of Ordination: 1941
Arch/Diocese of Victoria

Hernandez, Larry C.
(Inactive)
Year of Ordination: 1978
Arch/Diocese of San Antonio

Hernandez, Antonio
(Inactive)
Year of Ordination:
1992
Arch/Diocese of San
Antonio

Hernandez, Eduardo Rev.
Year of Ordination: 1980
Arch/Diocese of
Brownsville

Hernandez, Alfred Rev.
Year of Ordination: 1966
Arch/Diocese of San Antonio

Hernandez, Ricardo
Alfredo Rev.
Year of Ordination:
1966
Arch/Diocese of San
Antonio

Higgins, Patrick Rev.
Year of Ordination: 2010
Arch/Diocese of Corpus
Christi

Horstman, Keith (Inactive)
Year of Ordination: 1995
Arch/Diocese of Lansing

Hubertus, Albert H.
Rev. Msgr.
Year of Ordination:
1950
Arch/Diocese of San
Antonio

Hunt, III, H. Clay Rev.
Year of Ordination: 2009
Arch/Diocese of San
Antonio

Hutzler, James (Inactive)
Year of Ordination: 1970
Arch/Diocese of Amarillo

Hybner, Joseph M. Rev.
Msgr.
Year of Ordination:
1963
Arch/Diocese of
Victoria

Ibe, Robert Doak
(Inactive)
Year of Ordination: 1978
Arch/Diocese of Amarillo

Irlbeck, Tom (Inactive)
Year of Ordination: 1968
Arch/Diocese of Amarillo

Irwin, Michael T. Rev.
Year of Ordination:
1964
Arch/Diocese of Fort
Worth

Iven, David L. (Inactive)
Year of Ordination: 1959
Arch/Diocese of Oklahoma
City

Jamail, Michael A. Rev.
Msgr.
Year of Ordination: 1960
Arch/Diocese of Beaumont

Janak, Gary W. Rev.
Year of Ordination:
1988
Arch/Diocese of
Victoria

Janish, James Rev. Msgr.
Year of Ordination: 1969
Arch/Diocese of San
Antonio

Janysek, Scott Rev.
Year of Ordination: 2014
Arch/Diocese of San Antonio

Jarzombeck, Dennis
Rev.
Year of Ordination:
1979
Arch/Diocese of San
Antonio

Jarzombeck, OSB,
Casimir Rev.
Year of Ordination: 1960
Order of Benedictines

Johnson, Richard E.
(Inactive)
Year of Ordination: 1960
Arch/Diocese of Dallas

Johnson, Robert Rev.
Year of Ordination:
1951
Arch/Diocese of Fort
Worth

Johnson, Philip L. Rev.
Year of Ordination: 1964
Arch/Diocese of Fort
Worth

Joseph, Louis J. Rev.
Year of Ordination: 1955
Arch/Diocese of Corpus
Christi

Juarez, Rudy Rev.
Year of Ordination:
1980
Arch/Diocese of
Davenport

Juenke, Carlos (Inactive)
Year of Ordination: 1966
Arch/Diocese of San
Antonio

Kahlich, Daniel P. Rev.
Year of Ordination: 1966
Arch/Diocese of Victoria

Kajs, Larry (Inactive)
Year of Ordination:
1978
Arch/Diocese of
Brownsville

Kammerer, James
(Inactive)
Year of Ordination: 1997
Arch/Diocese of San
Antonio

Kelley, Daniel Rev.
Year of Ordination: 1995
Arch/Diocese of Fort Worth

Kennedy, William M.
Rev.
Year of Ordination:
1963
Arch/Diocese of
Galveston-Houston

Kennedy, Thomas Rev.
Year of Ordination: 2007
Arch/Diocese of Fort
Worth

Keyman-Ige, Isak Rev.
Year of Ordination: 2012
Arch/Diocese of San Antonio

Kieu, Kien Rev.
Year of Ordination:
2014
Arch/Diocese of San
Bernardino

King, William C.
(Inactive)
Year of Ordination: 1961
Arch/Diocese of Oklahoma
City

Kirkham, Richard Rev.
Year of Ordination: 2011
Arch/Diocese of Fort Worth

Kitz, OCD, Raphael
Rev.
Year of Ordination:
1960
Order of Carmelites

Klein, John (Inactive)
Year of Ordination: 1965
Arch/Diocese of San
Antonio

Klein, Lawrence J. Rev.
Year of Ordination: 1984
Arch/Diocese of Brownsville

Koday, Mishael Rev.
Year of Ordination:
2008
Arch/Diocese of
Brownsville

Kolb, Joseph C. Rev.
Year of Ordination: 1953
Arch/Diocese of Oklahoma
City

Korenek, Greg Rev.
Year of Ordination: 1983
Arch/Diocese of Victoria

Korioth, Henry F.
(Inactive)
Year of Ordination:
1961
Arch/Diocese of Dallas

Korson, Bernard
(Inactive)
Year of Ordination: 1964
Arch/Diocese of Grand
Rapids

Kosler, Timothy Rev.
Year of Ordination: 1971
Arch/Diocese of Victoria

Kotara, James M. Rev.
Year of Ordination:
1976
Arch/Diocese of San
Antonio

Kozlowski, Theodore
James Rev.
Year of Ordination: 1958
Arch/Diocese of Grand
Rapids

Kozlowski, OCD, Lawrence
Rev.
Year of Ordination: 1961
Order of Carmelites

Kramer, Richard A.
(Inactive)
Year of Ordination:
1968
Arch/Diocese of San
Antonio

Krenek, Fred (Inactive)
Year of Ordination: 1993
Arch/Diocese of Victoria

Kropp, Robert Owen
(Inactive)
Year of Ordination: 1964
Arch/Diocese of Oklahoma
City

Krueger, Frederick
(Inactive)
Year of Ordination:
1964
Arch/Diocese of
Oklahoma City

Kuehler, Norbert G. Rev.
Msgr.
Year of Ordination: 1955
Arch/Diocese of Amarillo

Kuehner, Jr., Joseph E.
(Inactive)
Year of Ordination: 1991
Arch/Diocese of Santa Fe

Kulleck, Thomas G.
Rev.
Year of Ordination:
1974
Arch/Diocese of
Brownsville

LaBranch, Derek R.
(Inactive)
Year of Ordination: 2007
Arch/Diocese of
Sacramento

Lagunilla, Ariel R. Rev.
Year of Ordination: 2006
Arch/Diocese of San Angelo

Lander, Mark C.
(Inactive)
Year of Ordination:
2000
Arch/Diocese of San
Bernardino

Laskowski, Lambert
(Inactive)
Year of Ordination: 1952
Arch/Diocese of Victoria

Leopold, Martin J. Rev.
Year of Ordination: 2001
Arch/Diocese of San Antonio

Leven, Marvin "Sam"
Rev.
Year of Ordination:
1959
Arch/Diocese of
Oklahoma City

Litsch, Thomas G.
(Inactive)
Year of Ordination: 1961
Arch/Diocese of Oklahoma
City

Litteken, Robert T.
(Inactive)
Year of Ordination: 1953
Arch/Diocese of Fort Worth

Lomasiewicz, Donald
E. Rev.
Year of Ordination:
1962
Arch/Diocese of Grand
Rapids

Lopez, Hector Rev.
Year of Ordination: 1973
Arch/Diocese of El Paso

Lopez, Edilberto "Beto" Rev.
Year of Ordination: 1997
Arch/Diocese of El Paso

Lopez, Mariano H. Rev.
Year of Ordination:
2011
Arch/Diocese of El Paso

Lopez, Nahum Rev.
Year of Ordination: 2010
Arch/Diocese of Lubbock

Lopez, Bruce D. Rev.
Year of Ordination: 1988
Arch/Diocese of Peoria

Lopez Guzman,
Ernesto Rev.
Year of Ordination:
2006
Arch/Diocese of
Lubbock

Lopez, Sergio Rev.
Year of Ordination: 1998
Arch/Diocese of Oakland

Lucas Coronel, Eliseo Rev.
Year of Ordination: 2001
Arch/Diocese of San
Bernardino

Lukoskie, Raymond M.
Rev.
Year of Ordination:
1958
Arch/Diocese of Peoria

Luschen, Timothy D. Rev.
Year of Ordination: 1988
Arch/Diocese of Oklahoma
City

Lynch, OCD, Denis
(Inactive)
Year of Ordination: 1958
Order of Carmelites

Lynes, James Rev.
Year of Ordination:
1979
Arch/Diocese of
Galveston-Houston

Macias, Salvador Rev.
Year of Ordination: 1982
Arch/Diocese of Oakland

Macias, Frank Rev.
Year of Ordination: 1994
Arch/Diocese of San Antonio

Maddox, Edward M.
Rev. (Inactive)
Year of Ordination:
1996
Arch/Diocese of Austin

Maldonado, Francisco Rev.
Year of Ordination: 1990
Arch/Diocese of Tucson

Marconi, Joseph Rev.
Year of Ordination: 2001
Arch/Diocese of Little Rock

Martinez, Mario
Enrique (Inactive)
Year of Ordination:
1977
Arch/Diocese of San
Antonio

Martinez, Robert L. Rev.
Year of Ordination: 1979
Arch/Diocese of Santa Fe

Martinez, Adam Rev.
Year of Ordination: 1985
Arch/Diocese of Austin

Martinez, Eusebio Rev.
Year of Ordination:
2003
Arch/Diocese of
Brownsville

Martinez Morales,
Gonzalo Rev.
Year of Ordination: 1985
Arch/Diocese of Fort
Worth

Mason, Mark E. Rev.
Year of Ordination: 1975
Arch/Diocese of Oklahoma
City

Matthews, James
Ronald Rev.
Year of Ordination:
1975
Arch/Diocese of
Alexandria

Matthiesen, Samuel Rev.
Year of Ordination: 2013
Arch/Diocese of San
Angelo

Matula, Lawrence J. Rev.
Year of Ordination: 1962
Arch/Diocese of Victoria

Mauer, Carl Rev.
Year of Ordination:
2001
Arch/Diocese of San
Antonio

McCarthy, Thomas
(Inactive)
Year of Ordination: 1967
Arch/Diocese of San
Antonio

McCarthy, Donald P. Rev.
Year of Ordination: 1959
Arch/Diocese of Salina

McCartney, James S.
Rev.
Year of Ordination:
1984
Arch/Diocese of
Lubbock

McDaniel, Raymond L.
Rev.
Year of Ordination: 2007
Arch/Diocese of Fort
Worth

McGrath, John R. Rev.
Year of Ordination: 1982
Arch/Diocese of Biloxi

McGuill, Martin Rev.
Year of Ordination:
1964
Arch/Diocese of Corpus
Christi

McKone, John E. Rev.
Year of Ordination: 2008
Arch/Diocese of Fort
Worth

McLaughlin, Gregory A.
Rev.
Year of Ordination: 1985
Arch/Diocese of Austin

Medina, Hector M. Rev.
Year of Ordination:
1984
Arch/Diocese of Fort
Worth

Meiller, Vaughn Rev.
Year of Ordination: 1976
Arch/Diocese of Austin

Melton, Thomas K. Rev.
Year of Ordination: 1959
Arch/Diocese of Oklahoma
City

Menasco, Edward Rev.
Year of Ordination:
1990
Arch/Diocese of
Oklahoma City

Menezes, Gervan Rev.
Year of Ordination: 2014
Arch/Diocese of Nashville

Mercado Uribe, Heriberto
Rev.
Year of Ordination: 2006
Arch/Diocese of Lubbock

Metrejean, Paul Rev.
Msgr.
Year of Ordination:
1963
Arch/Diocese of
Lafayette

Meza, Arturo Rev.
Year of Ordination: 1988
Arch/Diocese of Amarillo

Meza, Gonzalo E. Rev.
Year of Ordination: 2009
Arch/Diocese of San Antonio

Michalski, Louis
(Inactive)
Year of Ordination:
1962
Arch/Diocese of San
Antonio

Mikkelson, Scott Rev.
Year of Ordination: 1982
Arch/Diocese of Austin

Miller, Milton Peter
(Inactive)
Year of Ordination: 1982
Arch/Diocese of Lake
Charles

Miranda, Luke A. Rev.
Year of Ordination:
1956
Arch/Diocese of Fort
Worth

Molina, Joe Rev.
Year of Ordination: 1995
Arch/Diocese of El Paso

Montalbano, Joseph E. Rev.
Year of Ordination: 1955
Arch/Diocese of Alexandria

Mora Torres, Sergio
Rev.
Year of Ordination:
1994
Arch/Diocese of
Oakland

Morales, Guillermo Rev.
Year of Ordination: 1988
Arch/Diocese of Amarillo

Morales, Eduardo Rev.
Year of Ordination: 1996
Arch/Diocese of San Antonio

Morello, OCD, Anthony
Rev.
Year of Ordination:
1962
Order of Carmelites

Moreno, Moises Uazua
Rev.
Year of Ordination: 2010
Arch/Diocese of Knoxville

Morgan, Martin J. Rev.
Year of Ordination: 1970
Arch/Diocese of Tulsa

Murphy, Francis Rev.
Msgr.
Year of Ordination:
1966
Arch/Diocese of Grand
Rapids

Mussey, Gerald (Inactive)
Year of Ordination: 1964
Arch/Diocese of San
Antonio

Mutuku, Anthony Rev.
Year of Ordination: 2014
Arch/Diocese of Nashville

Naberhaus, William J.
(Inactive)
Year of Ordination:
1963
Arch/Diocese of
Oklahoma City

Naffate Ruiz, Lenin E.
Rev.
Year of Ordination: 2000
Arch/Diocese of San
Antonio

Nesvadba, Reginald R. Rev.
Year of Ordination: 1966
Arch/Diocese of
Galveston-Houston

Nevlud, Gregory Rev.
Year of Ordination:
1982
Arch/Diocese of San
Antonio

Neyland, Malcom L. Rev.
Year of Ordination: 1973
Arch/Diocese of Lubbock

Ngo, Khan Duy Rev.
Year of Ordination: 2011
Arch/Diocese of San
Bernardino

Nguyen, Peter
(Inactive)
Year of Ordination:
1990
Arch/Diocese of
Oklahoma City

Nguyen, Thu Van Rev.
Year of Ordination: 1992
Arch/Diocese of Fort
Worth

Nguyen, Hoa X. Rev.
Year of Ordination: 1998
Arch/Diocese of Fort Worth

Nguyen, Khiem Van
Rev.
Year of Ordination:
2011
Arch/Diocese of Fort
Worth

Nguyen, Paul Rev.
Year of Ordination: 2014
Arch/Diocese of Nashville

Nguyen, Tu Thanh Rev.
Year of Ordination: 2007
Arch/Diocese of San Antonio

Nguyen, Minh Toan
Rev.
Year of Ordination:
2008
Arch/Diocese of San
Bernardino

Nguyen, Anthony Tong
Ba Rev.
Year of Ordination: 2009
Arch/Diocese of San
Bernardino

Nguyen, Tien Tri Rev.
Year of Ordination: 1996
Arch/Diocese of Santa Fe

Nguyen, CMC, Bede
Tam Rev.
Year of Ordination:
2012
Congregation Mater
Coredemptrix

Nichols, Arland C.
(Inactive)
Year of Ordination: 1975
Arch/Diocese of San
Antonio

Nieto Ruiz, Jesus Rev.
Year of Ordination: 1994
Arch/Diocese of Oakland

Nolan, Patrick Clancy
(Inactive)
Year of Ordination:
1964
Arch/Diocese of San
Antonio

Nolan, John P. Rev.
Year of Ordination: 2012
Arch/Diocese of San
Antonio

Ochetti, Jerome M. Rev.
Year of Ordination: 2002
Arch/Diocese of San
Bernardino

Ochoa, Einer R. Rev.
Year of Ordination:
1985
Arch/Diocese of San
Antonio

O'Connor, Thomas P.
(Inactive)
Year of Ordination: 1968
Arch/Diocese of Dallas

Olguin Zuniga, Jacinto Rev.
Year of Ordination: 1974
Arch/Diocese of Laredo

Oliva, Jesus (Inactive)
Year of Ordination:
1978
Arch/Diocese of
Alexandria

Onyekozuru, Francis Rev.
Year of Ordination: 2013
Arch/Diocese of San
Angelo

Oropel, James Rev.
(Inactive)
Year of Ordination: 2007
Arch/Diocese of San
Bernardino

Orr, John R. (Inactive)
Year of Ordination:
1964
Arch/Diocese of San
Antonio

Ortega, Miguel Angel Rev.
Year of Ordination: 2009
Arch/Diocese of
Brownsville

Ortega Leon, H. Eduardo
Rev.
Year of Ordination: 1995
Arch/Diocese of Brownsville

Osorio, Celimo Rev.
Year of Ordination:
1987
Arch/Diocese of El Paso

Oswalt, M.Price Rev.
Year of Ordination: 1996
Arch/Diocese of Oklahoma
City

O'Toole, James P. Rev.
Year of Ordination: 1950
Arch/Diocese of Fort Worth

Pacheco, Saul Rev.
Year of Ordination:
2010
Arch/Diocese of El Paso

Pacheco, John D. Rev.
Year of Ordination: 2009
Arch/Diocese of Fort
Worth

Palacios, Joseph Rev.
Year of Ordination: 2012
Arch/Diocese of Lubbock

Pansza, Gilbert
(Inactive)
Year of Ordination:
2000
Arch/Diocese of Fort
Worth

Parra, Andres Rev.
Year of Ordination: 2005
Arch/Diocese of San Jose

Partida, Cesar Uriel Rev.
Year of Ordination: 2012
Arch/Diocese of Brownsville

Pavlicek, Jr., Edward
A. Rev.
Year of Ordination:
1983
Arch/Diocese of San
Antonio

Payne, OCD, John
Michael Rev.
Year of Ordination: 1970
Order of Carmelites

Paz, Lorenzo T. (Inactive)
Year of Ordination: 1997
Arch/Diocese of San
Bernardino

Pedroza De Leon,
Salvador Rev.
Year of Ordination:
1981
Arch/Diocese of Laredo

Pehl, Jeffrey Rev.
Year of Ordination: 1995
Arch/Diocese of San
Antonio

Peinemann, Michael Rev.
Year of Ordination: 2005
Arch/Diocese of San Antonio

Pemberton, Joseph Rev.
Year of Ordination:
1977
Arch/Diocese of Fort
Worth

Pemberton, James Rev.
Year of Ordination: 2005
Arch/Diocese of Fort
Worth

Pena, Raymundo J. Most
Rev.
Year of Ordination: 1957
Arch/Diocese of Brownsville

Pena, Richard Rev.
Year of Ordination:
1992
Arch/Diocese of San
Antonio

Pena, Luis Rev.
Year of Ordination: 1982
Arch/Diocese of Santa Fe

Pena, OCD, Joseph Mary
Rev.
Year of Ordination: 1967
Order of Carmelites

Pereida, Alex Rev.
Year of Ordination:
2008
Arch/Diocese of San
Antonio

Perez, Joel Rev.
Year of Ordination: 2012
Arch/Diocese of Laredo

Perez, M.Rene Rev.
Year of Ordination: 2003
Arch/Diocese of Lubbock

Perez, Raul Rev.
Year of Ordination:
2011
Arch/Diocese of San
Bernardino

Perez, Aurelio H. Rev.
Year of Ordination: 1986
Arch/Diocese of
Milwaulkee

Perez Galindo, Francisco
Rev.
Year of Ordination: 2000
Arch/Diocese of Amarillo

Perez-Villanueva,
Edgar H. Rev.
Year of Ordination:
2008
Arch/Diocese of Reno

Pesek, Anthony Rev. Msgr.
Year of Ordination: 1965
Arch/Diocese of San
Antonio

Peters, Daniel E. Rev.
Year of Ordination: 1989
Arch/Diocese of Rockford

Peters, John C. Rev.
Msgr.
Year of Ordination:
1974
Arch/Diocese of
Victoria

Petru, James (Inactive)
Year of Ordination: 1962
Arch/Diocese of Corpus
Christi

Petsch, Joseph P. Rev.
Year of Ordination: 1950
Arch/Diocese of San Antonio

Petta, Philip Rev.
Year of Ordination:
2011
Arch/Diocese of Fort
Worth

Petter, Henry V. Rev.
Year of Ordination: 1976
Arch/Diocese of Dallas

Pham, Toan N. Rev.
Year of Ordination: 2013
Arch/Diocese of San
Bernardino

Phan, Peter Rev.
Year of Ordination:
2011
Arch/Diocese of San
Bernardino

Picacio, John H. (Inactive)
Year of Ordination: 1968
Arch/Diocese of San
Antonio

Picton, CSSR, Tom Rev.
Year of Ordination: 1971
Order of Redemptorists

Piette, Gilbert M.
(Inactive)
Year of Ordination:
1979
Arch/Diocese of
Brownsville

Pillari, Moses of Jesus
Rev.
Year of Ordination: 2007
Arch/Diocese of San
Antonio

Pina, Martin Rev.
Year of Ordination: 1993
Arch/Diocese of Lubbock

Polizzi, Samuel J. Rev.
Year of Ordination:
1961
Arch/Diocese of
Alexandria

Ponce, Juan Manuel Rev.
Year of Ordination: 2000
Arch/Diocese of Santa
Rosa

Popp, Bernard F. Most Rev.
Year of Ordination: 1943
Arch/Diocese of San Antonio

Portele, Fred T.
(Inactive)
Year of Ordination:
1965
Arch/Diocese of
Galveston-Houston

Priest, Gerald A. Rev.
Msgr.
Year of Ordination: 1968
Arch/Diocese of Tyler

Puente, Jose Francisco Rev.
Year of Ordination: 2000
Arch/Diocese of San Antonio

Quintero, Haider Rev.
Year of Ordination:
2011
Arch/Diocese of
Amarillo

Quiroz Carrizales,
Francisco Rev.
Year of Ordination: 2014
Arch/Diocese of Laredo

Raaz, Paul Rev.
Year of Ordination: 1970
Arch/Diocese of San Antonio

Radke, Barnabas R.
Rev.
Year of Ordination:
2009
Arch/Diocese of
Amarillo

Ragsdale, Patrick Rev.
Msgr.
Year of Ordination: 1972
Arch/Diocese of San
Antonio

Rahm, SJ, Harold J. Rev.
Year of Ordination: 1950
Order of Jesuits

Ramon-Landry,
Kenneth Rev,
Year of Ordination:
1987
Arch/Diocese of Biloxi

Regan, Richard Rev.
Year of Ordination: 1985
Arch/Diocese of San
Angelo

Rehkemper, Robert C. Rev.
Msgr.
Year of Ordination: 1949
Arch/Diocese of Dallas

Reilly, Hugh J.
(Inactive)
Year of Ordination:
1957
Arch/Diocese of Dallas

Reyes, Leopoldo G.
(Inactive)
Year of Ordination: 1978
Arch/Diocese of Austin

Reyes, Lonnie Rev. Msgr.
Year of Ordination:
Arch/Diocese of Austin

Reyes, OCD, Ralph Rev.
Year of Ordination:
Order of Carmelites

Reyes, OCD, Raul Rev.
Year of Ordination: 1969
Order of Carmelites

Reyna, Cecilio Rev.
Year of Ordination: 1994
Arch/Diocese of Lansing

Reynoso Jauregui,
Oscar Rev.
Year of Ordination:
2005
Arch/Diocese of San
Bernardino

Rihn, Roy J. Rev. Msgr.
Year of Ordination: 1942
Arch/Diocese of San
Antonio

Ritter, Eric J. Rev.
Year of Ordination: 2003
Arch/Diocese of San Antonio

Rizo, Sergio Rev.
Year of Ordination:
1989
Arch/Diocese of Fort
Worth

Robinson, Ken Rev.
Year of Ordination: 1992
Arch/Diocese of Fort
Worth

Roden Lucero, Edward Paul
Rev.
Year of Ordination: 1982
Arch/Diocese of El Paso

Rodriguez, Arthur
(Inactive)
Year of Ordination:
2010
Arch/Diocese of
Amarillo

Rodriguez, Fernando
Edvin Rev.
Year of Ordination: 2007
Arch/Diocese of San
Antonio

Rodriguez, TOR, Florencio
Rev.
Year of Ordination: 1980
Arch/Diocese of Austin

Roldan, Jorge Rev.
Year of Ordination:
2014
Arch/Diocese of Salt
Lake City

Roman, Luis Rev.
Year of Ordination: 1968
Arch/Diocese of Arecibo
Puerto Rico

Rosendale, Glenn Rev.
Year of Ordination: 1976
Arch/Diocese of Amarillo

Ruano, Jorge (Inactive)
Year of Ordination:
1974
Arch/Diocese of San
Antonio

Rubio-Boitel, Fernando
Rev.
Year of Ordination: 1975
Arch/Diocese of Santa Fe

Ruiz, Raphael (Inactive)
Year of Ordination: 1965
Arch/Diocese of San Antonio

Ruppert, Donald R.
Rev.
Year of Ordination:
1978
Arch/Diocese of
Victoria

Ryan, William H. Rev.
Msgr.
Year of Ordination: 1948
Arch/Diocese of El Paso

Saenz, Augustinus Alex Rev.
Year of Ordination: 2011
Arch/Diocese of Corpus
Christi

Samour, Richard Rev.
Year of Ordination:
2012
Arch/Diocese of San
Antonio

Sanchez, Carlos Rev.
Year of Ordination: 1950
Arch/Diocese of
Guatemala City

Sanchez, William E. Rev.
Year of Ordination: 1983
Arch/Diocese of Santa Fe

Scantlin, Joseph S. Rev.
Year of Ordination:
1959
Arch/Diocese of Fort
Worth

Scheel, Daniel R. Rev.
Year of Ordination: 1969
Arch/Diocese of
Galveston-Houston

Schellenberg, James E. Rev.
Year of Ordination: 1977
Arch/Diocese of San Antonio

Schlecht, Richard Dean
(Inactive)
Year of Ordination:
1967
Arch/Diocese of
Oklahoma City

Schneider, Ronald F. Rev.
Year of Ordination: 1967
Arch/Diocese of Grand
Rapids

Schoellman, MM, Edward
R. Rev.
Year of Ordination: 1965
Order of Maryknoll

Schuster, Raymond
Rev.
Year of Ordination:
1993
Arch/Diocese of San
Antonio

Schwertner, Timothy Rev.
Year of Ordination: 1965
Arch/Diocese of Lubbock

Schwind, Christopher Scott
Rev.
Year of Ordination: 2013
Arch/Diocese of Amarillo

Seitz, Patrick K. Rev.
Year of Ordination:
1992
Arch/Diocese of
Brownsville

Seiwert, James K. Rev.
Year of Ordination: 2009
Arch/Diocese of San
Antonio

Sena, Sotero Rev.
Year of Ordination: 1981
Arch/Diocese of Santa Fe

Shaw, David Rev.
Year of Ordination:
1968
Arch/Diocese of Santa
Rosa

Sheehan, Michael J. Most
Rev.
Year of Ordination: 1964
Arch/Diocese of Santa Fe

Shirley, Richard J. Rev.
Msgr.
Year of Ordination: 1967
Arch/Diocese of Corpus
Christi

Siordia, Oscar Octavio
Rev.
Year of Ordination:
2006
Arch/Diocese of
Brownsville

Smaistrla, Benjamin Rev.
Year of Ordination: 1971
Arch/Diocese of
Galveston-Houston

Smith, Richard J. Rev.
Year of Ordination: 1967
Arch/Diocese of Corpus
Christi

Smith, OCD, Hilary
Rev.
Year of Ordination:
1959
Order of Carmelites

Sokolski, Richard J. Rev.
Year of Ordination: 1947
Arch/Diocese of Fort
Worth

Solis, Jr., Ralph Rev.
Year of Ordination: 1993
Arch/Diocese of El Paso

Sosa, Emilio Rev.
Year of Ordination:
2006
Arch/Diocese of San
Angelo

Sprigler, William Rev.
Year of Ordination: 1975
Arch/Diocese of New Ulm

Springer, Robert (Inactive)
Year of Ordination: 1966
Arch/Diocese of Dallas

Stafford, Thomas D.
(Inactive)
Year of Ordination:
1959
Arch/Diocese of
Oklahoma City

Stafford, James D. M. Rev.
Year of Ordination: 1967
Arch/Diocese of Oklahoma
City

Steffen, William J. (Inactive)
Year of Ordination: 1946
Arch/Diocese of Santa Fe

Stephens, Gerald N.
Rev.
Year of Ordination:
1963
Arch/Diocese of Fort
Worth

Stiles, Wallis J. Rev.
Year of Ordination: 1961
Arch/Diocese of San
Antonio

Strittmatter, Robert L. Rev.
Year of Ordination: 1966
Arch/Diocese of Fort Worth

Stuebben, Lawrence J.
Rev. Msgr.
Year of Ordination:
1955
Arch/Diocese of San
Antonio

Sweeney, Edward Rev.
Year of Ordination: 1988
Arch/Diocese of Amarillo

Swistovich, John Wesley
Rev.
Year of Ordination: 1998
Arch/Diocese of Fort Worth

Swize, Marion
(Inactive)
Year of Ordination:
1959
Arch/Diocese of San
Antonio

Sykora, Robert J.
(Inactive)
Year of Ordination: 1965
Arch/Diocese of Dallas

Tallman, Stephen J. Rev.
Year of Ordination: 1959
Arch/Diocese of Helena

Tejada, Denis (Inactive)
Year of Ordination:
1972
Arch/Diocese of El Paso

Tello-Curiel, Oscar Rev.
Year of Ordination: 2012
Arch/Diocese of San
Antonio

Thames, Robert W. Rev.
Year of Ordination: 1964
Arch/Diocese of Fort Worth

Thome, Edward A. Rev.
Year of Ordination:
1954
Arch/Diocese of
Gaylord

Thompson, PA, William T.
Rev. Msgr.
Year of Ordination: 1954
Arch/Diocese of Corpus
Christi

Thumma, Sunil Kumar Rev.
Year of Ordination: 2011
Arch/Diocese of San Angelo

Timoney, OCD,
Christopher Rev.
Year of Ordination:
1963
Order of Carmelites

Towner, James (Inactive)
Year of Ordination: 1954
Arch/Diocese of Oklahoma
City

Underdonk, Lawrence Rev.
(Inactive)
Year of Ordination: 1968
Arch/Diocese of San Angelo

Urrego Chavarria, Luis
Fernando Rev.
Year of Ordination:
2001
Arch/Diocese of
Sacramento

Valdez, John Rev.
Year of Ordination: 1991
Arch/Diocese of Amarillo

Valdez, Victor Rev.
Year of Ordination: 2014
Arch/Diocese of San Antonio

Valdivia Aguirre,
Adolfo Rev. Msgr.
Year of Ordination:
1981
Arch/Diocese of San
Antonio

Valencia, Mario Rev.
Year of Ordination: 2010
Arch/Diocese of Santa
Rosa

Valencia Garcia, Raul Rev.
Year of Ordination: 2003
Arch/Diocese of Tucson

Vallejo Rodriguez,
Gilberto Rev.
Year of Ordination:
2002
Arch/Diocese of San
Antonio

Van, Anton Quang Rev.
Year of Ordination: 2004
Arch/Diocese of San
Antonio

Vanderholt, James Rev.
Msgr.
Year of Ordination: 1957
Arch/Diocese of Beaumont

Vega, Aglayde Rafael
Rev.
Year of Ordination:
2006
Arch/Diocese of
Brownsville

Velasquez, Carlos B. Rev.
Year of Ordination: 1990
Arch/Diocese of San
Antonio

Vesbit, Stephen E. Rev.
Year of Ordination: 1962
Arch/Diocese of Saginaw

Vilano, Tony Rev.
Year of Ordination:
1996
Arch/Diocese of San
Antonio

Villa, Eduardo Rev.
Year of Ordination: 1980
Arch/Diocese of
Brownsville

Villanueva, Edgar H. Rev.
Year of Ordination: 2008
Arch/Diocese of Reno

Villegas, Gonzalo Rev.
Year of Ordination:
1992
Arch/Diocese of Tucson

Vu, CMC, Alphonsus Tri
Rev.
Year of Ordination: 2012
Congregation Mater
Coredemptrix

Wagner, John A. Rev. Msgr.
Year of Ordination: 1949
Arch/Diocese of San Antonio

Walden, Robert
(Inactive)
Year of Ordination:
1952
Arch/Diocese of San
Antonio

Waldow, Harold L. Rev.
Msgr.
Year of Ordination: 1970
Arch/Diocese of Amarillo

Wallis, Jonathan Rev.
Year of Ordination: 2007
Arch/Diocese of Fort Worth

Walsh, Daniel M. Rev.
Year of Ordination:
1959
Arch/Diocese of
Shreveport

Walterscheid, Kyle R. Rev.
Year of Ordination: 2002
Arch/Diocese of Fort
Worth

Wasielewski, Jr., Henry R. Rev.
Year of Ordination: 1964
Arch/Diocese of Phoenix

Watford, Marshall Rev.
Year of Ordination: 1969
Arch/Diocese of New Orleans

Weaver, Richard C. Rev.
Year of Ordination: 1964
Arch/Diocese of Dallas

Weber, Donald E. Rev.
Year of Ordination: 1958
Arch/Diocese of Grand Rapids

Weinzapfel, Thomas W. Rev. Msgr.
Year of Ordination: 1945
Arch/Diocese of Dallas

Weseley, Eugene L. Rev.
Year of Ordination: 1957
Arch/Diocese of Crookston

Wesselsky, Emil J. Rev. Msgr.
Year of Ordination: 1956
Arch/Diocese of San Antonio

Whalen, Peter
(Inactive)
Year of Ordination: 1967
Arch/Diocese of Brownsville

White, Lawrence E. Rev.
Year of Ordination: 1970
Arch/Diocese of Corpus Christi

White, James Rev.
Year of Ordination: 1969
Arch/Diocese of Tulsa

Wiggins, Vincent Rev.
(Inactive)
Year of Ordination: 1981
Arch/Diocese of San Angelo

Wilcox, James A. Rev.
Year of Ordination: 2013
Arch/Diocese of Fort Worth

Winkler, Edward Rev.
Year of Ordination: 1986
Arch/Diocese of Victoria

Wise, Louis E.
(Inactive)
Year of Ordination: 1963
Arch/Diocese of Dallas

Witkowski, Eugene A.
(Inactive)
Year of Ordination: 1955
Arch/Diocese of Fort Worth

Wood, Brian P. Rev.
Year of Ordination: 2012
Arch/Diocese of Lubbock

Wurth, OCD, M. Philip Rev.
Year of Ordination: 1960
Order of Carmelites

Yanta, John W. Most Rev.
Year of Ordination: 1956
Arch/Diocese of Amarillo

Young, James E. Rev.
Year of Ordination: 1974
Arch/Diocese of Tyler

Zientek, Benedict J.
Rev.
Year of Ordination:
1959
Arch/Diocese of Austin

Zientek, Boleslaus J. Rev.
Msgr.
Year of Ordination: 1959
Arch/Diocese of Austin

Zoeller, Benedict J. Rev.
Year of Ordination: 1965
Arch/Diocese of Oklahoma
City

Zumaya, Benigno David
Rev.
Year of Ordination:
1977
Arch/Diocese of San
Antonio

Zurovetz, Jerome G. Rev.
Year of Ordination: 1967
Arch/Diocese of Corpus
Christi

DECEASED ALUMNI

Aaron, James R. Rev.
Year of Ordination: 1957
Arch/Diocese of San Angelo
Year of Death: 1999

Abbey, James A. Rev.
Year of Ordination:
1929
Arch/Diocese of Dallas
Year of Death: 1942

Aguirre, Francisco Rev.
Year of Ordination: 1959
Arch/Diocese of
Brownsville
Year of Death: 1991

Alvarado, Joseph G. Rev.
Msgr.
Year of Ordination: 1939
Arch/Diocese of Corpus
Christi
Year of Death: 1990

Alvesteffer, Eugene F.
Rev.
Year of Ordination:
1965
Arch/Diocese of Grand
Rapids
Year of Death: 1998

Augustynowicz, Leon A.
Rev. Msgr.
Year of Ordination: 1936
Arch/Diocese of Dallas
Year of Death: 1965

Aviles, Joe Rev.
Year of Ordination: 1990
Arch/Diocese of San Antonio
Year of Death: 2008

Aycock, Leon R. Rev.
Year of Ordination:
1935
Arch/Diocese of
Alexandria
Year of Death: 1961

Baistra, Jorge Rev.
Year of Ordination: 1974
Arch/Diocese of San
Antonio
Year of Death: 2010

Baker, Joseph Michael Rev.
Year of Ordination: 1986
Arch/Diocese of Tucson
Year of Death: 2007

Barranger, Ralph F.
Rev.
Year of Ordination:
1961
Arch/Diocese of El Paso
Year of Death: 2002

Bartosh, Engelbert Rev.
Msgr.
Year of Ordination: 1939
Arch/Diocese of Corpus
Christi
Year of Death: 1991

Bartsch, Edward C. Rev.
Msgr.
Year of Ordination: 1949
Arch/Diocese of Victoria
Year of Death: 2010

Basso, John F. Rev.
Msgr.
Year of Ordination:
1930
Arch/Diocese of Corpus
Christi
Year of Death: 1966

Baumann, Hubert Rev.
Year of Ordination: 1939
Arch/Diocese of San
Antonio
Year of Death: 1977

Becker, Francis J. Rev.
Year of Ordination: 1963
Arch/Diocese of Dallas
Year of Death: 1991

Benavides, Albert J.
Rev.
Year of Ordination:
1970
Arch/Diocese of San
Antonio
Year of Death: 1984

Benish, William Rev.
Year of Ordination: 1972
Arch/Diocese of Austin
Year of Death: 2012

Berger, Joseph Rev.
Year of Ordination: 1959
Arch/Diocese of Corpus
Christi
Year of Death: 2013

Bernasconi, Gino V.
Rev.
Year of Ordination:
1950
Arch/Diocese of
Victoria
Year of Death: 2006

Bertrand, Joseph L. Rev.
Year of Ordination: 1960
Arch/Diocese of Beaumont
Year of Death: 2000

Bertrand, Ambrose Rev.
Year of Ordination: 1960
Order of Carmelites
Year of Death: 0

Billimek, Thomas M.
Rev.
Year of Ordination:
1980
Arch/Diocese of
Brownsville
Year of Death: 1983

Bily, Edmund J. Rev.
Msgr.
Year of Ordination: 1936
Arch/Diocese of San
Antonio
Year of Death: 1978

Bily, Vaclav J. Rev. Msgr.
Year of Ordination: 1939
Arch/Diocese of Victoria
Year of Death: 1990

Bily, Edward F. Rev.
Msgr.
Year of Ordination:
1951
Arch/Diocese of San
Antonio
Year of Death: 2006

Black, Allen M. Rev.
Year of Ordination: 1946
Arch/Diocese of Victoria
Year of Death: 1968

Blank, Severius Rev.
Year of Ordination: 1958
Arch/Diocese of Fort Worth
Year of Death: 2011

Blinka, Louis A. Rev.
Year of Ordination:
1930
Arch/Diocese of San
Antonio
Year of Death: 1946

Bockholt, Herbert Rev.
Msgr.
Year of Ordination: 1939
Arch/Diocese of
Brownsville
Year of Death: 1995

Boehme, Gerald F. Rev.
Year of Ordination: 1941
Arch/Diocese of San Antonio
Year of Death: 1964

Boensch, Gregory A.
Rev.
Year of Ordination:
1950
Arch/Diocese of Corpus
Christi
Year of Death: 2009

Bojniewicz, Walter C. Rev.
Year of Ordination: 1940
Arch/Diocese of Dallas
Year of Death: 1972

Bollich, Ronald W. Rev.
Year of Ordination: 1964
Arch/Diocese of Beaumont
Year of Death: 1996

Botik, William A. Rev.
Msgr.
Year of Ordination:
1944
Arch/Diocese of Dallas
Year of Death: 1998

Boyle, James M. Rev.
Msgr.
Year of Ordination: 1932
Arch/Diocese of San
Antonio
Year of Death: 1992

Breedlove, C. Lawrence Rev.
Year of Ordination: 1956
Arch/Diocese of Fort Worth
Year of Death: 2006

Brunner, James C. Rev.
Year of Ordination:
1954
Arch/Diocese of
Victoria
Year of Death: 2010

Bryce, Philip A. Very Rev.
Year of Ordination: 1955
Arch/Diocese of Oklahoma
City
Year of Death: 1996

Buchanan, Henry D. Rev.
Msgr.
Year of Ordination: 1921
Arch/Diocese of El Paso
Year of Death: 1979

Bujnowski, Loepold F.
Very Rev.
Year of Ordination:
1934
Arch/Diocese of Austin
Year of Death: 1976

Burger, Joseph W. Rev.
Year of Ordination: 1954
Arch/Diocese of Oklahoma
City
Year of Death: 2012

Cahill, Patrick Rev.
Year of Ordination: 1956
Arch/Diocese of Alexandria
Year of Death: 1982

Cann, James H. Rev.
Msgr.
Year of Ordination:
1931
Arch/Diocese of St.
Augustine
Year of Death: 1957

Cardenas, OCD, David
Rev.
Year of Ordination: 1961
Order of Carmelites
Year of Death: 2006

Carrillo, Victor M. Rev.
Year of Ordination: 1987
Arch/Diocese of San Antonio
Year of Death: 2009

Charcut, Paul Rev.
Msgr.
Year of Ordination:
1936
Arch/Diocese of Dallas
Year of Death: 1968

Clark, Robert E. Rev.
Msgr.
Year of Ordination: 1953
Arch/Diocese of Corpus
Christi
Year of Death: 1999

Collins, Thomas J. Rev.
Msgr.
Year of Ordination: 1948
Arch/Diocese of San Antonio
Year of Death: 1997

Costantino, Anthony
Rev. Msgr.
Year of Ordination:
1944
Arch/Diocese of San
Antonio
Year of Death: 2009

Curran, Robert J. Rev.
Year of Ordination: 1956
Arch/Diocese of Dallas
Year of Death: 1993

De Angelis, OSB, William
Rev.
Year of Ordination: 1948
Order of Benedictines
Year of Death: 1999

De Llano, Domingo
Rev.
Year of Ordination:
1966
Arch/Diocese of Corpus
Christi
Year of Death: 2013

De Luna, OFM, Thomas
Rev.
Year of Ordination: 1937
Order of Franciscans
Year of Death: 0

DeGuadalupe DeLuna,
Reynerlo Rev.
Year of Ordination: 1937
Arch/Diocese of San Antonio
Year of Death: 1993

Devers, Edward J. Rev.
Year of Ordination:
1938
Arch/Diocese of Dallas
Year of Death: 1973

Diab, Thomas P. Rev.
Year of Ordination: 1971
Arch/Diocese of San
Antonio
Year of Death: 2007

DiBenedetto, Peter P. Rev.
Year of Ordination: 1969
Arch/Diocese of Amarillo
Year of Death: 1995

Doerfler, Marvin G.
Rev. Msgr.
Year of Ordination:
1959
Arch/Diocese of San
Antonio
Year of Death: 2013

Donohue, Sean B. Rev.
Year of Ordination: 1985
Arch/Diocese of Victoria
Year of Death: 1989

Donovan, J. Paul Rev.
Year of Ordination: 1958
Arch/Diocese of Tulsa
Year of Death: 2011

Dougherty, Bernard M.
Rev.
Year of Ordination:
1932
Arch/Diocese of Corpus
Christi
Year of Death: 1952

Doyle, George A. Rev.
Msgr.
Year of Ordination: 1937
Arch/Diocese of
Brownsville
Year of Death: 1966

Dragon, Edmund S. Rev.
Year of Ordination: 1930
Arch/Diocese of San Antonio
Year of Death: 1961

Drees, Charles J. Rev.
Year of Ordination:
1937
Arch/Diocese of San
Antonio
Year of Death: 1968

Drozd, Anthony F. Rev.
Msgr.
Year of Ordination: 1934
Arch/Diocese of San
Antonio
Year of Death: 1987

Drummey, CSC, Francis
Rev.
Year of Ordination: 1931
Order of Holy Cross
Year of Death: 1935

Duesman, John Very
Rev.
Year of Ordination:
1939
Arch/Diocese of Fort
Worth
Year of Death: 1984

Dunne, Kevin A. Rev.
Msgr.
Year of Ordination: 1933
Arch/Diocese of Corpus
Christi
Year of Death: 1996

Dworaczyk, Edward J. Rev.
Year of Ordination: 1930
Arch/Diocese of San Antonio
Year of Death: 1965

Dworaczyk, Edmund
Rev.
Year of Ordination:
1961
Arch/Diocese of Corpus
Christi
Year of Death: 1970

Dworaczyk, Julius V. Rev.
Year of Ordination: 1946
Arch/Diocese of San
Antonio
Year of Death: 1993

Ehlinger, Harold J. Rev.
Msgr.
Year of Ordination: 1941
Arch/Diocese of San Antonio
Year of Death: 1974

Ehlinger, Paul J. Rev.
Msgr.
Year of Ordination:
1937
Arch/Diocese of San
Antonio
Year of Death: 1982

Eisele, Raymond A. Rev.
Year of Ordination: 1973
Arch/Diocese of Amarillo
Year of Death: 1982

Erdelt, Eugene E. Rev.
Year of Ordination: 1958
Arch/Diocese of Corpus
Christi
Year of Death: 1995

Fale, Richard A. Rev.
Year of Ordination:
1958
Arch/Diocese of
Milwaukee
Year of Death: 1987

Faust, Claude A. Rev.
Year of Ordination: 1939
Arch/Diocese of Austin
Year of Death: 1973

Fellman, Francis J. Rev.
Year of Ordination: 1928
Arch/Diocese of San Antonio
Year of Death: 1939

Fitzsimon, Laurence J.
Most Rev.
Year of Ordination:
1921
Arch/Diocese of
Amarillo
Year of Death: 1958

Foegelle, Peter L. Rev.
Msgr.
Year of Ordination: 1932
Arch/Diocese of San
Antonio
Year of Death: 1986

Forliti, Robert Rev.
Year of Ordination: 1940
Arch/Diocese of Dallas
Year of Death: 1996

Freeman, Robert E.
Rev. Msgr.
Year of Ordination:
1957
Arch/Diocese of Corpus
Christi
Year of Death: 2003

Gallagher, Patrick F. Rev.
Year of Ordination: 1937
Arch/Diocese of Dallas
Year of Death: 1959

Galle, Norbert Rev.
Year of Ordination: 1937
Arch/Diocese of San Antonio
Year of Death: 1969

Gallerano, Victor J.
Rev.
Year of Ordination:
1958
Arch/Diocese of
Galveston-Houston
Year of Death: 1988

Garcia, Camilo Rev.
Year of Ordination: 1930
Arch/Diocese of Corpus
Christi
Year of Death: 1984

Garcia, Ramon J. Rev. Msgr.
Year of Ordination: 1955
Arch/Diocese of San Antonio
Year of Death: 2012

Garcia, Jr., Ricardo
Rev.
Year of Ordination:
1992
Arch/Diocese of
Brownsville
Year of Death: 2011

Geary, Eugene P. Rev.
Msgr.
Year of Ordination: 1941
Arch/Diocese of El Paso
Year of Death: 1975

Gebhardt, John Rev.
Year of Ordination: 1981
Arch/Diocese of San Antonio
Year of Death: 1984

Geehan, Patrick Rev.
Msgr.
Year of Ordination:
1915
Arch/Diocese of San
Antonio
Year of Death: 1968

George, Dexter L. Rev.
Msgr.
Year of Ordination: 1947
Arch/Diocese of
Galveston-Houston
Year of Death: 1992

Gerbermann, John J. Rev.
Msgr.
Year of Ordination: 1932
Arch/Diocese of San Antonio
Year of Death: 1981

Gerbermann, Hugo
Mark Most Rev.
Year of Ordination:
1943
Arch/Diocese of San
Antonio
Year of Death: 1996

Gillespie, James J. Rev.
Year of Ordination: 1950
Arch/Diocese of Fort
Worth
Year of Death: 1985

Glorioso, Charles E. Rev.
Year of Ordination: 1957
Arch/Diocese of Alexandria
Year of Death: 1971

Goertz, Bernard C. Rev.
Year of Ordination:
1952
Arch/Diocese of Austin
Year of Death: 2012

Golden, John M. Rev.
Year of Ordination: 1941
Arch/Diocese of El Paso
Year of Death: 1945

Gomez, OFM Conv,
Francisco A. Rev.
Year of Ordination: 1976
Order of Franciscans
Year of Death: 1998

Gotwals, Stephen H.
Rev.
Year of Ordination:
1953
Arch/Diocese of El Paso
Year of Death: 1979

Gulczynski, John T. Rev.
Msgr.
Year of Ordination: 1936
Arch/Diocese of Dallas
Year of Death: 2004

Halata, William F. Rev.
Year of Ordination: 1953
Arch/Diocese of Victoria
Year of Death: 2000

Halfmann, Hubert J.
Rev.
Year of Ordination:
1951
Arch/Diocese of
Amarillo
Year of Death: 1976

Halfmann, Curtis T. Rev.
Year of Ordination: 1959
Arch/Diocese of Lubbock
Year of Death: 2012

Hamala, Joseph V. Rev.
Year of Ordination: 1944
Arch/Diocese of Victoria
Year of Death: 1992

Hammond, William M.
Rev.
Year of Ordination:
1951
Arch/Diocese of
Amarillo
Year of Death: 1971

Hanacek, John J. Rev.
Msgr.
Year of Ordination: 1936
Arch/Diocese of Victoria
Year of Death: 1994

Harris, George Rev.
Year of Ordination: 1965
Arch/Diocese of Brownsville
Year of Death: 2002

Hartnett, Donald A.
Rev. Msgr.
Year of Ordination:
1939
Arch/Diocese of Fort
Worth
Year of Death: 1999

Hartwig, Lawrence N.
Rev.
Year of Ordination: 1967
Arch/Diocese of Grand
Rapids
Year of Death: 1998

Heffernan, Donald Rev.
Year of Ordination: 1961
Arch/Diocese of San Antonio
Year of Death: 2013

Henke, Raymond Rev.
Year of Ordination:
1959
Arch/Diocese of San
Antonio
Year of Death: 2013

Henkes, Albert G. Rev.
Msgr.
Year of Ordination: 1932
Arch/Diocese of San
Antonio
Year of Death: 1986

Herbst, Henry S. Rev. Msgr.
Year of Ordination: 1940
Arch/Diocese of Victoria
Year of Death: 1994

Herzig, Charles E. Most
Rev.
Year of Ordination:
1955
Arch/Diocese of Tyler
Year of Death: 1991

Heyburn, Kevin J. Rev.
Msgr.
Year of Ordination: 1948
Arch/Diocese of San
Angelo
Year of Death: 2001

Higginbotham, Paul J. Rev.
Msgr.
Year of Ordination: 1950
Arch/Diocese of Fort Worth
Year of Death: 1995

Hildebrand, Joseph J.
Rev.
Year of Ordination:
1930
Arch/Diocese of San
Antonio
Year of Death: 1967

Hilscher, Henry V. Rev.
Year of Ordination: 1954
Arch/Diocese of San
Antonio
Year of Death: 1964

Hoelscher, James Rev.
Year of Ordination: 1959
Arch/Diocese of San Antonio
Year of Death: 2011

Hoffmann, Rudolph C.
Rev.
Year of Ordination:
1943
Arch/Diocese of
Victoria
Year of Death: 1979

Hoffmann, Patrick Rev.
Year of Ordination: 1968
Arch/Diocese of Amarillo
Year of Death: 2005

Hoover, William R. Rev.
Year of Ordination: 1955
Arch/Diocese of Fort Worth
Year of Death: 1996

Hubertus, Bruno J.
Rev. Msgr.
Year of Ordination:
1937
Arch/Diocese of San
Antonio
Year of Death: 1977

Hubertus, Gerald M. Rev.
Msgr.
Year of Ordination: 1964
Arch/Diocese of San
Antonio
Year of Death: 2003

Hug, Henry V. Rev.
Year of Ordination: 1932
Arch/Diocese of San Antonio
Year of Death: 1971

Hurtado, Jose R. Rev.
Year of Ordination:
1961
Arch/Diocese of
Phoenix
Year of Death: 1981

Janacek, Balthasar Rev.
Msgr.
Year of Ordination: 1950
Arch/Diocese of San
Antonio
Year of Death: 2006

Janak, Roman M. Rev.
Year of Ordination: 1946
Arch/Diocese of San Antonio
Year of Death: 1962

Janak, Hubert J. Rev.
Msgr.
Year of Ordination:
1941
Arch/Diocese of San
Antonio
Year of Death: 1996

Janda, Adolph P. Rev.
Year of Ordination: 1939
Arch/Diocese of San
Antonio
Year of Death: 1978

Jansky, Edward J. Rev.
Year of Ordination: 1930
Arch/Diocese of San Antonio
Year of Death: 1979

Janson, Eugene Rev.
Year of Ordination:
1976
Arch/Diocese of
Victoria
Year of Death: 2005

Janysek, Theodore T. Rev.
Msgr.
Year of Ordination: 1930
Arch/Diocese of San
Antonio
Year of Death: 1989

Jasek, Ladislaus A. Rev.
Year of Ordination: 1951
Arch/Diocese of San Antonio
Year of Death: 1958

Jedlowski, John J. Rev.
Year of Ordination:
1935
Arch/Diocese of El Paso
Year of Death: 1974

Jewitt, Bernard C. Rev.
Year of Ordination: 1959
Arch/Diocese of Tulsa
Year of Death: 2008

Jones, Jack Allen Rev.
Year of Ordination: 1970
Arch/Diocese of Santa Fe
Year of Death: 1976

Judge, Richard Rev.
Year of Ordination:
1958
Arch/Diocese of Fort
Worth
Year of Death: 1993

Juraschek, Erwin A. Rev.
Msgr.
Year of Ordination: 1946
Arch/Diocese of San
Antonio
Year of Death: 1993

Kahlich, Oswald B. Rev.
Year of Ordination: 1942
Arch/Diocese of San Antonio
Year of Death: 1979

Kalina, Francis Rev.
Year of Ordination:
1945
Arch/Diocese of San
Antonio
Year of Death: 1996

Kamel, Raphael Rev.
Msgr.
Year of Ordination: 1954
Arch/Diocese of Dallas
Year of Death: 1992

Kaminski, Benjamin C. Rev.
Year of Ordination: 1928
Arch/Diocese of San Antonio
Year of Death: 1974

Kapitz, Donald R. Rev.
Year of Ordination:
1973
Arch/Diocese of Santa
Fe
Year of Death: 2013

Kehoe, John J. Rev.
Year of Ordination: 1941
Arch/Diocese of El Paso
Year of Death: 1961

Kelly, Reginald Rev.
Year of Ordination: 1951
Arch/Diocese of Fort Worth
Year of Death: 1985

Kelly, John Edward
Rev.
Year of Ordination:
1980
Arch/Diocese of San
Antonio
Year of Death: 2009

Killian, William A. Rev.
Year of Ordination: 1958
Arch/Diocese of San
Antonio
Year of Death: 1975

Kircher, Edward H. Rev.
Year of Ordination: 1957
Arch/Diocese of Corpus
Christi
Year of Death: 2003

Koelsch, James R. Rev.
Year of Ordination:
1963
Arch/Diocese of
Oklahoma City
Year of Death: 1995

Kolodzie, Emmett B. Rev.
Year of Ordination: 1933
Arch/Diocese of San
Antonio
Year of Death: 1986

Kopczynski, Ignatius I. Rev.
Year of Ordination: 1922
Arch/Diocese of San Antonio
Year of Death: 1954

Kownacki, Robert P.
Rev.
Year of Ordination:
1963
Arch/Diocese of San
Antonio
Year of Death: 2006

Kram, Jr., Charles W. Rev.
Year of Ordination: 1975
Arch/Diocese of Victoria
Year of Death: 2000

Kraus, Alex J. Rev.
Year of Ordination: 1933
Arch/Diocese of Victoria
Year of Death: 1992

La Pierre, Hollis Rev.
Year of Ordination:
1950
Arch/Diocese of
Alexandria
Year of Death: 1975

Laurenson, George F. Rev.
Year of Ordination: 1963
Arch/Diocese of
Galveston-Houston
Year of Death: 1970

Lazek, Aleck Rev.
Year of Ordination: 1960
Arch/Diocese of Austin
Year of Death: 1997

Leopold, Wilbert Rev.
Year of Ordination:
1944
Arch/Diocese of San
Antonio
Year of Death: 1959

Leopold, Aloysius A. Rev.
Msgr.
Year of Ordination: 1930
Arch/Diocese of San
Antonio
Year of Death: 1982

Leyva, Joseph Rev.
Year of Ordination: 1971
Arch/Diocese of Victoria
Year of Death: 1983

Lopez, Jose A. Rev.
Msgr.
Year of Ordination:
1971
Arch/Diocese of San
Antonio
Year of Death: 2011

Lyssy, Thomas A. Rev.
Msgr.
Year of Ordination: 1952
Arch/Diocese of San
Antonio
Year of Death: 1990

Macunas, Theodore Rev.
Year of Ordination: 1964
Arch/Diocese of
Altoona-Johnston
Year of Death: 2006

Maher, Robert E. Rev.
Msgr.
Year of Ordination:
1971
Arch/Diocese of
Brownsville
Year of Death: 2012

Maneth, Albert V. Rev.
Msgr.
Year of Ordination: 1937
Arch/Diocese of San
Antonio
Year of Death: 1992

Manning, Joseph Leroy Rev.
Msgr.
Year of Ordination: 1940
Arch/Diocese of San Antonio
Year of Death: 2004

Matocha, John L. Rev.
Year of Ordination:
1947
Arch/Diocese of Corpus
Christi
Year of Death: 2013

Matula, Anthony J. Rev.
Msgr.
Year of Ordination: 1939
Arch/Diocese of Victoria
Year of Death: 1994

Matzner, John A. Rev.
Year of Ordination: 1946
Arch/Diocese of Dallas
Year of Death: 1977

Mazurkiewicz, Benedict
Rev. Msgr.
Year of Ordination:
1955
Arch/Diocese of Austin
Year of Death: 2010

McDole, Robert G. Rev.
Year of Ordination: 1958
Arch/Diocese of Oklahoma
City
Year of Death: 1983

McGill, Robert P. Rev.
Year of Ordination: 1958
Arch/Diocese of Dallas
Year of Death: 1968

McKnight, James F.
Rev.
Year of Ordination:
1939
Arch/Diocese of San
Antonio
Year of Death: 1946

McLane, Newton Rev.
Year of Ordination: 1956
Arch/Diocese of Dallas
Year of Death: 2000

Meany, Thomas L. Rev.
Msgr.
Year of Ordination: 1955
Arch/Diocese of Corpus
Christi
Year of Death: 2008

Menco, John F. Rev.
Year of Ordination:
1955
Arch/Diocese of Peoria
Year of Death: 1974

Metzger, Sydney M. Most
Rev.
Year of Ordination: 1926
Arch/Diocese of El Paso
Year of Death: 1986

Meurer, David C. Rev.
Year of Ordination: 1951
Arch/Diocese of San Antonio
Year of Death: 2000

Mey, Ernest A. Rev.
Year of Ordination:
1936
Arch/Diocese of El Paso
Year of Death: 1956

Miesch, Francis G. Rev.
Msgr.
Year of Ordination: 1941
Arch/Diocese of Fort
Worth
Year of Death: 1990

Mitchell, John E. Rev.
Year of Ordination: 1948
Arch/Diocese of Fort Worth
Year of Death: 1996

Moczygemba, Henry I.
Rev. Msgr.
Year of Ordination:
1949
Arch/Diocese of San
Antonio
Year of Death: 1995

Moeller, Louis B. Rev.
Msgr.
Year of Ordination: 1951
Arch/Diocese of San
Angelo
Year of Death: 2008

Montoya, Ernesto Rev.
Year of Ordination: 1989
Arch/Diocese of Santa Fe
Year of Death: 2001

Morales, Gonzalo Rev.
Msgr.
Year of Ordination:
1952
Arch/Diocese of Las
Cruces
Year of Death: 1984

Moran, William F. Rev.
Year of Ordination: 1956
Arch/Diocese of Dallas
Year of Death: 1986

Morkovsky, John L. Most
Rev.
Year of Ordination: 1933
Arch/Diocese of
Galveston-Houston
Year of Death: 1990

Morkovsky, Alois J.
Rev. Msgr.
Year of Ordination:
1924
Arch/Diocese of San
Antonio
Year of Death: 1990

Mosman, Fred J. Rev.
Msgr.
Year of Ordination: 1948
Arch/Diocese of Dallas
Year of Death: 1982

Murski, Edward J. Rev.
Year of Ordination: 1932
Arch/Diocese of San Antonio
Year of Death: 1970

Mysliwiec, Bronislaus
Rev.
Year of Ordination:
1941
Arch/Diocese of Dallas
Year of Death: 1981

Neilson, OCD, Joseph Rev.
Year of Ordination: 1962
Order of Carmelites
Year of Death: 2012

Neu, PA, Hubert J. Rev.
Year of Ordination: 1951
Arch/Diocese of Fort Worth
Year of Death: 2011

Nichol, James P. Rev.
Msgr.
Year of Ordination:
1928
Arch/Diocese of Kansas
City
Year of Death: 1979

Notzon, Marcel Rev.
Year of Ordination: 1930
Arch/Diocese of
Galveston-Houston
Year of Death: 1992

Nowak, Joseph Rev.
Year of Ordination: 1949
Arch/Diocese of San Antonio
Year of Death: 1969

O'Brien, Forrest Leon
Rev.
Year of Ordination:
1955
Arch/Diocese of
Oklahoma City
Year of Death: 1998

O'Brien, Daniel J. Rev.
Year of Ordination: 1975
Arch/Diocese of Victoria
Year of Death: 2009

Ordner, Charles Rev.
Year of Ordination: 1937
Arch/Diocese of Corpus
Christi
Year of Death: 1969

Ordner, Aloysius J. Rev.
Msgr.
Year of Ordination:
1933
Arch/Diocese of Corpus
Christi
Year of Death: 1979

O'Rourke, John Rev.
Year of Ordination: 1948
Arch/Diocese of Dallas
Year of Death: 2008

O'Shaugnessy, Michael A.
Rev.
Year of Ordination: 1950
Arch/Diocese of Victoria
Year of Death: 2013

Padalecki, Alphonse
B. Rev.
Year of Ordination:
1959
Arch/Diocese of
Victoria
Year of Death: 1992

Palmer, Harold F. Rev.
Msgr.
Year of Ordination: 1932
Arch/Diocese of Corpus
Christi
Year of Death: 1981

Parrini, Warren M. Rev.
Year of Ordination: 1953
Arch/Diocese of Rockville
Center
Year of Death: 2002

Pater, Frank J. Rev.
Msgr.
Year of Ordination:
1937
Arch/Diocese of
Brownsville
Year of Death: 1992

Pawlak, Edwin F. Rev.
Year of Ordination: 1968
Arch/Diocese of Amarillo
Year of Death: 2005

Pekar, Gilbert F. Rev. Msgr.
Year of Ordination: 1947
Arch/Diocese of
Galveston-Houston
Year of Death: 1997

Pesek, Leo E. Rev.
Msgr.
Year of Ordination:
1942
Arch/Diocese of San
Antonio
Year of Death: 1965

Petru, Julius A. Rev.
Year of Ordination: 1937
Arch/Diocese of Victoria
Year of Death: 2001

Petru, Stanley J. Rev. Msgr.
Year of Ordination: 1948
Arch/Diocese of Victoria
Year of Death: 2013

Pruski, Benedict A.
Rev. Msgr.
Year of Ordination:
1942
Arch/Diocese of San
Antonio
Year of Death: 1993

Psencik, Henry F. Rev.
Year of Ordination: 1932
Arch/Diocese of San
Antonio
Year of Death: 1989

Pugh, Charles M. Rev. Msgr.
Year of Ordination: 1960
Arch/Diocese of San Antonio
Year of Death: 2006

Pustka, Joseph A. Rev.
Msgr.
Year of Ordination:
1922
Arch/Diocese of San
Antonio
Year of Death: 1955

Quintana, OSB, Carlos
J. Rev.
Year of Ordination: 1949
Order of St. Benedict
Year of Death: 1998

Rachunek, Henry C. Rev.
Year of Ordination: 1962
Arch/Diocese of
Galveston-Houston
Year of Death: 2013

Regan, Patrick L. Rev.
Year of Ordination:
1938
Arch/Diocese of
Lafayette
Year of Death: 1969

Reile, SM, Louis A. Rev.
Year of Ordination: 1960
Order of Marianists
Year of Death: 2003

Reyna, Joseph A. Rev.
Year of Ordination: 1971
Arch/Diocese of San Antonio
Year of Death: 1997

Rice, James W. Rev.
Year of Ordination:
1976
Arch/Diocese of Austin
Year of Death: 1983

Rolf, Henry Otto Rev.
Year of Ordination: 1944
Arch/Diocese of San
Antonio
Year of Death: 1986

Romero, Cayetano Rev.
Year of Ordination: 1926
Arch/Diocese of San Antonio
Year of Death: 1978

Rosloniac, Leo Rev.
Msgr.
Year of Ordination:
1954
Arch/Diocese of Grand
Rapids
Year of Death: 2010

Rother, F. Stanley Rev.
Year of Ordination: 1963
Arch/Diocese of Oklahoma
City
Year of Death: 1981

Roy, James Rev.
Year of Ordination: 1961
Arch/Diocese of Alexandria
Year of Death: 2009

Roy, Kenneth Rev.
Year of Ordination:
1978
Arch/Diocese of
Alexandria
Year of Death: 2009

Schiel, Lambert J. Rev.
Year of Ordination: 1926
Arch/Diocese of San
Antonio
Year of Death: 1969

Schlitt, Robert I. Rev.
Year of Ordination: 1956
Arch/Diocese of Oklahoma
City
Year of Death: 2002

Schmidt, Robert E. Rev.
Msgr.
Year of Ordination:
1944
Arch/Diocese of
Victoria
Year of Death: 1989

Schmidtzinsky, Victor G.
Rev. Msgr.
Year of Ordination: 1941
Arch/Diocese of Victoria
Year of Death: 2005

Scholl, Gerard M. Rev.
Year of Ordination: 1962
Arch/Diocese of Fort Worth
Year of Death: 2002

Seidler, Andrew J. Rev.
Year of Ordination:
1964
Arch/Diocese of Dallas
Year of Death: 1979

Sides, Clyde Gary Rev.
Year of Ordination: 1973
Arch/Diocese of Amarillo
Year of Death: 1998

Silverman, J. Robert Rev.
Msgr.
Year of Ordination: 1967
Arch/Diocese of San Antonio
Year of Death: 2004

Smith, Robert J. Rev.
Year of Ordination:
1971
Arch/Diocese of Santa
Fe
Year of Death: 1989

Smith, Ralph J. Rev. Msgr.
Year of Ordination: 1936
Arch/Diocese of San
Antonio
Year of Death: 1992

Smith, Charles Rev.
Year of Ordination: 1992
Arch/Diocese of San Antonio
Year of Death: 1995

Smith, Peter J. Rev.
Year of Ordination:
1951
Arch/Diocese of
Brownsville
Year of Death: 2002

Smith, Sherrill J. Rev.
Msgr.
Year of Ordination: 1955
Arch/Diocese of San
Antonio
Year of Death: 2012

Smyth, William J. Rev.
Year of Ordination: 1947
Arch/Diocese of Dallas
Year of Death: 1973

Speck, James A. Rev.
Year of Ordination:
1950
Arch/Diocese of Winona
Year of Death: 2009

Staff, Gus P. Rev. Msgr.
Year of Ordination: 1930
Arch/Diocese of San
Antonio
Year of Death: 1981

Stryk, Jerome J. Rev.
Year of Ordination: 1944
Arch/Diocese of Victoria
Year of Death: 1999

Stuebben, George H.
Rev. Msgr.
Year of Ordination:
1954
Arch/Diocese of San
Antonio
Year of Death: 2006

Sullivan, Darius J. Rev.
Year of Ordination: 1957
Arch/Diocese of Dallas
Year of Death: 1991

Swierz, OCSO, M. Lawrence
Rev.
Year of Ordination: 1934
Order of Trappists
Year of Death: 0

Szapka, Edward J. Rev.
Msgr.
Year of Ordination:
1938
Arch/Diocese of Tyler
Year of Death: 2005

Taylor, OSB, Martin H.
Rev.
Year of Ordination: 1960
Order of Benedictines
Year of Death: 1988

Tengler, Alvin J. Rev. Msgr.
Year of Ordination: 1949
Arch/Diocese of Corpus
Christi
Year of Death: 2009

Thompson, E. Joseph
Rev.
Year of Ordination:
1962
Arch/Diocese of
Oklahoma City
Year of Death: 2002

Thurmond, Benton A. Rev.
Msgr.
Year of Ordination: 1946
Arch/Diocese of Victoria
Year of Death: 2009

Till, Joseph R. Rev.
Year of Ordination: 1949
Arch/Diocese of San Antonio
Year of Death: 1992

Titus, John Rev.
Year of Ordination:
1955
Arch/Diocese of
Oklahoma City
Year of Death: 1963

True, David H. Rev.
Year of Ordination: 1988
Arch/Diocese of Oklahoma
City
Year of Death: 2006

Tucek, James I. Rev. Msgr.
Year of Ordination: 1947
Arch/Diocese of Dallas
Year of Death: 1990

Tuohy, Daniel Rev.
Year of Ordination:
1934
Arch/Diocese of Corpus
Christi
Year of Death: 1956

Tyl, Albert R. Rev.
Year of Ordination: 1954
Arch/Diocese of Fort
Worth
Year of Death: 2005

Ullrich, Robert J. Rev.
Year of Ordination: 1953
Arch/Diocese of Corpus
Christi
Year of Death: 1995

Valenta, Marcus A.
Rev.
Year of Ordination:
1929
Arch/Diocese of San
Antonio
Year of Death: 1984

Valiquette, Vincent J. Rev.
Year of Ordination: 1956
Arch/Diocese of Peoria
Year of Death: 1977

Vance, Leslie A. Rev. Msgr.
Year of Ordination: 1976
Arch/Diocese of San Antonio
Year of Death: 2013

Vann, Joseph W. Rev.
Year of Ordination:
1947
Arch/Diocese of Dallas
Year of Death: 1953

Vigil, Edwin Rev.
Year of Ordination: 2007
Arch/Diocese of San
Antonio
Year of Death: 2011

Vinclarek, Emil T. Rev.
Year of Ordination: 1941
Arch/Diocese of San Antonio
Year of Death: 1996

Wangler, Alex C. Rev.
Msgr.
Year of Ordination:
1941
Arch/Diocese of San
Antonio
Year of Death: 2003

Weber, Armand J Rev.
Year of Ordination: 1928
Arch/Diocese of San
Antonio
Year of Death: 1984

Weinzapfel, Joseph J. Rev.
Year of Ordination: 1954
Arch/Diocese of Fort Worth
Year of Death: 1996

Wiewell, John M. Rev.
Msgr.
Year of Ordination:
1937
Arch/Diocese of Fort
Worth
Year of Death: 1996

Wilkes, James Rev.
Year of Ordination: 1950
Arch/Diocese of Corpus
Christi
Year of Death: 2012

Wilson, Robert W. Rev.
Year of Ordination: 1957
Arch/Diocese of Fort Worth
Year of Death: 2008

Wolf, Vincent J. Rev.
Msgr.
Year of Ordination:
1938
Arch/Diocese of Fort
Worth
Year of Death: 1997

Zagar, John T. Rev.
Year of Ordination: 1961
Arch/Diocese of Oklahoma
City
Year of Death: 2003

APPENDIX III

BIBLIOGRAPHY

Author's Notations on Text and Sources

"Rev." indicates an ordained clergyman; "Very Rev." indicates that he is/was a monsignor; "Most Rev." indicates that he is/was a bishop.

About the main sources:

25 Years a Seminary, compiled and written by the staff of *The Bulletin*, a seminary publication, was published in 1940 by the Archdiocese of San Antonio. Contributors were seminarians who were, at that time, studying at St. John's. None of the material is cited as to its source. Presumably, the work is based on oral accounts by eye-witnesses.

Called to Serve, by Rev. James Vanderholt (Rector of Assumption: 1975-1981), published by St. John's and Assumption Seminaries Alumni Association, is also undocumented. Though he offers a listing of his sources in the back of the book (with notations), he does not cite them directly in the text.

Priest Forever, written under the direction of Rev. Alois Goertz, et al., also published by St. John's and Assumption Seminaries Alumni Association in 1966, cites its sources in the "Introduction" (p. 5), but sources are not cited in the body of the book.

Breaking Ground, an unpublished work by Rev. Matthew Gilbert is his memoir of the beginnings of St. John's Seminary.

The DeAndrein is a newsletter published over many decades by the Congregation of the Mission. It is mostly a compilation of "news notes" from within the Vincentian Community. Authors of the articles are noted in citations within this book if they were given.

The Interviews come from the cherished (and perhaps, not so cherished) memories and experiences of the persons interviewed. The materials gleaned from the interviews are very valuable. However, our memories are *our* memories. Others might remember the same event differently.

Books, Periodicals and Articles

"Assumption Seminary: A reflection of the universal church," *Today's Catholic*, Oct. 1, 1993. "Enrollment Increases!," *Today's Catholic*, October 11, 1985.

"Seminary Changes," *The Alamo Messenger,* Friday, March 20, 1970.

"St. John's Minor Seminary Closing," *San Antonio Express/News,* Saturday, May 6, 1972.

"Residence hall blessed, new faculty welcomed," *Today's Catholic*, Oct. 3, 2003.

Assumption Seminary Newsletter, Summer, Vol. VII, 1995.

Assumption Seminary Newsletter, Winter, Vol. I, 1990.

Author Unknown, The Student Diary 1952-1953.

Author Unknown, Journals: 1981-1985.

Barnes, Msgr. Gerald, "75th Year for Assumption," *Today's Catholic*, Jan. 9, 1990

Callahan, CDP, Sister Generosa, *The History of the Sisters of Divine Providence*, Bruce Press, Milwaukee, WI, 1955.

Cruz, Msgr. David R., *The Human Face of God*, Pleasant Word Publications, Enumclaw, WA, 2007.

Gilbert, M. J., Rev. (Ed.), *Diamond Jubilee Archdiocese of San Antonio 1874-1949*, Schneider Printing Company, San Antonio, TX.

Gilbert, Rev. M. J., "The Early Years". Assumption Seminary Archives (unpublished bound manuscript).

Gilbert, Rev. Matthew, "Breaking Ground" Assumption Seminary Archives (Unpublished bound manuscript).

Goertz, Very Rev. Alois J, et al., *Priest Forever . . . History of St. John's and Assumption Seminaries San Antonio, Texas 1915-1965*, Published by St. John's and Assumption Seminaries Alumni Assocation, San Antonio, TX, 1966.

Herzig, Very Rev. Charles, compiler, "The Last Year 1968-1969" (unpublished collection).

Herzig, Very Rev. Charles, compiler, Daily Bulletins: 1971-1972 (collection of St. John's daily bulletins).

McMorrough, Jordan, "New hall a symbol of increased vocations," *Today's Catholic*, August 31, 2007

McMorrough, Jordan, "Assumption Seminary announces new $26 million capital campaign," *Today's Catholic*, Feb. 7, 2003.

Pruss, Teri, "Assumption Seminary: Offers the Whole Works," *Today's Catholic*, April 4, 1985.

Richelieu, David Anthony, "Archdiocese gets OK to demolish 1925 building," *San Antonio Express-News,* Nov. 16, 2000.

Richilieu, David Anthony, "Survey would assess historic S.A. buildings" *San Antonio Express-News,* Nov. 18, 2000

Sowa, Carol Bass, "Msgr. Larry Stuebben--The Busy Life of a 'Retired" Priest'", *Today's Catholic,* April 25, 2008.

Staff of "The Bulletin", Editors, *25 Years a Seminary Silver Jubilee St. John's Seminary San Antonio, Texas 1915 - Oct. 2-1940.*

The DeAndrein, Various Volumes, Published in house by the Vincentians at Perryville, MO (Archived at DePaul University, Chicago, IL).

United States Conference of Catholic Bishops, *Program for Priestly Formation* (available online at USCCB.org).

Vanderholt, Father James, "Rector recalls time at Assumption Seminary," *Today's Catholic,* August 17, 2007.

Vanderholt, Very Rev. James, *Called to Serve . . . History of St. John's an Assumption Seminaries San Antonio, Texas 1915-1990,* Published by St. John's and Assumption Alumni Association, San Antonio, TX, 1990.

Internet Sites

"MARGIL DE JESUS, ANTONIO, *Handbook of Texas Online* (http://www. tshaonline.org/ handbook/ online/articles/ fma45), accessed December 10, 2012. Published by the Texas State Historical Society Fehrenbach, T. R., accessed Feb 27, 2013

"Nun's new challenge: Mexican American Cultural Center" www. thefreelibrary.com

"Mexican American Cultural Center evolves into Catholic college"

"Obituary of Msgr. Edward F. Bily," *San Antonio Express-News*, 21 Apr 2006

"Plenary Councils of Baltimore," en.wikipedia.org/wiki/ Plenary_**Councils_of_Baltimore**

Antonian High School, San Antonio, TX, www.**antonian**.org

Central Catholic High School, www.cchs-satx.org

Diocese of San Bernadino, CA Website, "Biography of Bishop Barnes"

Francis J. Furey, General History of Assumption Seminary

Hermanas Josefinas website, www.hermanasjosefinas. org. mx

John Yanta, John Yanta http://en.wikipedia.org/wiki/John_Yanta

Kacmarcik, Frank, www.hmml.org/arca2010/artist.htm

Kacmarcik, Frank, mail.architexturez.net/+/Design-L.V1/ archive/msg21319.shtml, accessed on February 25, 2013

Kacmarcik, Frank, cad.edu/125/alumni/brother-frank-kacmarcik

Leven, Stephen A., en.wikipedia.org/wiki/**Stephen**_Aloysius_**Leven**

Louis J. Franz, C.M., "VINCENTIAN FATHERS," Handbook of Texas Online(http:// www.tshaonline.org/handbook/online/ articles/ixv01), accessed May 02, 2012. Published by the Texas State Historical Association

Michael J. Sheehan, http://en.wikipedia.org/wiki/Michael_Jarboe_Sheeh

Moye Center, Castroville, Texas, www.moyecenter.org

Oblate School of Theology Website, http://www.ost.edu/OblateSite/ OST/about-ost.htm

O'Neil Ford, en.wikipedia.org / wiki/ O'Neil Ford

Personnel Catalogues, V1948 (1948).Personnel Catalogues.Paper 84.

Prairie View A & M University, en.wikipedia.org/wiki/Prairie_ View_A%26M_ University

Raymundo Joseph Pena, http://en.wikipedia.org/wiki/Raymundo_ Joseph_ Pe%C3%B1a

Re: Msgr. David Garcia, crs.org/ newsroom/expert./profile-garcia; www.catholicidaho. org/; mynotredame.nd.edu).

Robert_Emmet_Lucey, assumptionseminary.org/history.aspx

Rother Deserves to Be State's First Saint, http:// w w w . e n i d n e w s . c o m / o p i n i o n / x 1 6 4 3 1 9 9 9 8 / Rev-Stanley-Rother-as-state-s-first-saint-advisable

Rother, Rev. Stanley, *en.wikipedia.org/wiki/ **Stanley_Rother***

Sheehan, Archbishop Michael, www.archdiocesesantafe.org/ ABSheehan/ ABSheehan.html

Sidney M. Metzger, http://en.wikipedia.org/wiki/Sidney_Matthew_ Metzger

St. Catherine Labouré, en.wikipedia.org/wiki/Catherine_Laboure

St. Lawrence High, Wikipedia Encyclopedia, en.wikipedia.org/ wiki/ **St._Lawrence_ Seminary_**High_School

St. Lawrence High School, www.capuchinfranciscans.org/ and www.stlawrence seminary.org

Steven P. Ryan, S.J., "JESUITS," Handbook of Texas Online (http://www.tshaonline.org/ handbook/ online/articles/ixj02), accessed May 09, 2012

Tehuacana, Texas, www.texasescapes.com/CentralTexasTowns North/Tehuacana-Texas/

The DeAndrein, Vols. 14-32, The Institutional Repository at DePaul

Trinity University, www.trinity.edu/

Vincentian Personnel Catalogues. V 1940, 1947-1960. Via Sapientiae: http://via.library. depaul.edu

Virgilio Elizondo, http://en.wikipedia.org/wiki/Virgilio_Elizondo

Young, Christine, "Sister Jacinta Millán retires, would do it all again," Intermountain Catholic [Diocese of Salt Lake City, UT], June 19, 2009, www.intermountaincatholic

Interviews

Barnes, Most Rev. Gerald R.	Sep-13
Boulette, Msgr. Michael	Jun-12
Brinkman, Paul	10-Jul-12
Christian, Msgr. Lawrence	Jun-13
Cruz, Msgr. David	7-May-13
Cullen, CSB, Sr. Mary Teresa	13-Feb-12
Eichoff, Rev. Paul	17-May-12
Elizondo, Msgr. Virgilio	Jul-13
Gaalaas, Msgr. Patrick	18-May-12
Henke, Msgr. James	Jun-13
Hubertus, Msgr. Albert	2-Jul-12
Janish, Msgr. James	Jun-13

McGraw, Rev. Robert	Nov-13
Mondragón, Sor Guadalupe	Jul-13
Morgan, Rev. Martin	17-May-12
Morkovsky, CDP, Sr. Mary Christine	Jul-13
Morkovsky, Robert L.	9-Jul-12
Pehl, Msgr. Jeff	27-Jun-12
Rihn, Msgr. Roy	9-Feb-12
Rippinger, OSB, Rev. Joel	Sep-13
Stuebben, Msgr. Lawrence	13-Feb-12
Vance, Msgr. Les	3-Jul-12
Vanderholt, Msgr. James	8-Nov-12
Wagner, Msgr. John	Nov-12
Walker, SSND, Sr. Addie Lorraine	Jun-13
White, Rev. James D.	Jun-13